Touch Not The Unclean Thing

The Text Issue and Separation

✝

David H. Sorenson, D. Min.

☆
Northstar Baptist Ministries
Duluth, MN

© 2001 David H. Sorenson

Library of Congress Control Number: 2001132441
ISBN: 0-9711384-0-0

First Edition 2001
Second Edition 2001
Third Edition 2002

Northstar Baptist Ministries
1820 West Morgan Street
Duluth, MN 55811-1878

davidsorenson@juno.com

TABLE OF CONTENTS

Preface v

Chapters

1. Introduction 1
2. The Three Major Positions 15
3. Basic Terminology of the Textual Debate 34
4. The Double Stream of Biblical Texts 43
5. Early History of the Received Text 76
6. Additional History of the Critical Text 95
7. Dating, Weighting, and Counting 128
8. The Scriptural Principle of Separation from Apostasy .. 143
9. Applying the Principle of Separation to the Textual Issue .. 162
10. What about Erasmus, King James, and His Translators? .. 186
11. The Issue Today 213

Appendices

A. Problems in the New American Standard Bible 227
B. Problems in the New International Version 236
C. Problems with the New King James Version 240

D.	Weakened Doctrine in the Critical Text	245
E.	Evidences of a Historical Connection Between the Waldenses and the King James Version	256

Selected Bibliography 262

General Index 279

Scripture Index 291

Vita 295

PREFACE

The foundation for Bible-believing Fundamentalists is the Bible itself. As the psalmist wrote, "If the foundations be destroyed, what can the righteous do?" (Ps. 11:3). The defense of the Word of God as the inerrant, providentially preserved and infallible Word of God is a crucial issue of our day. There have been many good books written on the subject of the Bible translation/textual issue. Many of them, however, are so technical or arcane in nature that most readers cannot readily grasp the issue. Others are simply incorrect in their assertions and conclusions. As I have sought to develop this material, I have endeavored to be both factually and historically accurate as well as practical—putting the truth on a shelf where almost anyone can reach it.

I would like to thank my wife and church for tolerating the considerable amount of time which has been spent on this project. I also would like to thank Dr. Dell Johnson. He has provided many insights of which I had not originally considered. Thank you, Dr. Johnson.

The reader may note on several occasions throughout this book that some reference citations are placed as page numbers in parentheses (e.g., 191) in the text. The number in parentheses refers to the page number of the last reference cited as a footnote. This has been done when these citations are all from the same source. This prevents unnecessary footnotes at the bottom of the page and is in accordance with Turabian's *A Manual for Writers of Term Papers, Theses, and Dissertations* (sixth edition, 1996).

*****

The reader will also note throughout this book that the author has routinely capitalized the term *Deity* when referring to the Deity of Christ. Traditional grammar normally does not capitalize the term *deity* in that context. However, the author has sought to magnify the fact that Jesus Christ is God against the incipient erosion of that sacred truth by apostates who question or deny it.

CHAPTER ONE

INTRODUCTION

This book is being written by a Fundamental Baptist. Its intended readership is other Fundamentalists. Evangelicals and theological Liberals, unencumbered with the biblical conviction of separation, may proceed at their own peril. They are not the audience to whom I write. (As a separatist, I write from that conviction.) Thus, the scope of this volume is from a Fundamental Baptist perspective for those of like mind.

My intent is to be kind toward those who do not share the position which will be developed in this volume. Moreover, it is my express intention to be kind toward those who heretofore have not agreed with the Received Text position. I did not always hold this position and for fifteen years sat where many still sit in the seat of the critical text position. Therefore, I can empathize with them. Though the truth at times can be sharp, I have attempted to soften what may be the unkind edge of historical truth.

Many good people in good churches and good educational institutions alike are confused regarding the Bible translation controversy and particularly the undergirding textual issue. Many have never studied the issue at all. Others know only what they picked up in passing from a book or a lecture on the subject. I intend to be as accurate as possible in presenting both sides of this highly controversial issue and shall carefully avoid naming contemporary names of other fundamental individuals or institutions unless and only as it is necessary to clarify or certify a controversial point.

Author's Background

As a third-generation Fundamentalist, I understand the background of my audience and the need to clearly explain this highly controversial topic. My grandfather, Olaf P. Lovik, was a Fundamental Baptist pastor during the first half of the twentieth century. My father, Henry C. Sorenson, was also a Fundamental, separatist Baptist pastor for fifty years. The latter went through some of the great separatist controversies of the Northern Baptist Convention and the Conservative Baptist Association, eventually separating from both. I attended and graduated from separatist, Fundamental institutions of higher learning.[1] I have been involved only with Fundamental, separatist Baptist associations and fellowships throughout my entire ministry. Hence, I think that I understand the movement where I am and from whence I came.

During the years of my seminary training, the "default" position in which I was trained was that of the critical text and its concomitant use of various modern translations of the Bible, the New American Standard Bible in particular. There were upward of fifteen years in which I routinely referred to the New American Standard Bible in study. I even at times used it from the teaching lectern or the pulpit. I had been trained that any translation of the Bible was acceptable (in theory) as long as it was a "good" translation. Little or nothing was said regarding the significant differences between the two principal textual bases.

Hence, by training, I was indoctrinated in the critical text position and taught to be extremely wary of anything which approached using only the King James Version of the Bible as one's biblical base. I thus can honestly say that I have sat where many presently sit on this controversial issue.

In a later chapter, considerable attention will be given to the double stream of Bible translations which exist in the world today. However, at this juncture it will be helpful for some readers to realize that there

---

[1] Pillsbury Baptist Bible College and Central Baptist Theological Seminary of Minneapolis. This book is an adaptation of the author's doctor of ministry major project submitted to Pensacola Theological Seminary.

are really only two types of Bibles. (Our focus will be upon the English-speaking world and the New Testament in particular. However, the issue remains the same in any other language.) There accordingly are two distinct Greek texts from which the New Testament is translated. The one used since antiquity is commonly called the "Received Text" and is the source from which the King James Version of the Bible has been translated. The other Greek text is relatively modern in its creation and is commonly referred to as the "critical text"—sometimes called the "eclectic text." From this modern textual base, *almost* all modern Bible translations have been made including the New International Version, the New American Standard Bible, and other less used versions.

The Essence of Fundamentalism

By way of introduction, it is appropriate to carefully, though briefly define, what Fundamentalism is. The term *Fundamentalist* is of relatively modern derivation. This designation came into being as a modern movement having its roots in the independent Bible conferences of the latter part of the nineteenth century. The term *Fundamentalist* was popularized by Curtis Lee Laws of the Northern Baptist Convention in 1920 when he referred to those adhering to the *fundamentals* of the Christian faith as "Fundamentalists." Historically, there are three characteristics which have come to define the Fundamentalist movement, particularly as it pertains to fundamental Baptists.

The first characteristic of Fundamentalism is that of being **orthodox in doctrine**. Webster's dictionary defines the word *orthodox* as "being sound in doctrine, especially religious doctrine." Hence, Fundamentalism has always adamantly supported the foundational, cardinal, essential truths of historic New Testament Christianity. Fundamentalists take the Bible at face value. By way of contrast, in the latter half of the nineteenth century theological Liberalism (i.e., Modernism) had permeated most major Protestant and Baptist denominations in the Western world. Such foundational truths as the verbal inspiration of Scripture, the inerrancy of Scripture, the Deity of Christ, the blood atonement of

Christ, and the bodily resurrection of Jesus Christ (to name a few) were either questioned or directly denied altogether. Bible-believing Christian leaders at the end of the nineteenth century and the beginning of the twentieth century reacted strongly against the gathering darkness of apostasy by emphasizing the great "fundamental" truths of the Scripture. Thus, orthodoxy in doctrine has always been the cornerstone of the Fundamentalist position.

The second characteristic of Fundamentalism has been that of **separation from apostasy**. As theological Liberalism (i.e., apostasy) little by little gained control of the prominent denominations in America, those who considered themselves as Fundamentalists eventually separated from the apostasy of their denominations. In the Northern Baptist Convention later to be called the American Baptist Convention many leaders sought to take back the denominational structure from the Liberals who were in control of it. Notable in this effort was W. B. Riley of the First Baptist Church of Minneapolis. Sadly, Riley never was able to win the battle against apostasy in the NBC.

However, many other pastors and churches saw the handwriting on the wall and in several steps separated from the Northern Baptist Convention. They came out and formed several new separatist groups such as the General Association of Regular Baptist Churches (GARBC) and the Conservative Baptist Association of America (CBA). In the case of the latter, it soon lost any stomach for a separatist position and numerous pastors led their churches out of the CBA. In recent years there has been a separatist movement from within the GARBC as some pastors and churches have been troubled by the lack of a separatist position in its national movement.[2]

For the most part, there are no organized movements within large national church groups advancing separation today. However, there are thousands of local churches around the nation which in recent decades have been formed specifically as independent churches and separatists from what they view as apostate denominations or associations. In short,

---

[2]Jerry Huffman, "Michigan Church Leaves GARBC," *Calvary Contender* (Huntsville, Ala.: Calvary Baptist Church), 15 May 2000, 2.

historic Fundamentalism has always believed and practiced separation from apostasy.

Finally, the third characteristic of Fundamentalism has been that of **separation from the world** and its underlying societal system: its philosophies, its value, and its entertainments. This latter characteristic for the most part is not germane to the greater scope of this volume and so will not be embellished upon further. However, suffice it to say that all true Fundamentalists to one degree or another certainly advocate separation from the world on a personal level.

Hence, it should be apparent from the discussion above that a significant portion of the Fundamentalist position is that of separation, especially from apostasy. Both the *summum bonum* and the touchstone of being a Fundamentalist is thus.

Connecting the Principle of Separation to the Translational/Textual Issue

In the early 1980s, a pastor friend gave me a copy of a book written by David Otis Fuller entitled *Which Bible?* I received it with skepticism. It cut across the grain of everything I had been taught in seminary on the issue of Bible translations. However, as I read what Fuller wrote, I came to understand that there were two Greek texts. Moreover, as I began to further study the issue, it became increasingly clear that the critical text had connections with apostasy which made me, as a Fundamentalist, quite ill at ease. The more I learned about the underlying critical texts, the people involved therewith, and the translations emanating therefrom, the more the involvement of the doctrine of separation began to come into view.

This book will attempt to document the historic lineage of the two primary textual bases. On the one hand, the history of the Received Text, and particularly one strain thereof, will be found to be associated with our persecuted, martyred brethren in separatist churches across the face of history. On the other hand, the lineage of the critical text will be shown to be linked to apostasy at virtually every step of its history. As will become apparent as this volume develops, there has been a dual stream of Bibles down through the ages. There have been two textual bases, two philosophies regarding the Bible, two types of text criticism, and two resultant types of Bibles. As this book unfolds, it should be apparent to any true Fundamentalist that one lineage is linked with apostasy and the other with true believers. Hence, the doctrine of the Bible becomes central.

Core Issue

The core issue at hand is bibliology. Bibliology is the study of the doctrine of the Scriptures. All Fundamentalists believe that the Bible is the inspired Word of God. Furthermore, any orthodox statement of bibliology will speak of the verbal, plenary inspiration of the Scriptures. The word *verbal* advances the thought that the Holy Spirit of God inspired every word in the Bible. Thus, the very words of the Bible, in their microcosm, are inspired. The word *plenary* refers to the collective whole of the Bible. That is the macrocosm thereof. Not only has God inspired the individual words of the Bible, He also has inspired the sum total thereof. The word *inspiration*, as found in 2 Tim. 3:16, literally means "God-breathed."[3] God, through His Holy Spirit, breathed out His very words to the various scriptural penmen as they wrote the various books of the Bible. Verbal plenary inspiration of the Bible is truly one of the foundational tenets of historic Fundamentalism. In 2 Pet. 1:21, the Apostle wrote, "For the prophecy came not in old time by the will of man: but holy men of God spake *as they were* moved by the Holy Ghost." The word translated as *moved* (φερω or *phero*) has the sense of being "led along," "carried," or "moved." The thought is how the Holy Spirit so led or moved the minds of the inspired writers that what they wrote were in fact the very words of God.

Bibliology therefore is the foundation of all faith and practice. If the Bible has flaws or is in error, the very foundation of faith is at risk.

---

[3] All Scripture quoted in this book is from the King James Version, 1769 edition.

Introduction

Fundamental Baptists have always posited that the bedrock foundation of all which they believe (their faith) and all that they do (their practice) is predicated upon God's Word.[4] As David wrote, "If the foundations be destroyed, what can the righteous do?" (Ps. 11:3).

As this volume will later demonstrate, the critical text and its resultant translations have altered the Word of God which was received and used by Bible-believing churches throughout the ages. Though the claim is often made that the critical text and its modern translations do not eliminate any major doctrines, the truth is that they have *eroded* them in numerous places. Ominously, the doctrine which is most eroded is that which pertains to the person of our Lord. Bibliology is a core issue indeed. But is not Christology a crucial issue as well?

Some have protested that making an issue of the Bible translation controversy is needlessly divisive. Many in Fundamentalist circles wish the whole issue would just go away. More than one fundamental Baptist pastor or leader has announced that the Bible translation issue (much less the underlying debate regarding the textual issue) is a nonissue; therefore, to make it an issue is to be divisive.

Is this issue divisive? Indeed it is—and it ought to be! Crucial doctrinal issues are at stake and they go to the heart of all Bible doctrine. Many in Charismatic and New Evangelical circles complain that doctrine divides. It certainly does. It divides truth from error. However, once the layers of worn clichés claiming there are no real issues are pealed away and the incipient apostasy connected with the critical text is revealed, the problem becomes evident. This is an issue Fundamentalists must address.

Fundamentalists have historically believed in *verbal* inspiration and not *thought* inspiration. However, as the debate regarding the textual issue continues, those supporting the critical text come perilously close to the position of "thought" inspiration. As the bramble of textual variants are endlessly addressed in the apparatus (footnotes) of the critical

---

[4]True faith and practice are not based upon the history of Fundamentalism, specific leaders, or their schools. These things are the beginnings of traditionalism. Rather, faith and practice must be anchored in the Word of God.

text, the concept of the very words being inspired seems to fade. The impression left is that only the thought is important, not the words.

However, the Sacred Writ declares that "**every** word of God *is* pure" (Prov. 30:5). Likewise, Jesus said, "Heaven and earth shall pass away: but my **words** shall not pass away" (Luke 21:33). The apostle Paul wrote, "Wherefore comfort one another with these **words**" (1 Thess. 4:18). *Verbal* inspiration is the foundation of the doctrine of bibliology. If the words of God lose importance, Fundamentalism has slipped its moorings. Ironically, this author is not aware of any Fundamental Baptist who would admit that the words of God are not important. Yet, in defending the critical text and its resultant translations, these Fundamentalists lose many words which seem to fall through the cracks of *modern* textual criticism.

As will be carefully developed later in this volume, there are essentially only two major Greek texts available today (the Textus Receptus and the modern critical text). From the Received Text (Textus Receptus) comes the King James Version. From the critical text comes almost all modern versions. Contrary to claims that the differences between these two texts (and their resultant translations) are insignificant, there are vast differences between the two Greek texts (and their translations). There are approximately 8,000 word differences between the Textus Receptus and the modern critical text. More than 2,800 of the words in the Textus Receptus are omitted in the modern critical text. This is approximately the number of words found in 1 and 2 Peter.[5] Or, to put it another way, the modern critical text with its modern translations has deleted the verbal equivalent of 1 and 2 Peter. How can this be considered an inconsequential issue? If we believe in *verbal* inspiration, we had best be concerned about thousands of words missing from the text of the New Testament received and used by God's people for eighteen hundred years.

The New International Version is a popular manifestation of the modern critical text. However, the NIV has either deleted or seriously

---

[5]David Cloud, *Myths about the Modern Bible Versions* (Oak Harbor, Wash.: Way of Life Literature 1999), 35.

questioned **45** entire verses as compared to the time-honored King James Version. Moreover, in the NIV there also are **147** other verses with significant portions missing.[6] A similar disparity exists for the New American Standard Bible along with most other modern English translations.[7]

This is not a nonissue. If it is divisive, then so be it. The integrity of the Word of God is at stake. Moreover, as will be summarized later in this book, serious doctrinal issues are indeed affected by the modern critical text. Though major doctrines may not have been omitted, they certainly have been diminished and watered down. The problem is that most Fundamentalists who still cling to the critical text and its concomitant translations simply have not done their homework. For the most part, they are unaware of the apostasy and major problems connected to the critical text from its origin to the present hour.

Confusion

A study has indicated that as recently as 1998 there was record of 293 English translations of the complete New Testament plus twenty-three more abridged New Testaments.[8] Furthermore, this same study noted at least 135 English translations of the complete Bible with an additional 99 abridged Bibles not included.[9] There undoubtedly have been more translations added since then. Some of these translations are quite obscure. Some are out of print. However, some are quite popular such as the King James Version, the New International Version, the

---

[6] Ibid., 36.

[7] The reason for such deletions is simple. The underlying Greek text used by these translations (the modern critical text) has deleted them.

[8] D. A. Waite, *Defending the King James Bible* (Collingswood, N.J.: Bible for Today, 1998), 203-212.

[9] Ibid., 198-203.

New American Standard Bible, and the New King James Version. Most "laymen" are unaware that the several well-known versions mentioned above are not all from the same Greek text. Modern Bible publishing companies often gloss over the fact that there is more than one Greek text. Others use creative advertising to "market" their Bibles. For example, some publishers at times advertise their particular version as being based upon the *earliest* and *best* Greek manuscripts. Others advertise their version as being based upon the text that "scholars recommend." Most Christian laymen have no idea what the "best" Greek texts are. Moreover, many are influenced by the claims of the earliest and the best or what "scholars" recommend.

Sincere Christians often are either unaware that there is more than one Greek text or confused about the matter. Of the several popular versions mentioned above, the King James Version and the New King James Version are based upon the Received Text while the New International Version and the New American Standard Bible are based upon the critical text. The vast majority of modern Bible translations are based upon the critical text. Only a handful are based upon the Received Text. Of these, the King James Version towers above them all in its historic heritage as a translation.

However, the reality of it is that there are really only two types of Bibles. On the one hand is the tried and true anvil of the King James Version. It is based upon the traditional, historic, Received Text of the Greek New Testament. For almost 400 years, it has stood head and shoulders above most other translations. On the other hand, particularly in the last one hundred years, almost every other translation of the Bible into the English language has been based upon the relatively recent, modernistic critical text of the Greek New Testament.[10] As this book will document, notwithstanding the hundreds of versions of the Bible, there really are only two types. The conviction of this author is that one

---

[10]The reader will note that the writer has used a "charged" term in the word *modernistic*. However, as this volume unfolds, that term in connection with the critical text will be found to be historically and theologically accurate. Its use does not necessarily connote an *a priori* prejudice.

Introduction

reflects the providential preservation of God and the other a human effort. Moreover, as this volume will unfold, it will become evident that the men involved in the development of the critical text for the most part have been apostate.

Controversy

To say that there is controversy on the Bible translation issue is an understatement. Good brethren disagree on this issue. Unfortunately, the controversy has become contentious for many. Because I have been on both sides of the issue, I believe that I have insight into why there is such disagreement.

There is no question that most Fundamental Baptist brethren who hold the opposing position are good men. Though this volume will document the apostasy connected with the critical text, I am not in any way implying that Fundamental Baptist brethren who hold to a critical text view are organizationally connected with that apostasy. There are Fundamental institutions of higher learning which uphold the critical text position. Though the leadership of these schools ought to know better, in many cases they have never carefully studied the other side of the issue. Their graduates therefore are at risk of moving in a direction which violates biblical principles as well as the professors who may move the position of the institution.

That brings to bear a major reason for the controversy. Many on the side of the critical text position have never carefully studied the entire issue. When I was in seminary, both sides of the issue were never presented. Moreover, it seemed evident that my seminary professors had never studied the opposing view. With all due respect, in the mid-twentieth century, there had not been a great deal of material written on the issue. That is no longer the case. At the time of this writing, there are literally scores of books clearly defining and defending the Received Text position. Notwithstanding the plethora of information presently available, many holding the critical text position have simply never carefully studied the opposing view—the Received (or Preserved) Text position.

A classic illustration of this strange phenomenon is a recent book which was published to be an enlightenment on the issue.[11] *From the Mind of God to the Mind of Man* is a compilation of articles written by eleven authors and reviewed by eight academicians from several Fundamentalist institutions of higher learning. The book purports to be neutral on the issue, but clearly is an apologetic for the critical text. The eleven authors of the various articles profess to give a comprehensive analysis of the translational-textual controversy and include extensive bibliographies. However, almost all of the books listed in the bibliographies of this work are either favorable to the critical text position or are reference works neutral on the subject. Almost none of the well-written, well-documented books of evident scholarship which support the Received Text position are included. The point to be made is simple. Most proponents of the critical text position have either never studied the other side of the issue or have a prejudice against it to such a degree that they ignore anything written thereon.

One author in the above-mentioned book used an interesting illustration to advance his thesis that this issue should really be a nonissue. (That position essentially equates to a choose-whichever-text-or-translation-you-please view. Or put another way, the critical text and its resultant translations are quite acceptable.) The illustration advanced was of a new roadway being reconstructed over an ancient roadbed. The story told how that the new roadway varied from the old by a foot or two. The application was therefore made to the textual controversy to the effect that even if the modern critical text varies from the ancient Received Text here and there, it is still substantially the same.[12]

The illustration intimates that there very well might be errors in the Bible be they ever so small. Moreover, the implication is that one should

---

[11] James B. Williams, ed., *From the Mind of God to the Mind of Man* (Greenville, S.C.: Ambassador—Emerald International, 1999).

[12] "Let's Meet the Manuscripts," in Williams, *From the Mind of God*, 92.

rest assured that small errors in the Bible are nothing of which to be concerned. But even the illustration the author chose reveals the error of this logic. Before entering the ministry years ago, I was trained in engineering. Survey baselines for industrial construction projects were allowed a deviation of only one tenth of an inch per mile. For a roadway to be off by a foot or two as it approached a bridge would be disastrous. Moreover, every succeeding mile would amplify the original deviation so that ten miles down the road, the roadway might be off by ten feet when it met the next bridge. The implications in regard to Scripture are clear. That another Fundamentalist would hold such a cavalier view of the Word of God is astounding to this writer.

The contention of this author is that the Word of God is inerrant in its original inspiration and that God has providentially preserved an infallible transmission of it to this very hour. Jesus said, "For verily I say unto you, Till heaven and earth pass, one jot or one tittle shall in no wise pass from the law, till all be fulfilled" (Matt. 5:18). Exod. 20:1 says, "And God spake **all** these words." If we believe in verbal inspiration and the inerrancy of the Word of God, we must be concerned about every word in the Bible. Though this issue is indeed controversial (and even divisive), the integrity of the Word of God is at stake for this generation and those to come. God certainly can and will overcome human folly. But it ought to be our duty to stand for the truth even if it is controversial or divisive. The issue at hand is the Word of God: its integrity, accuracy, and trustworthiness.

Review Questions for Further Study

1. What is the first essence of Fundamentalism?

2. What is the second characteristic of Fundamentalism?

3. What is the core issue in the Bible translation debate?

4. Does inspiration pertain to the very words of the Scripture?

5. How many basic Greek New Testaments are used today?

6. How many types of Bibles really exist?

7. Why are so many people confused on this issue?

8. What is really at stake in the debate?

CHAPTER TWO

THE THREE MAJOR POSITIONS

In addressing the translational and textual controversy, it will be helpful to realize that there are three major views or positions.[1] These three are (1) the King James only position, (2) the critical text position, (3) and the preserved text position. In this chapter, each of these will be examined in *summary* fashion.

The King James Only Position

The King James Only position of the translation controversy advances the view that the King James Version of the Bible as a *translation* is inspired. Therefore, the King James Version as a *translation* is the exclusive Word of God in this age. Though there are several varieties of this position, its most prominent advocate is Peter Ruckman.

---

[1]There are actually more than three views on the issue. But we will address only the three *major* positions. A fourth position which holds interest for some is the Majority Text position. In 1985, a Greek text was published by Zane Hodges and Arthur Farstad entitled the Majority Text. Then in 1991, *another* Majority Text was published by Maurice Robinson and William Pierpont. However, to date, no major translations have been based upon either. Both are essentially creations known only amongst academicians. Moreover, how can one consider a Greek text which was created less than twenty years ago as being the Word of God? If one of these variations of the Majority Text is the Word of God, then the church of Jesus Christ did not have it until at least 1985.

Ironically, the Majority Text position has been produced using the same rationalistic principles of modern textual criticism. It essentially begins with the premise that the true Word of God has been lost and must be reconstructed by scientific means. This is the same philosophy and approach that Rationalists have used in composing the modern critical text. Thus, the Majority Text is an "escape hatch" for those who have come to realize the problems in the critical text, but are not willing to embrace the Received Text. Many view the latter position as too radical for their own comfort.

Among other things, he holds the view that the King James Version *as an English translation* is superior to the Greek readings of any Greek text.[2] Other proponents of the King James only position advance the view that the King James Version was re-inspired in A.D. 1611 and thus supercedes even the original Greek manuscripts (the autographa) of the New Testament.

In their view, the King James Version as a *translation* is therefore the inspired Word of God in this age. Ed Devries, former editor of the *Baptist Information Service*, is a strong proponent of the King James only position. In electronic correspondence to this author in August 1998, Devries wrote that if other nations wish to know God's Word, they need to learn English and the King James Version in particular to actually have the Word of God in their hands. In their view, God has blessed the English speaking world with the issuance of the Word of God in its native tongue. This is the King James Version. Thus, according to them, the King James Version is the absolute Word of God. Translation therefrom into another language might be good to help others hear the gospel, but the autographa for today is the King James Version. Its translators, in their view, were inspired even as the original scriptural penmen such as Peter, Paul, Luke, Moses, and David were. Those holding this view will translate the Bible into other languages only from the King James Version and not from any Greek or Hebrew text. According to them, the only true source of the Word of God is the King James Version of A.D. 1611.

Most holding this view do not seek to base their position upon Scripture or even history as such. Rather, it is founded upon a circular rationale which goes something like this: "The Bible is the inspired Word of God. The Bible I hold in my hand is the King James Version. Therefore, the King James Bible is the inspired Word of God. Accordingly, when the King James Version translators accomplished their translation in A.D. 1611, they were inspired. Thus, the result of their

---

[2]Peter S. Ruckman, *The Christian's Handbook of Manuscript Evidence* (Pensacola, Fla.: Pensacola Bible Institute, 1970), 128, 131.

work, the King James Version, is inspired and is the exclusive manifestation of the Word of God in this age."

To their credit, those who hold such a view have a fierce loyalty to the Word of God. Never will one of these be accused of questioning the inerrancy or the infallibility of the Bible. However, their loyalty to and defense of the King James Version as the Word of God, though admirable, is simply not based in either historical fact or scriptural foundation.

Here is why. Though the advocates of the King James only position refer continually to the Authorized Version of 1611, the Bible they hold forth and use is not the King James Version of 1611. The King James Version of the Bible in America at present is in fact the 1769 edition. (There were also eight other revisions and editions of the King James Version between 1611 and 1769: 1612, 1613, 1629, 1631, 1638, 1717, 1762, 1745. All of these essentially were to correct typographical errors or to modernize spelling or punctuation. They were revisions nevertheless.)

In 1769, Benjamin Blayney completed a comprehensive modernization of the King James Version by permission of the Church of England.[3] Those who do not favorably view the King James Version are quick to point out that Blayney's revision changed the 1611 King James Version in 75,000 places.[4] (What such critics fail to point out is that the overwhelming majority of those changes were simply modernizations of spelling and punctuation marks.) The truth is that there are only 136 substantial changes between the King James Version of 1611 and 1769. D. A. Waite (the author of this research) defined "substantial change" as words which were not merely of updated spelling, but actually sound differently. They thus are different words.[5] Or to put it another way, the

---

[3]Balmer H. Kelly and Donald G. Miller, eds., *Tools for Bible Study* (Richmond: John Knox Press, 1956), 119-20.

[4]W. Edward Glenny, "Defining the Terms," in *The Bible Version Debate*, ed. Michael Grisanti, (Minneapolis: Central Baptist Theological Seminary, 1997), 59.

[5]D. A. Waite, *The Authorized Version 1611 Compared to Today's King James Version* (Collingswood, N.J.: Bible for Today, 1985), 4.

1769 edition of the King James Version (which is the present common American edition) has been revised in 136 places in distinction to the 1611 edition.

Some examples of these changes are as follows. The 1769 edition in Isa. 47:6 changes the word "the" to "thy." In Isa. 49:13, the 1769 edition changes the word "God" to "Lord." In Isa. 57:8, the 1769 edition changes the words 'made . . . a" to "made thee a." Examples of other changes include the change in Ezek. 3:11 where "thy people" was changed to "the children of thy people." New Testament examples include "the shearer" being changed to "his shearer" in Acts 8:32, or "sacrifice" being changed to "sacrifices" in 1 Pet. 2:5.[6] These examples are not speculation or opinion but rather unforgiving facts.

That being the case, the advocates of the King James only position have a severe problem. Most of them hold the view that the King James Version of 1611 as a *translation* was inspired and thus has no need for further *translational* revision. However, the King James Bible which they use is in fact the 1769 edition of the KJV. That edition differs in substance from the 1611 original in 136 places. However, the vast majority of those who take a King James only position use the 1769 edition.

Another problem facing those advocating a King James only position is the difference between the Oxford Edition of the 1769 edition and the Cambridge Edition thereof. The Cambridge Edition is the one used in England. The Oxford Edition is the more commonly used one in the United States. These two editions differ in their rendering of Jer. 34:16.[7] The Cambridge edition (of the 1769 KJV) reads as follows: "But ye turned and polluted my name, and caused every man his servant, and every man his handmaid, whom **ye** had set at liberty at their pleasure, to return, and brought them into subjection, to be unto you for servants and for handmaids." The Oxford Edition (of the 1769 edition)

---

[6]Ibid., 6-13.

[7]It should be noted that some editions of the Oxford Bible have corrected this problem.

reads thus: "But ye turned and polluted my name, and caused every man his servant, and every man his handmaid, whom he had set at liberty at their pleasure, to return, and brought them into subjection, to be unto you for servants and for handmaids."

As it turns out, the Cambridge Edition is the correct translation of the traditional Masoretic Hebrew Text. Moreover, the King James only position is almost entirely an American phenomenon. What is ironic, however, is that *many* King James only advocates use the Oxford Edition of the 1769 KJV.

Therefore, the historical facts do not bode well for brethren holding this view. To summarize, the edition of the King James Version almost universally used in the world today is the 1769 edition by Benjamin Blayney. It contains 136 substantial and specific translational changes as documented by D. A. Waite. Therefore, the King James Bible used by these brethren has been changed 136 times from the one which they hold inviolate. Furthermore, the edition of the KJV which virtually all Americans use is the Oxford Edition. However, that differs from the Cambridge Edition at Jer. 34:16. The Cambridge Edition (the British one) offers the correct translation of the traditional Masoretic Hebrew Text.

These brethren, advancing a King James only position, are to be commended for their love of the Word of God. Their separatist instincts have correctly sensed that modern Bible translations are connected with apostasy. However, they have essentially gone too far down the right road. Moreover, they advance a confused and unorthodox view of inspiration. They have concluded the KJV to be the best English translation, but they have gone farther than the historical and scriptural evidence allows.[8] There is no scriptural or historical evidence that God re-inspired any set of biblical translations. Only the original manuscripts (the autographa) of the Bible were directly inspired by the Holy Spirit.

---

[8]Ironically, the single historical parallel to the King James Only position is the Roman Catholic view that the Latin Vulgate *translation* was inspired.

The Critical Text Position

A second and radically different position regarding the textual and translational debate might be called the *critical text position*. Before launching into the philosophy, history, and approach of the critical text position, it will be helpful to first pause and consider some basic history.

Background

When the various books of the Bible were written, they were done so in manuscripts, which, as the name implies, were handwritten copies. These original documents of the various biblical books are called "autographs." Their collective sum is called the "autographa." This term applies to both the Old as well as the New Testaments. However, because the largest portion of the controversy surrounds the text and translations of the New Testament, this will be our focus in this book.

Whether it was the writing of Moses, David, and Jeremiah of the Old Testament or Paul, John, and Peter of the New Testament; not one of these original manuscripts remains. The firm conviction of this writer is that God has providentially ordained for the autographa not to survive. The reason is simple. Mankind (including believers) has repeatedly demonstrated that they will worship ancient religious relics or artifacts. God's clear intention in His Word is that people believe and obey His Word. However, if the autographa (the original manuscripts) remained to this day, men would undoubtedly worship the artifact rather than the God thereof. Hence, God allowed these inspired original documents to disappear with the passing of time.

During the middle of the fifteenth century, mechanical printing was invented. Hence, prior to that time all biblical manuscripts were copied by hand. Usually those involved were scribes whose profession it was to carefully and accurately copy documents. Thus, all existing manuscripts of biblical books are handwritten copies. (The technical term for a copied manuscript is an "apograph.") These manuscripts were produced on ancient writing materials. They varied from carefully prepared, leathern animal skins, called parchments, to a material called papyri. The latter was used primarily in Egypt. The name derives from the papyrus plant which was an aquatic reed growing in the Nile River. These plants would be split into long narrow piths and beaten flat. Then, the flattened papyrus piths would be woven into a crude sheet of paper. This was called *papyri*. In some ways, papyri resembled paper, but it was crude and not particularly long lasting. But papyri was also the more economical material. However, because of Egypt's dry climate in Egypt, biblical manuscripts have been found there in varying degrees of preservation. Most of them are not well preserved. Thus, all extant (existing) biblical manuscripts to this day are made either of parchment or papyri.

Furthermore, hand-copied manuscripts were prone to unintentional slips of the pen by scribes. Thus, no two manuscripts are identical. However, it should be pointed out that accuracy was the professional goal and standard of most scribes, especially when they were copying Scripture. Hence, there is a high degree of accuracy in the majority of the manuscripts. However, scribes would on occasion make variant spellings or unintentionally leave out a word. There also were other discernable types of scribal variants of this nature which will not be noted here. But the majority of manuscripts contained only minor variants.

Ironically, as early as the second century, there were scribes who intentionally modified their copying to suit preconceived theological biases. Even in the lifetime of the apostle Paul, he warned the Corinthian church, "For we are not as many, which corrupt the word of God" (2 Cor. 2:17). Even at that early stage of church history, it is apparent that there was intentional tampering with the Scriptures. John Burgon, an erudite textual expert of the nineteenth century, wrote: "It seems that corruption arose in the very earliest age. . . . Thus, it appears that error crept in at the very first commencement of the life of the Church."[9] Burgon wrote further that many intentional corruptions of New Testament books were made within one-hundred years of the date of their

---

[9] John Burgon and Edward Miller, *The Causes of the Corruption of the Traditional Text of the Holy Gospels* (London: MacMillan Co., 1897), 3-4.

inspired writing, especially among a minority of unreliable manuscripts.[10]

Existing Manuscripts

Today, there are more than 5,650 manuscripts of the Greek New Testament.[11] The vast majority of these contain only portions of the New Testament. In some cases, they represent less than a single page of a given book. In a later section, extensive details will be given as to how there are several "families" of these extant (existing) manuscripts.

Because there are literally thousands of New Testament manuscripts and because no two of them are exactly alike, an academic discipline called "textual criticism" has been borrowed from the secular world and applied to biblical manuscripts. Textual criticism is the "science" of comparing manuscripts with manuscripts to find what appears to be scribal errors. Then the "text critics," by consensus, seek to determine what they think the actual reading should be. However, *modern* text criticism has developed a quixotic labyrinth of techno-speak rules (to be presented in a later chapter). Moreover, some of the "conventional" norms of modern text criticism borders upon the bizarre. Furthermore, almost all *modern* text critics will be found to be either apostate in their theology or to freely associate with apostates or apostate institutions.

The work of modern text critics has produced what is commonly called the "critical text." (This is also at times called the "eclectic text.") What is significant about the critical text position is that virtually all modern English translations of the New Testament derive from it.

---

[10]Ibid., 200-201.

[11]Kurt Aland and Barbara Aland, eds., *Kurzgefasste Liste der grieschen Handscriften des Neuen Testaments* (Hawthorne, N.Y.: Walter de Gruyter, 1994), 72-84.

Modern Textual Criticism

The critical text position therefore advances the view that the text of the New Testament must be "reconstructed" from extant (existing) manuscripts by scientific means. B. B. Warfield wrote in 1881, "We cannot doubt but that the leading principles of method which they have laid down will meet with speedy universal acceptance. They [Westcott and Hort] furnish us for the first time with a really *scientific* method"[12] (emphasis added). Of note is that a major, American, Fundamental theologian, Warfield, rejoiced that textual criticism now furnished a *really scientific method* for determining the text of the New Testament.

Yet, discerning Christians should immediately put up their antenna at such a comment. Do we need "science" and "scientists" to determine the Word of God? Moreover, as this volume will develop, much of the "science" of modern text criticism is in reality "science falsely so called."[13] Nevertheless, in the *modern* critical text position, the text scientist (i.e., the textual critic) becomes a *de facto* judge over the Word of God. Though this is often denied, the reality of what they say and do suggests otherwise. The considered judgment of the text critics becomes the criteria for determining what should be (or should not be) included in the New Testament. This should be particularly troubling for a Fundamentalist Christian when the lineage of the critical text becomes known.

The Alexandrian Textual Family

Returning to the matter of the thousands of extant (existing) manuscripts, it is important to understand that there are two distinct

---

[12] Benjamin Warfield, *Presbyterian Review* 3 (1882): 355; quoted in Theodore P. Letis, *The Ecclesiastical Text* (Philadelphia: Institute for Renaissance & Reformation Biblical Studies, 1997), 17.

[13] See 1 Tim. 6:20.

lineages of Greek texts of the New Testament.[14] These are what are generally known as (1) the "Received Text" family and (2) the "Alexandrian text" family.[15] The Received Text is whence the King James Version has been translated. The Alexandrian text forms the lion's share of the critical text whence almost all modern translations derive. In the Alexandrian family of Greek texts, two specific manuscripts are the major portion. One is known as Codex Sinaiticus, the other as Codex Vaticanus. (The word *codex* is a Latin term and means a bound volume such as a modern book. This is in distinction to a scroll.)

Codex Sinaiticus, as might be imagined, was found in St. Catherine's Greek Orthodox monastery at Mount Sinai. This Alexandrian manuscript had been in a waste basket ready to be burned by the local monks. Constantine von Tischendorf "discovered" this ancient manuscript there in 1844. It was determined to be about 1,500 years old and he thought it was the oldest extant (existing) manuscript ever found. It also came to be know by the Hebrew letter א—pronounced as *aleph*, the first character of the Hebrew alphabet.

Codex Vaticanus refers to an ancient manuscript kept in the Vatican library. Though it certainly was known to the Roman Catholic hierarchy and had been general knowledge during the Reformation, it had fallen out of memory to modern textual critics until the middle of the nineteenth century. As Tischendorf traveled the Mediterranean world searching for ancient manuscripts, he learned of this ancient manuscript as well. Vatican records show that Vaticanus had been in the possession of its library at least since A.D. 1475, when the first catalogue of the

---

[14]Some textual experts suggest that there are three or possibly four textual families. However, there is no question that the two primary textual groupings are the Received-Text family and the Alexandrian family. Some have suggested there is a "Western" text type, though it is minor and obscure. Moreover, no major translations have been based thereon. A fourth textual type, the "Caesarean," has been alleged, but has never been proved to exist. For all practical purposes, there remain two major textual types—the Received Text family and the Alexandrian text family.

[15]There are several other synonyms for these two groups. These will be addressed in the next chapter.

Vatican library was made.[16] This ancient Alexandrian manuscript was judged by Tischendorf to have been copied in the middle of the fourth century (about A.D. 350). It thus was one of the oldest and possibly the oldest manuscript of the New Testament at that time. This manuscript came also to be known simply as *B*. Thus, Aleph and B became the primary sources of the critical text soon to be created. Several scholars have determined that 99 percent of the critical text is comprised of B and Aleph.[17] Moreover, manuscript B (Vaticanus) occupies the majority of that 99 percent. Hence, these two Alexandrian manuscripts form the essence of the modern critical text.[18]

Sinaiticus and Vaticanus

Let us pause briefly and preview the sources of these two prominent manuscripts. They are noteworthy. There is little question by any textual critic that Sinaiticus and Vaticanus were produced in Alexandria, Egypt. This famous city has special significance for early church history because there originally was a large colony of Jews which had settled there. It also was a major center of Greek and Platonic philosophy in the Roman world. From this center of Greek philosophy, major heresies such as Gnosticism developed. It was also from Alexandria, Egypt, that the heresy of Arianism sprang. A key element of Arianism was a denial

---

[16] Edward F. Hills, *The King James Version Defended* (Des Moines: Christian Research Press, 1956), 116.

[17] D. A. Waite, telephone interview by author, October 1999.

[18] "It is common today to read that a given modern translation (see the preface of the NIV) or Greek text is based upon an 'eclectic' text. This is to give the impression that the 'best readings' from many sources were used including the TR. This must be exposed as being totally misleading. When the critical text was first produced by Westcott and Hort, so also today the primary pillar is B and it is only departed from with great reluctance." Jack Moorman, *Forever Settled: A Survey of the Documents and History of the Bible* (Johannesburg, South Africa: privately printed, 1985; reprint, Collingswood, N.J.: Bible for Today, 1997), 84 (page citations are to the reprint edition).

of the Deity of Christ. To that extent, the Arians were similar to the modern Jehovah's Witnesses.

An early church leader born and raised in Alexandria was Origen. His impact was greatest in the first half of the third century. Though brilliant and influential, Origen has been accused of having a great corrupting influence on both the early church and the New Testament itself. It was Origen who first taught that infants were to be baptized for the forgiveness of sins. He fostered numerous other heretical teachings which will be documented in a later chapter. Origen has also been called the father of Arianism.[19]

Another key name in early church history was Eusebius, who lived from A.D. 265 to 340. He is renowned as the father of church history because of his ten-volume work *Ecclesiastical History*. He too lived and labored in Alexandria, Egypt. Eusebius was a disciple of Origen who vigorously taught and defended his predecessor's position.[20]

So what does all of this have to do with the critical text? Constantine the Great commissioned Eusebius to produce a version of the Bible based upon Origen's manuscripts. Because the quality of materials and the professional character of the work of the scribes who produced it, Vaticanus is thought by some to have been one of the manuscripts produced for Constantine at Alexandria. Though there is not definitive proof of this, the original quality of the materials and the professional style of copying suggest this.

Therefore, the central pillar of the critical text (B) very well may have been produced by Eusebius, whose theology was built upon that of Origen. His work likely was for the apostate Constantine the Great. In any event, both Vaticanus (B) and Sinaiticus (Aleph) were produced at Alexandria, Egypt, at the time when the apostasy of Eusebius and Origen was the prevailing philosophical culture of the religious academia of the city. Thus, the conclusion can be drawn that the two main pillars of the critical text had their origins in the midst of an apostate

---

[19]Ibid., 68.

[20]Ibid., 69.

religious center. That should hold significance for modern Fundamentalists.

Modern textual critics have therefore labored to reconstruct, by *scientific* means, what they think was the original New Testament text.[21] They, by consensus, have sought to collate the numerous extant Greek manuscripts of the New Testament to that end. Notwithstanding that there are more than 5,500 fragments of New Testament manuscripts, the modern critical text uses only about one percent of that total.[22] (B is the primary content seasoned liberally with Aleph. About fifty other manuscripts are sprinkled into this eclectic mix.) Because of that, the modern critical text is actually a synthesis of about fifty manuscripts. Its proponents therefore refer to it as an "eclectic" text.[23] Curiously, though the vast majority (99 percent) of extant (existing) manuscripts support the Received Text, they are set aside and discounted as not having significant textual value.[24]

Westcott and Hort

In the last half of the nineteenth century, two British scholars and textual critics by the names of B. F. Westcott and F. J. A. Hort eagerly set out to produce a new Greek text of the New Testament. Their work would be based almost entirely upon Vaticanus (B) and Sinaiticus

---

[21] Those who have produced the two published Majority Texts of the latter portion of the twentieth century have followed the same rationalistic procedures.

[22] Chapter 7 will provide further data and documentation for this figure.

[23] Webster's dictionary defines *eclectic* as follows: "Containing, or made up of what is chosen or selected."

[24] The ostensible rationale for ignoring 99 percent of the evidence is that (1) extant MSS of the Received Text are of a later date than the Alexandrian texts. Also (2) text critics note that since most MSS supporting the Received Text have such similarity, they must have had a common source. Rather than seeing this as an evidence of preservation of the Received Text, the critics altogether reject these MSS as evidence.

(Aleph), with Vaticanus being their predominant source. From the extensive work of these two textual critics came the popularization of the modern critical text. Their work was completed in England in 1881. However, these two textual "scientists" were in fact apostates. Some recent Fundamentalists in America have vociferously denied that. Nevertheless, there is definitive evidence to document their liberal theology. In chapters 6 and 9 of this volume, documentation of these allegations will be made. However, Westcott and Hort never once announced a belief in the verbal inspiration of the Scriptures in their voluminous writings. As subtle Liberals of the day, they used theological terminology which sounded orthodox. However, the private correspondence and ancillary writings of these men will document them as classical, theological Modernists. As will be shown later, Westcott and Hort did not believe in verbal inspiration or inerrancy. They did not believe in a *physical* resurrection of Jesus Christ. Neither did they believe in the *substitutionary* atonement of Jesus Christ. This apostasy and other examples of their Liberalism will be addressed in later chapters. However, it is from these two that the fountainhead of the modern critical text has sprung.

Twentieth Century Critics

When crossing the divide into the twentieth century, those who continued work on the critical text were by no means Fundamentalists either. Such text critics as Kurt Aland, Eberhard Nestle, and Bruce Metzger were all theological Liberals in one degree or another. Furthermore, Carlo Martini, who also was one of the primary editors of the United Bible Societies' Greek text, is a Roman Catholic cardinal! As will be documented later, the United Bible Societies organization has been connected with apostasy, cooperation with the Vatican, and the World Council of Churches from its beginning in 1946. The UBS is the primary publisher of the critical text of the Greek New Testament today. From that critical text comes most modern translations.

The critical text as a popular entity has existed for only about 130 years. From its inception, it has been a synthetic text created by collating together numerous and often disparate Greek manuscripts. It certainly is not the text of the New Testament used by the church of Jesus Christ prior to the twentieth century. Tyndale, Luther, Calvin, and Knox did not use it. The critical text differs from the traditional, historic Received Text in numerous places. Many entire verses have been deleted and there are hundreds of words which have been added or deleted. Proponents of the critical text deny that any doctrine has been eliminated by it. However, what they do not say is that significant doctrinal passages of the New Testament have been *eroded* or *diluted* in the critical text. Perhaps the worst of these is the diminution of the person of Jesus Christ.

Often overlooked by its proponents is taking the concept of the critical text to its logical conclusion. Therefore, consider this. If the critical text represents the superior and true text of the New Testament, then God allowed most of it to be hidden in the Vatican library and a Greek Orthodox monastery for approximately 1,500 years. If that is the case, the Bible used by all the reformers and great Christian leaders prior to about A.D. 1900 was an inferior text. Moreover, God used theological Liberals and apostates in the nineteenth and twentieth centuries to cobble together the true text.

Most Fundamentalists who support the critical text position never think through the logical conclusions of their own position. The reason likely is that for many of them, they are unaware of the apostasy connected with the critical text from its inception to its present stage of evolution.[25] It undoubtedly will change again in the twenty-first century. Notwithstanding, most Fundamental institutions of higher learning steadfastly support the critical text view.

---

[25]The word *evolution* is used by design. The simple truth is that the critical text continues to evolve. The UBS text is presently in its fourth edition, which means that it has changed four times in the fifty-plus years the UBS has existed. Moreover, the Nestle-Aland text, a similar alternative text created by textual critics Eberhard Nestle and Kurt Aland, is in its 27th edition.

The Preserved Text Position

Between the two widely disparate views summarized thus far (the relatively recent King James only position and the naturalistic critical text position) lies a third view. This may be best described as the preserved text position (also known as the Received Text position). This view simply holds that God has providentially preserved His Word through the traditional Received Text. Moreover, this text is that which has been used by virtually all orthodox, Bible-believing churches from the second century to the present. Ninety-nine percent of all extant (existing) New Testament Greek manuscripts support the Received Text.[26] This is *prima facie* evidence that God has preserved His Word in this lineage.

Preservation through Believing Churches

The considered judgment of this writer is that God has providentially preserved the New Testament through *believing* churches down through the centuries. As this volume will document, believing churches as early as the second century used and translated the traditional Received Text into their vernacular.[27] This will be documented for Syrian churches using the Peshitta translation and pre-Waldensian churches using the Itala translation. Also, believing European churches used the Gothic translation in the early fourth century. This was based upon the traditional Received Text and assumed its long use for its translational base. All of these early translations of the New Testament in the early pre-Catholic era of church history follow the distinctive readings of the traditional Received Text rather than the Alexandrian texts.

---

[26]D. A. Waite, *Defending the King James Bible* (Collingswood, N. J.: Bible for Today, 1992), 41.

[27]Frederick Henry Scrivener, *A Plain Introduction to the Criticism of the New Testament*, 2d ed. (Cambridge, England: Deighton, Bell, & Co., 1874), 2:43.

Moreover, the Waldensians in particular existed as distinct, separatist churches in southern Europe prior to and through the Reformation.[28] They continued to use their own translations of the New Testament (linked to the second century) even at the time of the Reformation.[29] More evidence will be developed regarding this in appendix E.

Preservation through the Received Text

In any event, the New Testament of the King James Bible was translated from the traditional Received Text. This text is commonly called "received" because up until about 120 years ago, it was received by *all* orthodox, Bible-believing churches of whatever variety they might have been. Desiderius Erasmus first published the Received Text in 1516. In his lifetime, he continued to refine and edit his work, producing five editions thereof. Frenchman Robert Estiennes (sometimes called Stephanus in Latin or, Stephens in English) continued Erasmus's work in refining and editing the publishing of the Received Text in Paris, France. He published four editions thereof in the mid-sixteenth century. Theodore Beza then continued the work with his fifth edition being published in 1598. In 1633, the Elzivir brothers of Leiden, Holland, published their second edition of the Greek New Testament. In the preface of it, they made this comment in Latin, "*textum . . . ab omnibus receptum,*" which translates into English as "text . . . now received by all."[30] That has come to be shortened to *textus receptus* which in Latin simply means "the Received Text." As a proper name,

---

[28]Emilio Comba, *History of the Waldenses of Italy from Their Origin to the Reformation*, trans. Teofilo E. Comba (London: Truslove & Shirley, 1889), 188.

[29]William Stephen Gilly, *Waldensian Researches during a Second Visit to the Vaudois of Piemont* (London: C. J. G. & F. Rivington, 1831), 8.

[30]The full context of that phrase was, "You have therefore the text now received by all in which we give nothing changed or corrupt." Hills, *King James Version Defended*, 208.

the "Textus Receptus" (TR) therefore has come to be a general synonym for the Received Text. The King James Version is the direct descendant of this and is by far the best English translation thereof.

It is ironic and unfortunate that most proponents of the critical text position ignore the preserved text position (a.k.a., the Received Text position). More often than not, they lump the preserved text position in with the King James only position. In some cases this is out of ignorance. In other cases, it seems to be done with malice. Notwithstanding, the preserved text position is frequently equated with the King James only position because it is so much easier to attack the latter. It seems that some therefore, in effect, create a red herring by combining both positions. They then construct a straw man, assuming the preserved text position to be part of the King James only position, and commence to demolish it from their false premise. However, what is invariably presented is an attack on the King James only position.

The following chapters will present greater detail and documentation of both the critical text position as well as the preserved text position. Thus far, the case has been presented in summary fashion.

Review Questions for Further Study

1. What are the three major positions in the textual debate?

2. Is the King James Version as a *translation* inspired?

3. What are the original manuscripts of the Bible called?

4. What is the conventional abbreviation for the word "manuscripts?"

5. What two basic types of variations are found in some manuscripts?

6. What is the basic premise of the critical text position?

7. In the matter of Greek manuscripts, what are the two major families?

The Three Major Positions

8. In the Alexandrian family of manuscripts, what are the two major manuscripts?

9. What percentage of existing Manuscripts today are used in the critical text?

10. What is the essence of the preserved text position?

11. What does the Latin term *Textus Receptus* mean?

12. From what textual family is the King James Version translated?

CHAPTER THREE

BASIC TERMINOLOGY OF THE TEXTUAL DEBATE

In presenting the first two chapters of this book, we have endeavored to either avoid technical terminology or briefly define it in passing. Though the purpose of this book is not to deal with the subject matter on a technical level, there is a certain amount of basic terminology which will appear. Furthermore, most literature on the subject will use these terms regularly. The purpose of this brief chapter therefore is to categorize this basic terminology. We will also define each expression and point out how that many of these terms are more or less synonymous with each other. Authors often will use some of these terms interchangeably, which, if there is not some point of reference, makes the situation all the more confusing for the reader. Thus, in this chapter, care will be taken to explain a little more about some of the basic terms used in the textual debate.

Manuscript Terms

As mentioned in an earlier chapter, all scriptural documents were originally written by hand. Hence, they are called **manuscripts**. The basic abbreviation for manuscripts, when plural in number, is the three letters *MSS*. The abbreviation for manuscript, when singular in number, is *MS*. However, more often than not the plural abbreviation *mss* is used.

The **original manuscript** (MS) of a given book of the Bible is called an **autograph**. The sum total of the original manuscripts of the Bible are sometimes referred to as the **autographa**. The latter is essentially a hypothetical term because there probably was never a time when all the original manuscripts (autographs) were ever collected together in one place and at one time. But the term does appear occasionally. A related term which occasionally crops up is the word ***apograph***. As mentioned earlier, this refers to a copy of an original manuscript. Thus, because there are no longer autographs in existence, all the manuscripts which are known to exist are actually apographs.

Here and elsewhere, you will often come across the word ***extant***. That is an academic word which simply means "existing." Thus, you will read from time to time of **extant** manuscripts. It simply means existing manuscripts. Another term mentioned earlier is the word ***codex***. This is a Latin word and refers to a document which is bound to the left as one views the document from the front. It essentially refers to a book as we think of it in modern terms. In distinction, most Old Testament manuscripts were in the form of scrolls and some New Testament manuscripts were also produced in this fashion. However, as time passed, documents began to be bound in book fashion. That term is *codex* (the plural of codex is codices). A number of significant manuscripts in the textual debate have this designation such as Codex Vaticanus, Codex Alexandrinus, and others.

Another term found in the history of the New Testament is ***lectionaries***. These are technically not Bible manuscripts. However, they are of value because they do contain significant quotations of Scripture. Lectionaries were used especially in the Greek Orthodox Church as service books. Like some modern hymn books with Bible readings in the back, lectionaries were books which among other things had extensive readings from the Bible. Almost all lectionaries support the Received Text.

Manuscript Types

We touch upon this section simply because one particular type of manuscript material is routinely referred to by its type (papyri). Paper as we know it today was unknown in ancient times, at least in the Mediterranean world of biblical times. Thus, materials for writing were completely different from those to which we are accustomed today. The pre-dominant material for writing through biblical times was called

parchment. Parchments were animal skins which had been stretched, dried, and appropriately cured. The animal skin of choice was often that of a calf. The term appears once in the Bible in 2 Tim. 4:13 wherein the Apostle Paul instructed Timothy, "The cloke that I left at Troas with Carpus, when thou comest, bring *with thee*, and the books, *but* especially the parchments." The word translated as "parchment" (μεμβρανα) is pronounced as "membrana" in English and is whence the word *membrane* derives.[1] This was the most typical type of writing material used in New Testament manuscripts. The word *vellum* is occasionally used to refer to parchments of a particularly high grade.

However, a term which is used frequently, particularly by those of the critical text position, is that of *papyri*. As mentioned briefly earlier, papyri was a type of writing material which was created from the pith of papyrus plants. The papyrus plant grew extensively along the Nile River in Egypt. Of interest is that baby Moses was hidden amongst "bulrushes" along the Nile River. The Hebrew word for such is גמא and is pronounced as "gomeh."[2] This is the Hebrew word for *papyrus*.

By New Testament times, Egyptian artisans had devised a means of extracting the pith of the papyrus plant in long strips. Quantities of these were then woven together and smoothed into a material which roughly resembled paper. This was called papyri and was more economical than parchment. However, papyri was not as durable as parchment. Nevertheless, because of its relative abundance in Egypt, papyri was used as a material there for writing or copying documents. A significant quantity of New Testament manuscripts have been copied onto papyrus. Accordingly, these are referred to as "the papyri." The abbreviation for papyri is simply the letter *p*. Usually, there is some sort of superscript number appended to this abbreviation. This is a means devised by text critics to keep track of the various extant papyri manuscripts. Because of the paper-like character of papyri manuscripts, most have not passed the test of time. Moreover, it is only because of the hot

---

[1]*Thayer's Greek-English Lexicon of the New Testament* (1969), s.v. "μεμβρανα."

[2]*Gesenius's Hebrew-Chaldee Lexicon of the Old Testament* (1967), s.v. "גמא."

and dry climate of Egypt that any have survived at all. Most of these are quite fragmentary in nature. Some papyri support the Received Text, while others are related to the Alexandrian text. The latter only stands to reason because of the geography involved. However, because some papyri manuscripts support the critical text position, those of that persuasion make a great deal of comment about them.

Manuscript Lettering

As one reads literature about the textual debate, he will come across terms such as *uncials* and *minuscules* among others. We have not used these terms in this book and with few exceptions will not. However, they are standard vocabulary used by textual historians. The word *uncials* simply refers to writing in all upper-case letters. (An example of this is as follows: THIS IS UNCIAL TYPE OF LETTERING.) This was the preferred form for official documents in the first millennium after Christ. Almost all manuscripts which are written in uncial letters are upon parchment. Another term which is essentially synonymous with *uncial* is *majuscule*. The latter likewise refers to manuscripts written in capital letters.

At about the beginning of the second millennium, scribes began to copy manuscripts with "minuscule" lettering. This simply refers to lower-case letters. This usually was in a "cursive" or connected "script" style of writing. The advantage of using minuscule lettering was that it took up less space. Moreover, scribes could write them much faster than the larger and more formal uncials. Thus, from the ninth century on, minuscules gained popularity amongst scribes and came to be used exclusively by the beginning of the second millennium. Most extant manuscripts of the Received-Text family have been copied using minuscule lettering.

Terms Related to the Received Text

As one reads the literature regarding the textual and translational debate of the Bible, it will be helpful to understand that there are a number of terms which are either synonymous with each other or are closely related. Authors sometimes use these terms interchangeably. In other cases, an author with a bias for or against one position or the other will use certain terms predominately. Human nature is such that terms which carry some sort of pejorative connotation are often used to describe an opponent's position. This is undoubtedly true for proponents of both the critical text position as well as the preserved text position.

Let us here, however, consider some for the basic terms which are more or less synonymous with the preserved text. Perhaps the most common term of this position is that of the **Received Text**. More will be said about this in a later chapter; however, it essentially has the following idea. Down through the centuries, the text which was received or accepted by most all groups came to be known as the "Received Text." The Latin form of that is *textus receptus*. After the mid-seventeenth century, the term *textus receptus* came to be capitalized as the proper title of the published or printed Greek text (in distinction to older manuscripts or scrolls). Though there is a slight distinction between the terms *Received Text* and *Textus Receptus*, for all practical purposes, they are essentially synonymous. The abbreviation for Textus Receptus is *TR*. Accordingly, the Received Text is referred to as "the TR" in some circles.

There are other terms which are generally synonymous to the term *Received Text*. Some prefer to use the term ***traditional text***. This again is essentially a synonym. However, it conveys (and properly so) the idea that the Received Text has been the text which traditionally has been the Greek text used by virtually all Bible-believing groups until the past century. Therefore, some have also used the term ***the historic text*** in referring to the Received Text. It certainly has been the text which was used up until the end of the nineteenth century.

A term which is at times used to refer to the Received Text by some not particularly sympathetic to it is the ***Byzantine Text***. This stems from the fact that many of the extant manuscripts of the Received Text were copied in the region of Byzantium (Constantinople), Greece. Because the Greek Orthodox Church through the ages has used Greek as its primary language, they never had any need to translate the New Testament. However, they have always used a text which supports the Received Text. Thus, the term *Byzantine* generally refers to the Greek Orthodox Church because of its headquarters in Constantinople (Byzantium). Those who use this term often do so as essentially a pejorative term.[3]

Some prefer to refer to the Received Text as the **Ecclesiastical Text**. The word *ecclesiastical* usually implies the institutional church. Therefore, those who have a "Protestant" perspective and draw their traditions from the Reformation may refer to the Received Text as such. Theodore Letis is one such example.[4]

Another term generally synonymous with the Received Text is that of the **majority text**. This is because the vast majority of extant manuscripts support the Received Text. This sometimes is cause for confusion because there are two modern published texts called *The Majority Text*. One is edited by textual editors Arthur Farstad and Zane Hodges. The other is edited by Maurice Robinson and William Pierpont. These Greek text is similar to the Received Text, but is somewhat more eclectic than the traditional Textus Receptus.[5] It however is not

---

[3]W. Edward Glenny, "Defining the Terms," in *The Bible Version Debate*, ed. Michael Grisanti, (Minneapolis: Central Baptist Theological Seminary, 1997), 41.

[4]Theodore Letis, *The Ecclesiastical Text* (Philadelphia: Institute for Renaissance & Reformation Biblical Studies, 1997).

[5]As noted earlier, the Majority Text of both Farstad and Hodges as well as that of Robinson and Pierpont were developed following the same rationalistic philosophy as that of the critical text. In each case, the presumption is that the text of the New Testament has been lost and therefore must be found by *scientific* means. Many of the same rationalistic norms and principles of textual criticism used to develop the critical text have been used to produce the two above-mentioned editions of the Majority Text.

widely used nor are any significant translations based upon it. This text is essentially known only in academic circles.[6]

Needless to say, the Received Text is also coming to be called the **Preserved Text**. There is both scriptural as well as historic evidence that God has preserved His Word. All of the evidence of the preservation of the text points to the Preserved Text. This proposition will be more fully developed in the coming chapters.

Therefore, the Received Text is also known as the Textus Receptus, the traditional text, the historic text, the Byzantine Text, the Ecclesiastical Text, the majority text, and the preserved text.[7] They all are essentially the same thing though some of the terms may have a prejudicial bias for or against the Received Text. In this book, for the most part, we will use the terms *Received Text* or *Preserved Text*.

Terms Related to the Critical Text

Even as there are synonyms for the Received Text, there are also several for the modern text which is still evolving through textual criticism. The most common name for this text is simply the **critical text** because it has been (and continues to be) reconstructed by text critics. Because the critical text is a blend of numerous and at times disparate text types, it is sometimes referred to as the **eclectic text**. The latter thought once again simply refers to a synthesis of several constituent parts. The critical text is based primarily upon Alexandrian text types in Codices Vaticanus and Sinaiticus.[8] However, there are a few

---

[6] The preface to the New King James Version notes that Majority Text readings were consulted in some cases.

[7] Several other more arcane and technical synonyms of the Received Text are the Syrian text, the Antiochan text, the common text, and the *koine* text. However, use of these terms is confined to largely academic circles.

[8] The Alexandrian text type will be described in some detail in chapters 4 and 6 of this book.

Basic Terminology of the Textual Debate

Received Text readings interjected here and there. There also are included a few obscure Western text readings as well.[9] Thus, the critical text is a synthesis of all of these and therefore "eclectic." As noted in an earlier chapter, the primary pillars of the critical text are the Codices **Vaticanus** and **Sinaiticus**. These are also called **B** and **א (aleph)** respectively.[10]

On occasion in this volume, this writer will use the term *modern* or even *modernist* in reference to the critical text. The term *modern* is accurate in that the critical text has primarily existed only since the end of the nineteenth century. Also, the term *modernist* is accurate as well. Almost all of the major editors and text critics involved in the production of the modern critical text have been theological Modernists (Liberals).[11] Thus, as the reader comes across the terms *critical text, eclectic text*, or *modern text*; he should be aware that they are all more or less synonymous. Also, the terms *Vaticanus, Sinaiticus, B,* or *Aleph* are also directly related to the modern critical text.

Review Questions for Further Study

1. What is the basic abbreviation for the term *manuscript*?

2. What does the word *apograph* mean?

---

[9] This is another textual type found largely only in technical literature pertaining to modern textual criticism. The term *western* refers to manuscripts which relate to the western or Roman Church in distinction to Byzantine or eastern manuscripts.

[10] The terms *Vaticanus* and *Sinaiticus* will be discussed more fully in chapters 4, 6, and 9 of this book. However, Vaticanus simply refers to the famous manuscript found in the Vatican library and Sinaiticus refers to the famous manuscript found in a monastery at the foot of Mount Sinai. *Aleph* is the first letter of the Hebrew alphabet and was used as a symbol or abbreviation for Codex Sinaiticus. B likewise was a symbol and abbreviation for Codex Vaticanus.

[11] Documentation of this will take place in chapters 6 and 9 of this book.

3. What does the word *codex* mean?

4. What are the two basic types of manuscript writing materials?

5. What are some basic synonyms for the Received Text?

6. What are some basic synonyms for the critical text?

CHAPTER FOUR

THE DOUBLE STREAM OF BIBLICAL TEXTS

The Double Stream

As the greater perspective of the Bible translation debate has unfolded, it is apparent that there is a double stream of thought throughout. Though there are scores of different Bible translations, there are primarily only *two types*. As we have already briefly discussed, there are essentially *two major textual bases*. As we will soon see, there are *two distinct philosophies* undergirding these two textual bases. Finally, there are *two distinct types of textual criticism* which have caused the division between the two textual bases.

The Received Text	The Critical Text
1. Based in belief of Providential Preservation	1. Based in scientific reconstruction of the text
2. Guided by usage of believing churches	2. Guided by the philosophy of rationalism
3. Major translation: the King James Version	3. Most modern translations (e.g., NIV, NASB, etc.)

This should not be surprising. Down through the ages there often has run a dichotomy of history. There always have been the people of God and the people of the world. There always have been truth and error. There always have been obedience to God as well as disobedience to Him. And, there have always been those who were willing to separate from apostasy and those who were not.

A similar dichotomy exists in the translational and textual controversy of this present day. One stream of Bibles has always been associated with belief and the other has largely been connected with apostasy. One textual base has been associated with persecuted martyrs and the other with institutional unbelief. One has an undergirding philosophy rooted in faith while the other is rooted in Rationalism. As this chapter will unveil, there are two distinct streams in the Bible translation controversy. Let us therefore look at (1) the two types of Bibles, (2) the two textual bases, (3) the two undergirding philosophies, and (4) the two types of textual criticism.

The Two Types of Bibles

As has already been touched upon in the preceding chapters, there are really only two *major* types of Bibles. Though there are hundreds of English translations of the New Testament and scores of translations of the entire Bible, they all essentially fall into one of two categories. There are those Bibles which are based upon the historic Received Text and those based upon the modern critical text. These are essentially the only two alternatives. Let us look more closely.

English Bibles Based upon the Received Text

There have been a number of English Bibles based upon the historic Received Text. William Tyndale produced his early English translation of the New Testament from the Received Text in 1525. It was the first modern English translation of the New Testament based upon the Greek New Testament. (Wycliffe's English translation of the Bible in 1382 was based upon the Latin Vulgate and therefore was a translation of a translation.) Tyndale died at the stake as a martyr for Jesus Christ for the crime of translating the Bible into English.

Other translations followed Tyndale's such as the Coverdale Bible completed in 1535. Though not having the linguistic credentials of Tyndale and actually only revising his work, Coverdale's translation was still related to the Received Text.[1] Following Coverdale, the Matthew Bible was released in England in 1537. Taking the pen name of Thomas Matthew, the actual editor and translator was John Rogers who had been an assistant to Tyndale. Again, this translation was based upon the Received Text. The Matthew Bible was followed by the Great Bible of 1539. The impetus behind this was again William Coverdale, who essentially updated printing errors of the Matthew Bible.

From Geneva, Switzerland, came a fresh English translation of the Bible in 1560 called the Geneva Bible. This Bible was translated under the influence of Theodore Beza and William Whittingham, brother-in-law of John Calvin. Again, this Bible was translated from the Received Text. It was the first English Bible to be printed with verse divisions. The Geneva Bible also contained marginal notes supporting the Puritan and dissident position against the Church of England. (The Geneva Bible was that which the Pilgrims brought to the New World when they landed at Plymouth Rock.)

However, because the marginal notes in the Geneva Bible were critical of the Church of England, the Bishops' Bible was produced in 1568 with the blessing of both the Church of England as well as the Crown. Though this Bible for a short time was the official "authorized version" of the Church of England, it remained largely the domain of the church leadership. Most lay people still used the Geneva Bible. Once again, the Bishops' Bible was translated from the Received Text.[2]

---

[1]The Coverdale Bible was also essentially a translation of a translation using the Latin Vulgate, Luther's German Bible, and Zwingli's Zurich Bible as additional resources.

[2]Those who advance the critical text position will quickly reply that the Received Text was all these early translators knew. They will claim that neither Sinaiticus nor Vaticanus had been as yet discovered. However, Erasmus and the Reformers in Switzerland were very much aware of Vaticanus and categorically rejected it as having any virtue. Documentation for this will be provided in a later chapter when this will be dealt

These Bible translations were all produced prior to the seventeenth century.[3] With the exception of Wycliffe's translation and the Catholic Douay Version, all of these Bibles were translated (or revised) from the traditional, historic Received Text.

However, the Bible translation which has endured for almost four hundred years is the Authorized King James Version. It quickly rose head and shoulders above the Bishops' Bible and the popular Geneva Bible. Though it has gone through a number of revisions to update spelling, punctuation, and other publishing errata, it held virtual monopoly status in the English-speaking world for three hundred years. And, notwithstanding the explosion of Bibles from the critical text in the last one hundred years, the venerable King James Bible remains one of the most popular Bibles in the English-speaking world today. It was translated from the Received Text.

The next chapter will document that Bibles used by other Bible-believing peoples elsewhere in the world prior to the heyday of English translations also used the Received Text as their textual base. These include the early Syrian church whose roots can be traced directly to the church at Antioch in Syria which also was the home church of the Apostle Paul.

---

with more extensively.

Furthermore, Reformation-era textual editor Theodore Beza never even used his own famous early-dated manuscripts known generally as Bezae (D) in his preparation of Greek editions of the Textus Receptus. He rejected them because they did not follow the received, Traditional Text. See Kurt and Barbara Aland, *The Text of the New Testament: An Introduction to the Critical Editions to the Theory and Practice of Modern Textual Criticism,* 2d ed. (Grand Rapids: W. B. Eerdmans, 1989), 128.

[3]The Rheims-Douay Version was an English translation produced in France in 1582. However, it was an effort by the Jesuits to place an official Catholic Bible into England.

Waldensian Bibles

The Waldenses of northern Italy, southern France, and Switzerland used translations of the Bible based upon the Received Text from the second century up to and including the time of the Reformation. The Waldenses were Bible-believing peoples who were separatists and in many ways similar to modern separatist Baptists.[4] The Bible they originally used, the Itala (or sometimes called the Italic), was translated from the Received Text.[5] Moreover, there were many Waldenses over the centuries who were martyred by Rome for their biblical and separatist position. Related groups in southern France as well as central Europe used translations of the Bible based upon the Received Text throughout the dark ages.

Modern Versions

Turning our focus to the contemporary scene is instructive. In this day, the Bible used *almost* exclusively by Fundamentalists is the Received-Text-based King James Version. (There also is a certain percentage of Fundamentalists who use modernist, critical-text-based translations.) Some of these Fundamentalists do not altogether understand the textual issue. However, their spiritual and separatist instincts cause them to shun these modern versions. As we shall soon see, there very well may be more to that aversion than just traditionalism or a that's-the-way-we-have-always-done-it type of conservatism.

---

[4]Because of the long history of the Waldenses, some over time became sacramental and suffered some of the same spiritual declension which seems to inevitably afflict all groups which originally were sound. However, there remains considerable evidence that the Waldensian movement in the main was orthodox and embodied the essence of regenerate New Testament Christianity.

[5]Frederick Nolan, *An Inquiry into the Integrity of the Greek Vulgate: or, Received Text of the New Testament* (London: F. C. & J. Rivington, 1815), xvii-xviii.

In contrast, the Bibles used by virtually all modern New-Evangelicals and Liberals are everything but the King James Version. That is interesting! Some using modern versions would claim that they simply are better educated and more open to change than narrow, old-fashioned Fundamentalists. However, there very well may be a connection between being a New Evangelical (or Liberal) and the type of Bible used. The connection may well go to the essence of New Evangelicalism's *new mood* of being relevant, up-to-date, and in step with modern culture.

Though Fundamentalists who use or promote the critical text may resent being associated with New Evangelicalism, the simple fact is that *almost* all New Evangelicals use critical-text-based translations such as the New International Version or the New American Standard Bible. In contrast, *almost* all Fundamentalists use the King James Bible publicly. They may favorably view the scientifically-reconstructed critical text, even using it for their own personal reference, but the Bible they use in the pulpit is the received-text-based King James Version. The reason may very well be that the Holy Spirit has *providentially* led them to do so. If there is a controversy regarding the true text of the New Testament (and there is), then it would only seem apparent that the Holy Spirit would lead His people into the truth thereof.[6] Regardless, the simple fact remains that *almost* all Fundamentalists use the King James Version in public and *almost* all New Evangelicals and Liberals use critical-text-based translations. That likely is not coincidental!

The Two Textual Bases

Though there are several other minor textual groups discussed by modern textual criticism, they are obscure. Outside of textual academia, they are unknown. For all intents and purposes, there are only two major textual groups from whence the New Testament is translated. At the

---

[6]John 16:13.

risk of being redundant, let us again note that those two major textual groups are the Alexandrian textual family and the traditional, Received Text family. The Alexandrian textual group is the predominant source of the modern critical text. The Received Text is that lineage of manuscripts which trace back to the earliest days of *believing*, orthodox Christianity. These are the overwhelming majority of existing Greek manuscripts of the New Testament. Moreover, the majority of the manuscripts of the Received Text are so virtually unanimous in their consistency that modern text critics have dismissed them as having a common source.[7] They do. His name is the Holy Spirit. One such critic states, "Even with their minor variations, the Byzantine manuscripts are a chorus of witnesses all singing the same song."[8] His conclusion therefore is that the vast number of almost identical manuscripts of the Received Text are to be treated as "essentially one witness."[9] Therefore, the thousands of manuscripts of the Received Text are reduced to the evidence of one (and incorrectly viewed as an inferior one at that) as far as proponents of the critical text are concerned.

The Alexandrian Textual Family

By way of contrast, the chief Alexandrian manuscripts (which make up the essence of the critical text) are disparate in their readings. There is no consistency. They at times contradict each other.[10] Vaticanus and

---

[7] Zane Hodges, "The Greek Text of the King James Version," in David Otis Fuller, ed., *Which Bible?* (Grand Rapids: Grand Rapids International Publications, 1970), 34.

[8] William H. Smallman, "Printed Greek Texts," in *From the Mind of God to the Mind of Man,* ed. James B. Williams (Greenville, S.C.: Ambassador—Emerald International, 1999), 174.

[9] Ibid.

[10] Jakob Van Bruggen, *The Ancient Text of the New Testament* (Winnipeg: Premiere Publishing, 1976), 31.

Sinaiticus alone show over three thousand variants between themselves in just the gospels alone.[11] Moreover, Tischendorf himself claimed that Aleph itself contains "15,000 changes made by contemporary or later hands."[12] There are wide differences between it and the Received Text. However, this is the stuff which makes the modern textual critic think the Alexandrian texts are superior. Such is the tortuous system of logic which defies common sense.

The modern critical text is essentially Alexandrian with the predominance of Vaticanus and Sinaiticus. However, in their attempt to reconstruct the New Testament text, modern textual criticism has in fact created a synthetic text. This accordingly is a text which has never before existed in history. Burgon noted this more than one-hundred years ago.[13] More recent analysts have made the same observation. For example, Harvard professor M. M. Parvis wrote in 1973, "When we reconstruct the 'original text,' we are not reconstructing but rather we are constructing something that never before existed in heaven and earth."[14] Moreover, J. K. Elliott, who certainly is not a Fundamentalist, made similar comment in 1988: "The recent printed editions of the Greek New Testament, which we can buy, give a text which never existed as a manuscript of the New Testament. They are all recon-

---

[11]Herman Hoskier, *Codex B and Its Allies: A Study and an Indictment* (London: Bernard Quaritch, 1914), vi.

[12]D. A. Waite, *Defending the King James Bible* (Collingswood, N.J.: Bible for Today, 1992), 59.

[13]John Burgon, *The Revision Revised* (original publisher unknown, 1883; reprint, Collingswood, N.J.: Dean Burgon Society, n.d.), 6.

[14]M. M. Parvis, "The Goals of New Testament Textual Studies," *Studia Evangelical* 6 (1973): 406; quoted in Theodore Letis, *The Ecclesiastical Text* (Philadelphia: Institute for Renaissance & Reformation Biblical Studies, 1997), 149.

structions based on their editor's choice of readings from manuscripts they had at their disposal, or which they elected to concentrate on."[15]

The Alexandrian Texts and Modern Translations

To complete this thought, let us mention one more time that *almost* all modern versions of the Bible are translated from the Alexandrian-based critical text. This book is being written at the beginning of the twenty-first century. Its author has been in the ministry as a Fundamental, independent Baptist for approximately thirty years at the time of this writing. It has been the experience of this writer that virtually all New-Evangelical or Liberal pulpits of which he is aware use anything but the King James Version. In the city of approximately 100,000 people in which this author lives, there is not a single New-Evangelical or Liberal church using the King James Version. Rather, they *all* use Bibles based upon the critical text. The same pattern holds true across the nation. This phenomenon is part of the uniform, insignia, and ensign of their movement. Lest one should doubt this, let him check out any church belonging to the National Association of Evangelicals or the National Council of Churches and see which type of Bible they use. Fundamentalists for the most part tend to use the King James Version based upon the historic Received Text. Robert Gromacki has noted that the King James Version is regarded as *the* text of Fundamentalism.[16] New Evangelicals and Liberals tend to use modern translations based upon the critical text (whose roots are the Alexandrian text).[17]

---

[15]J. K. Elliott, "The Original Text of the Greek New Testament," *Fax Theologica* 8 (1988), 6; quoted in Letis, *The Ecclesiastical Text*, 149.

[16]Robert Gromacki, *New Testament Survey* (Grand Rapids: Baker Book House, 1974), preface.

[17]Ironically, W. Edward Glenny, who formerly taught at the Fundamentalist Central Baptist Theological Seminary, is a strong proponent of the critical text. However, he has left that institution to teach at Northwestern College, a New-Evangelical institution.

Two Undergirding Philosophies

It should be clear by now that there must be a reason for such widely held views concerning Bible translations and the double stream of undergirding Greek texts. These differences can be categorized into two distinctly different undergirding philosophies. Briefly, those two philosophies can be summarized as follows. (1) The historic Received Textual position is based in belief. (2) The modern critical textual position is based in rationalism. Let us proceed to see if these assessments can be documented.

The Historic Received Textual Position Is Based in Belief

A foundational premise of the Received Text position is that God has providentially preserved His Word. Let us examine this assertion further.

Providential Preservation

The Received Text position begins with the premise that God has not only inspired His Word in its original writing, but that He has providentially preserved it. This is in clear distinction to the critical text position. Accordingly, some holding the latter view assert the Bible contains no indication that God has preserved His Word.[18]

Claims to the contrary notwithstanding, there indeed is Scripture clearly pointing to the preservation of God's Word. For example, Jesus said, "Heaven and earth shall pass away, but my words shall not pass away" (Matt. 24:35). Some allege that Jesus was simply foretelling that His words would be fulfilled.[19] That is to be sure. However, Jesus

---

[18]W. Edward Glenny, "The Preservation of Scripture," in *The Bible Version Debate*, *ed.* Michael Grisanti, (Minneapolis: Central Baptist Theological Seminary, 1997), 95.

[19]Ibid., 87.

clearly said that His *words* would not pass away. First, the context of the verse lends itself to this view. The heavens and earth indeed someday will pass away. See 2 Pet. 3:12-13. The earth in its present form will not last in perpetuity. However, in distinction to that, Jesus said that His words would. Second, the etymology of the word translated as "pass away" (παρερχομαι) is instructive. Thayer's *Greek-English Lexicon of the New Testament* lists a number of possible ways in which the word might be translated. One sense is to perish. Another is to go away.[20] Jesus in effect said that though the heavens and earth will perish, His words will not. Or to put it another way, though the heavens and earth will go away, His words will not. Common sense dictates that if the plain sense makes sense to seek no other sense. In the eschatological context of Matthew 24, verse 35 clearly bespeaks the preservation of the *words* of Christ.

The same critics object that these are His *spoken* words and not His *written* Word.[21] Thus implied is that though His spoken words may last forever, His written Word will not! However, what these selfsame critics seem to miss is that the Holy Spirit inspired the very word's of Jesus which He saw fit to record as Scripture. To infer that the written Word of God is anything less than eternal is inconceivable. The Psalmist wrote, "Concerning thy testimonies, I have known of old that thou hast founded them for ever" (Ps. 119:152). The word translated as founded (יסד pronounced as *yaw-sad'*) also has the sense of established.[22] David clearly implied that God's Word is established forever. Morever, the Holy Spirit inspired Him to write, "For ever, O LORD, thy word is settled in heaven" (Ps. 119:89). The word translated as settled (נצב pronounced as *naw-tsab'* in the Niphal stem) has the sense to be stationed,

---

[20]*Thayer's Greek-English Lexicon of the New Testament* (1969), s.v. "παρερχομαι."

[21]W. Edward Glenny, "The Preservation of Scripture," in *The Bible Version Debate*, ed. Michael Grisanti, 88.

[22]*Gesenius's Hebrew-Chaldee Lexicon of the Old Testament* (1967), s.v. "יסד."

or to stand.²³ God's Word has been stationed or will stand in heaven forever. If that does not imply preservation, what does? It is eternally preserved there. Is it too hard for God to preserve it here? Likewise, Ps.119:160 says, "Thy word *is* true *from* the beginning: and every one of thy righteous judgments *endureth* for ever." To be sure, the word *endureth* in the text was interpolated by the translators. But there clearly is an ellipsis in the text. (An ellipsis is a word left out by the original writer, but is clearly implied.) God's righteous judgments, without a doubt, is an eloquent synonym for His Word. David, under the inspiration of the Holy Spirit, wrote that it would continue forever. That is the doctrine of preservation!

Isa. 40:8 says, "The grass withereth, the flower fadeth: but the word of our God shall stand for ever." The word translated as "shall stand" (קוּם, pronounced as *koom*, qal stem) also has the sense to be established or to persist.²⁴ The prophet, in essence, wrote that God's Word will persist forever.

The psalmist also eloquently wrote, "He hath remembered his covenant for ever, the word *which* he commanded to a thousand generations" (Ps. 105:8). The context here is of the covenant which God made to Abraham. Yet, that is a part of the written Word of God. The inspired Psalmist described how that covenant will stand for a thousand generations. If we assume a generation to represent thirty years, thirty thousand years are then in view. That is considerably longer than recorded history. The likely thought rather is a metaphor referring to *forever*. Regardless, even though only a portion of God's Word is in direct view, are we to believe that the rest of it will not be preserved

---

²³Ibid., s.v. " נצב."

²⁴Ibid., s.v. "קוּם."

either? The Bible clearly teaches that God has promised to preserve His Word.[25]

Moreover, the fact that the Bible exists today is *prima facie* evidence that God has preserved it. History is replete with examples of attacks against the Bible down through the ages, yet it has stood the test of time. Roman emperors ordered Scripture to be burned and large quantities of Bibles were. Yet, it continued. The Roman Catholic hierarchy hid it away in its cloisters, yet it continued. Catholic authorities burned at the stake men who translated the Scripture into vernacular tongues, yet it continued. Most are aware of the anecdote told of Voltaire who sneered that the day was coming when the only place one could find a Bible would be in a museum. Yet, his home today houses a Bible society.[26] The Communists banned and burned untold numbers of Bibles. Yet, even in places such as the former Soviet Union, the Word of God abounds. There is no question that whether it is the Old Testament or the New Testament, God has preserved His Word.

Was that preservation miraculous? In some cases, perhaps so. However, it would rather seem that God has chosen to *providentially* preserve it. The word *providence* or *providentially* does not appear in the Bible in this context. Webster's dictionary defines it as "divine guidance or care."[27] Thus, the greater thought is that God, through His own guidance and protection, has preserved His Word through the ages. A basic tenet of the Christian life is that God providentially protects His people. He also providentially guides His people. And, He providentially reveals His will.

---

[25]Sadly and ironically, the faculty of Central Baptist Theological Seminary discount every one of these passages seeking in one way or another to explain them in some fashion other than that of the providential preservation of God's Word (Grisanti, ed., *The Bible Version Debate*, 87-92).

[26]Josh McDowell, *Evidence That Demands a Verdict* (San Bernadino, Calif.: Campus Crusade for Christ International, 1972), 22.

[27]*Webster's New Collegiate Dictionary* (1953), s.v. "providence."

Few devout Christians would deny that God providentially leads in important matters of His work. Most Fundamental brethren believe that God, for example, has providentially restored Israel to their land (if only partially). Most would agree that God has providentially raised up institutions of higher learning to train young men for the gospel ministry. Most missionaries believe that God has providentially guided them to their field of service. Moreover, while there, most of them believe that God has provided providential protection over them. Most men in the ministry today would agree that God in some way providentially called them into the ministry. The Bible surely teaches that God will provide providential guidance to us as we seek His face in prayer (see Prov. 3:5-6).

Therefore, is it unreasonable, much less unscriptural, to believe that God has providentially preserved His Word through the ages? After having inspired and inscripturated it, did He just cast it into the world and leave it to its own devices? I think not! If God will providentially guide and protect His people in their day-to-day lives, surely He has providentially protected and preserved His Word. That providential protection is usually not openly miraculous. Rather, it is discreetly supernatural. God likewise has worked behind the scenes to insure the accurate transmission and preservation of His Word.

When our Lord ascended back to heaven, He left three spiritual agencies in His physical absence. One is the local church of the New Testament. Another is the indwelling presence of His Holy Spirit. And, finally, He left the New Testament of His written Word. The Received Text position (also known as the preserved text position) *believes* that God has providentially preserved His Word to this hour. This is evident from both Scripture as well as history. In a coming section, we will touch upon how He has done so. However, suffice it to say at this point that God has providentially preserved His Word.

The Guidance of the Holy Spirit

In John 16:13, Jesus said, "Howbeit when he, the Spirit of truth, is come, he will guide you into all truth." Prior to our Lord's ascension, He promised His disciples that upon His departure, He would provide to them a greater ministry of the Holy Spirit. Notice that Jesus here described the Holy Spirit as the Spirit of *truth*. (Recall how that Jesus described His Word as *truth* in John 17:17.) Is it therefore unreasonable to believe that the Holy Spirit will guide His people to the truth of the right textual base for the Bible?

Moreover, that Spirit of truth will guide us into *all* truth. Several words bear a closer look. The word translated as guide (οδηγεω, pronounced as *hod-ayg-eh'-o*) can also have the sense to lead.[28] That in itself implies providential guidance of the Holy Spirit into questions of spiritual concern. Moreover, Jesus promised that the Spirit of truth would guide us into *all* truth. The word so translated as "all" (πας, pronounced as *pas*) also has the sense of "each" or "every."[29] The question of which New Testament text is correct surely is a matter of spiritual truth. It surely comes under the umbrella-promise of the Holy Spirit guiding us to a right understanding of "each and every" truth. Therefore, the promised guidance of the Holy Spirit must surely apply to the question of which biblical text is correct.

The Received Text position (also known as the preserved text position) also *believes* that God through the agency of the Holy Spirit has guided those searching for the true biblical text. Can we believe anything less? Has not our Lord promised that the Holy Spirit will guide us into *all* truth? Is there not a question here? Is there not the issue of truth involved? Indeed there is. Therefore, the Received Text position

---

[28]*Thayer's*, s.v. "οδηγεω."

[29]Ibid., s.v. "πας."

believes that the Spirit of God has and will guide His people in this regard.[30]

Preservation through the Church

The third element of the Received Text position is that the Holy Spirit has providentially worked through the believing church to preserve the true text of the New Testament. Some proponents of the critical text position will say that God *may* have preserved His Word, but He did not say *how* He would do so. To the contrary, the New Testament does provide insight into *how* God has promised to preserve His Word. Paul wrote to Timothy, "But if I tarry long, that thou mayest know how thou oughtest to behave thyself in the house of God, which is the church of the living God, the pillar and ground of the truth" (1 Tim. 3:15). The Apostle makes it clear that the church is both the foundation as well as the support of the truth.

The word translated as pillar (στυλος, pronounced as *stoo'-los*) refers to an architectural support such as a load-bearing column.[31] One illustration which comes to mind is that of a lighthouse. The structure of the light is that which upholds it and supports it. Is not this a careful illustration of the relationship of the church and the Word of God? The word translated as ground (εδραιωμα pronounced as *hed-rah'-yo-mah*)

---

[30] Some proponents of the critical text may claim that the Holy Spirit has led them as well. However, the actual working editors of the critical text are steeped in rationalistic philosophy and *scientific* reconstruction of the text. Their entire philosophical base is not inclined to such a Fundamentalist notion of seeking the leading of the Holy Spirit.

One writer of the critical text persuasion wrote, "One does not solve a problem of divergent textual readings by prayer or by the inner illumination of the Holy Spirit; but only by an extensive knowledge and skill in the science of textual criticism." See George Eldon Ladd, *The New Testament and Criticism*. (Grand Rapids: W. B. Eerdmans Publishing Co., 1967), 81.

[31] *Thayer's*, s.v. "στυλος."

refers to a foundation.[32] The church is therefore that pillar which supports the truth. The church of Jesus Christ is both the foundation as well as the pillar of support which holds forth the truth.

Jesus said in John 17:17, "thy word is truth." Therefore, truth as a concept certainly can be equated to the Word of God. Moreover, David wrote, "the judgments of the LORD *are* true . . . altogether" (Ps. 19:9). Can any disagree that the truth upheld by the church does not include the Word of God? It rather is the focal point thereof.

The church, like a lighthouse, shines forth the light of the Word of God upon a dark world. Lighthouses serve two purposes: (1) to warn of danger or (2) to point to safety. The local church does both through the preaching of the Word. It warns of the danger of hell ahead. It also points to the safety of heaven through our Lord Jesus Christ. The connection of the local church to the truth of the Word of God should be only too apparent.

However, there very well may be a deeper truth. That is, the church is the structure which God has ordained to uphold the truth of the Word of God down through the centuries. The view of this writer is that God has used *believing* churches down through the ages as the primary structure by which the New Testament has been preserved. That certainly was true in the first century. The same remains true today. And as we shall see, it has been the case through the course of history. Thus, the contention of this writer is that the church is the pillar and ground by which the truth of the Word of God has been preserved.

The Modern Critical Textual Position
Is Based in Rationalism

In distinction to the foundational premise of the Received Text, the critical text begins with altogether different premises. Let us therefore examine these more fully.

---

[32]Ibid., s.v. "εδραιωμα."

The Logic of the Critical Text

There are several strains of thought within the modern critical text position. Some are more conservative than others. However, the critical text position essentially follows this logic. (1) The original documents of the New Testament (the autographs) may or may not have been inspired and inerrant.[33] (2) Moreover, the autographa has been lost. (3) What exists today are conflicting copies (apographs) of those manuscripts, all of which have some degree of errors included therein. (4) Therefore, through textual criticism, the original text hopefully can be reconstructed by scientific means.[34]

Modern textual criticism accordingly has become the supreme court determining what is the Word of God and what is not. Little or no regard is paid to what the church has historically used, believed, and upheld as Scripture. Rather, the committees of modern textual critics issue their verdicts whether a given word, verse, or portions of a chapter should be a part of the Bible.[35] Truly, the collective judgments of text critics have determined the composition of the critical text of the New Testament. Modern text critics are the supreme court justices and none are Fundamental Baptists. Moreover, those of this position clearly teach that we must rely upon the findings of these text critics.[36]

As a related thought, Zane Hodges has summarized what (in his view) is the essence of the critical text position in relationship to the Received Text. (1) The oldest manuscripts do not support the Majority Text (i.e., the Received Text). (2) The Majority Text (i.e., the Received Text) is a revised, and hence secondary form of the Greek text. (3) The readings of the Majority Text (i.e., the Received Text) are repeatedly in-

---

[33]As will be documented in chapters 6 and 9, most of the major text critics of the past 275 years have either ignored inspiration and inerrancy or denied it altogether.

[34]Smallman, "Printed Greek Texts," in Williams, *From the Mind of God*, 171.

[35]Van Bruggen, *The Ancient Text*, 10.

[36]Minnick, "Let's Meet the Manuscripts," in Williams, *From the Mind of God*, 85.

ferior to those of the earlier manuscripts.[37] Hodges thus proceeds to show that each of these premises is false.[38]

The Rationalism of the Critical Text

As will be documented further in chapter 6, the foundation of modern textual criticism is rooted in rationalism. In 1915, James Orr writing about *textual criticism* said, "Higher criticism extends its operations into the *textual field*, endeavoring to get behind the text of the existing sources, and to show how this grew from simpler beginnings to what now is. Here, also, there is wide opening for arbitrariness.... *A chief cause of error in its application to the record of a supernatural revelation is the assumption that nothing supernatural can happen.* This is the vitiating element in much of the newer criticism"[39] (emphasis has been added).

Notice the perception of this author in 1915. To paraphrase the comment above in plain language, Orr said that *both* higher criticism (i.e., Rationalism) and modern textual criticism assume there is nothing supernatural about Scripture. He called this the vitiating (i.e., the corrupting) aspect of the new biblical criticism which includes modern textual criticism. In chapter 6, documentation will also be given showing that most of the major textual critics from Griesbach[40] to Westcott

---

[37]Zane C. Hodges, "The Greek Text of the King James Version" in Fuller, *Which Bible?* 27-34.

[38]Ibid., 25-38.

[39]James Orr, "Criticism of the Bible," *International Standard Bible Encyclopedia*, 1939 ed.

[40]Letis, *The Ecclesiastical Text*, 9.

and Hort[41] to Bruce Metzger[42] were trained in German Higher Rationalism.

The Subjectivity of the Critical Text

As the conclusions and methodology of *modern* textual criticism are studied, it becomes clear that the judgments of the text critics are often highly subjective. Here are comments of one strong advocate of the critical text: "A textual critic is initially little more than a reporter. He reports the wording of these variants. Following this initial reporting, a textual critic becomes an interpreter of this data. He interprets it by comparing the variants (called 'collation') in order to determine which, in his view, most likely reflect the wording of the original documents."[43]

Another author seeking to explain the principles of modern text criticism writes, "The most general rule is that reading is preferred which best explains the origin of the other(s)."[44] Without elaborating here, clearly implied in such textual decisions is the subjective judgment of the text critic. As early as 1882, N. M. Wheeler of Lawrence University challenged Benjamin Warfield's advocacy of textual reconstruction by text criticism. He asked, "Must we ask the critics every morning what is the latest conclusion in order to know what is that Scripture inspired of God?"[45] The well known English textual critics, Westcott and Hort, advanced a pretentious term called *conjectural emendation* in respect to text critics making judgment calls. In everyday language,

---

[41]D. A. Waite, *Heresies of Westcott and Hort* (Collingswood, N.J.: Bible for Today, 1998), 5.

[42]David Cloud, *Unholy Hands on God's Holy Word* (Oak Harbor, Wash.: Way of Life Literature, 1985), 31.

[43]Minnick, "Let's Meet the Manuscripts," in Williams, *From the Mind of God*, 71.

[44]Smallman, "Printed Greek Texts," in Williams, *From the Mind of God*, 174.

[45]Letis, *The Ecclesiastical Text*, 15.

it simply meant an educated guess.[46] The eminent Dutch scholar, Jakob Van Bruggen writes, "In modern textual criticism the eclectic method is generally followed: per *reading* a decision is made on the basis of a complicated structure of considerations. Subjectivity is not out of question with this method. Thus they will just have to arrive at a text by majority-vote."[47]

Let us paraphrase this translation from Dutch into simpler English. Van Bruggen essentially said that though modern textual critics use a complicated system of rules, in the final analysis, their decisions are subjective. That is, they base their decisions upon what *they* think. When a committee is involved in such decisions (as it often is), its decision is by simple majority vote. Therefore, there is not unanimity of opinion even within the ranks of text critics.

The Contradictions of the Critical Text

Not surprisingly, major text critics frequently contradict each other. Textual historian Jack Moorman comments that there is "hopeless confusion" in the myriad of textual variants in the critical text.[48] British text critics Westcott and Hort were the popular fountainhead of the modern critical text. However, though their work remains largely intact as the standard for the modern critical text, more recent text critics routinely differ with them. Kenneth W. Clark, a proponent of the critical text commented, "The textual history that the Westcott-Hort text represents is no longer tenable in the light of newer discoveries and fuller

---

[46]Ibid., 18-19.

[47]Van Bruggen, *The Ancient Text*, 11.

[48]Jack Moorman, ed., *Forever Settled: A Survey of the Documents and History of the Bible* (Johannesburg, South Africa: privately printed, 1985; reprint, Collingswood, N.J.: Bible for Today), 1997 (page citation is to the reprint edition), 56.

textual analysis."[49] Or, as Ernest Colwell, another a critical text proponent, said, "In the early years of this century Kirsopp Lake described Hort's work as a failure."[50] (Lake was also a proponent of the critical text.)

Edward Hills makes the comment, "If we make the Bodmer and Chester Beatty Papyri our chief reliance, how do we know that even older New Testament papyri of an entirely different character have not been destroyed by the recent damming of the Nile and the consequent flooding of the Egyptian sands?"[51] Hills also points out the contradictory assessments of various leading text critics.[52] This all may seem confusing, and that is exactly the point. There is contradiction and confusion throughout the history of the critical text. The leading proponents of the critical text position even today routinely disagree. It seems that their only point of agreement is that they want nothing to do with the Received Text used by Bible-believers down through the centuries.

---

[49]Ibid., 199.

[50]Ibid.

[51]The Bodmer and Chester Beatty Papyri were papyrus manuscripts found in the twentieth century which are thought to be of relatively early origins. Hills, *The King James Version Defended*, 225.

[52]Ibid., 126. "Concerning the relationship of the Alexandrian New Testament text to the Western New Testament text there has been a difference of opinion dating back to the early days of New Testament textual criticism. Some critics have believed that the Western text was the earlier and the Alexandrian text came into being as a refinement of this primitive Western text. Among those who have thought this are Griesbach (1796), Hug (1808), Burkitt (1899), A. C. Clark (1914), Sanders (1926), Lake (1928), Glaue (1944), and Black (1954). Other critics have regarded the Alexandrian text as prior and have looked upon the Western text as a corruption of this purer Alexandrian text-form. Some of those who have held this view are Tischendorf (1868), Westcott and Hort (1881), B. Weiss (1899), Ropes (1926), Lagrange (1935), and Metzger (1964)."

The Uncertainty of the Critical Text

As one becomes conversant with the critical text, it will be apparent that it abounds with textual variants. (These are differences in the various manuscripts used to compose it.)[53] Moreover, as one begins to try and sort out the thousands of textual variants, it becomes a bottomless pit of confusion and subjective second guessing. Furthermore, the textual apparatus (the footnotes at the bottom of each page of the critical text) changes periodically as various "authorities" of textual criticism disagree on respective variants. Rather than building faith, the endless minutia and disagreement over variants in the critical text lead to doubt and tend to shake one's faith in the integrity of the Word of God. As this writer in years past waded through the arguments, both pro and con, over a given variant reading, he came away shaking his head wondering what was the true reading. Yet, the very nature of the critical text and its attempt to "reconstruct" the Word of God lends itself to such doubts. Is God the author of confusion? Is He the author of doubt?

It should be apparent to this point that the critical text is mired in the quicksand of uncertainty. In the twentieth century, the United Bible Societies organization has produced four editions of its critical-text-based Greek New Testament. However, there were more than five-hundred changes made in the text between its second and third editions. Moreover, the same committee of five editors produced both editions.[54]

---

[53]Proponents of the critical text will quickly respond that there are variants in the Received Text as well. Indeed there are. However, the difference is in the *degree* of variations. There is a remarkable degree of consistency in the manuscripts which support the Received Text. In contrast, there is also a remarkable degree of disagreement in manuscripts which support the critical text. Herman Hoskier has documented over 3,000 places in which Aleph and B disagree in the Gospels alone. (Hoskier, *Codex B*, 59.) To the contrary, modern text critic Kurt Aland considers the thousands of manuscripts supporting the Received Text to be doctored or as it were "mimeographed" because of their uniformity and consistency (Waite, *Defending the King James Version*, 52).

[54]Wilbur Pickering, *The Identity of the New Testament Text* (Nashville: Thomas Nelson, 1977; reprint, Collingswood, N. J.: Bible for Today. n.d.), 18 (page citation is to the reprint edition).

Regarding establishing the New Testament text with certainty, one text critic is so bold as to assert, "We have already suggested that to achieve this goal is well-nigh impossible."[55] This same author also said, "It is generally recognized that the original text of the Bible cannot be recovered."[56] Another textual critic of the twentieth century wrote, "We have made little progress in textual theory since Westcott-Hort; that we simply do not know how to make a definitive determination as to what the best text is."[57] To conclude that there is maximum uncertainty in the critical text is an understatement.

Does the Critical Text Contain the Word of God?

In the past century, a form of apostasy called "Neo-orthodoxy" developed in Europe. It was a variation of older theological Liberalism. However, it was devious in that it routinely used orthodox terminology but imparted a different sense to these terms. One of its tenets was that the Bible *contains* the Word of God rather than *is* the Word of God. No true Fundamentalist would ever take such a position. Moreover, this writer is not aware of any Fundamentalist advocating the critical text position who would say, "The Bible *contains* the Word of God." However, having said that, Fundamentalists who hold the critical text position come perilously close to that view. The very nature of the critical text lends itself thereto.

With the thousands of admitted variants of the critical text and the uncertainty of which is right, many holding this position are reduced to only claiming that the critical text does not make any major doctrinal changes from the historic Received Text. (That claim will be addressed

---

[55]Robert Grant, *A Historical Introduction to the New Testament* (New York: Harper & Row, 1917; reprint, 1963, 51 (page citation is to the reprint edition).

[56]Ibid., 19.

[57]E. J. Epp, "The Twentieth Century Interlude in New Testament Textual Criticism," *Journal of Biblical Literature*, XCIII (1974): 403.

in appendices A, B, and D. However, we will allow that assertion to stand for now for the sake of discussion.) It is sad that one rarely hears those of the critical text position talk about the "words of God" (see Ps. 12:6; 119:103; or Prov. 30:5-6). Rather, more vague terms such as thoughts, revelation, or the autographa are used.

The Critical Text De-emphasizes the Precise Words of God

Notice the following quotation. "In our defense and propagation of the faith the key issue is not whether today we know the *precise form of the words* recorded in the autographa. To make that our focus moves us away from God to concentrate on the process by which His revelation has come to us. The key issue is that God has spoken in the autographa and He has spoken with authority and without error and we are responsible to respond to Him"[58] (emphasis mine). The author quoted above would turn us away from the "precise form of the words of God." This comes perilously close to the view that the Bible *contains* the Word of God. With all due credit, the author of this quotation likely would deny such a view. However, the point is that the critical text position comes very close to that view by the very nature of its philosophy.[59]

---

[58]Glenny, "The Preservation of Scripture," in Grisanti, *The Bible Version Debate*, 82.

[59]Most working editors of the critical text accept the Neo-orthodox position. It is assumed by them.

The Critical Text Was Developed by Bizarre Rules

As *modern* textual critics seek to reconstruct the text of the New Testament, they profess to do so by scientific means.[60] Therefore, "textual science" becomes the criteria of determining the Word of God. Listed below are four principles by which modern textual science operates. (1) The more difficult reading is preferred, presuming that scribes would simplify rather than complicate the text. (2) The shorter reading is preferred, presuming that scribes would include more possible variants rather than exclude any possible word from the sacred text. (3) In parallel or quoted passages, the divergent reading is preferred, being more difficult and explainable by the given data. (4) Other more subjective factors prefer the style and vocabulary of a given biblical author and of the immediate context of a passage, and resist any known preferences of a given scribe or corrector.[61]

With all due respect, the view of this writer is that these rules of *transciptional probabilities* are a bizarre labyrinth of techo-speak which borders upon psycho-babble. Yet, this is the "scientific" basis that modern textual criticism follows in making textual judgments. Moreover, as will be documented in chapter 6 and 9 of this book, virtually all major modern text critics have been or are theological Liberals. Textual scientists (text critics) become the authority. Though Fundamentalists who hold a critical text position deny that the textual critic sits in judgment of the Word of God, that in fact is exactly what they do.[62]

---

[60]Smallman, "Printed Greek Texts," in Williams, *From the Mind of God*, 171.

[61]Ibid., 174.

[62]Ibid., 171.

The Double Stream of Biblical Texts

Two Types of Textual Criticism

As we have traced the double stream of Bibles, we have thus far noted that there are *two types of Bibles, two textual bases,* and *two undergirding philosophies* for approaching the biblical text. Let us conclude this chapter by considering one final area of concern: *the two types of textual criticism.*

As modern textual criticism has been criticized, proponents of the critical text position will quickly point out that those involved in the editing and publication of the Received Text engaged in textual criticism. Indeed they did. Textual criticism in its generic form is merely investigating and analyzing biblical texts and seeking to arrive at the proper reading should a variant arise. (It should be recalled that there are relatively few variants in the Received Textual family compared to the enormous number of disparate variants in the Alexandrian and critical textual family.) However, in studying the textual analysis done over the past four hundred years, it is evident that there are two distinct and widely differing types of text criticism: (1) those based in *belief* following the usage of the church through previous centuries versus (2) those based in *rationalism* in modern scientific textual criticism.

Textual Criticism Based in Belief

A brilliant scholar who lived in the sixteenth century by the name of Desidierus Erasmus was the first to publish the Greek New Testament in printed form. He initially did so in A.D. 1516 with four more editions following in 1519, 1522, 1527, and 1535. His printed Greek New Testament was that of the Received Text. Erasmus did not have a great number of manuscripts at his disposal, but he had traveled across Europe extensively and had examined many biblical manuscripts from Italy to Britain and most points in between. In his day, he was the foremost authority of biblical manuscripts. (As will be documented in a coming section, Erasmus was well aware of Vaticanus and other Alexandrian manuscripts and rejected them out of hand.) Over the final twenty years of his life, Erasmus continued to edit and refine his initial publication of his Greek New Testament. During the course of those years, he came into contact with considerably more manuscripts than the ten which he initially used.[63] The work of Erasmus as a textual editor was not on the same plane as modern textual critics. He sought only to transmit the preserved Word of God. Unlike modern textual critics, he was not trying to reconstruct a lost New Testament by "scientific" means.

After the death of Erasmus in 1536, Robert Stephens (also known as Robert Estienne in French or Robert Stephanus in Latin) continued to analyze manuscripts available to him and published four more editions of the Greek New Testament from France. He also worked exclusively from the Received Text. (Because Erasmus was well aware of Vaticanus, it may be assumed that Stephens was as well.) After the death of Stephens, Theodore Beza continued to edit and refine the work of his predecessors and published a printed Greek New Testament from Switzerland. He too worked only with the Received Text. It was from Beza's fifth edition of 1598 that the King James translators primarily worked.[64]

Opponents of the Received Text position will quickly point out that each of these Renaissance scholars practiced textual criticism. And that they did. However, in each case, these scholars were all strong believers in the verbal inspiration of the Bible and its infallibility. Moreover, their basic rule when dealing with the relatively few variants found in the manuscripts of the Received Text was that the Received Text had been providentially preserved by God.[65] They therefore fell back on the usage of the text by *believing* churches in the centuries long before the

---

[63]Preserved Smith, *Erasmus: A Study of His Life, Ideals, and Place in History* (New York: Dover Publications, 1923; reprint, 1962), 163 (page citation is to the reprint edition).

[64]Frederick Henry Scrivener, *The New Testament in Greek: According to the Text Followed in the Authorized Version Together with the Variations Adopted in the Revised Version* (London: Cambridge University Press, 1881), vii.

[65]Hills, *The King James Version Defended*, 62.

Reformation. When necessary, they therefore labored to use the reading before them which reflected the usage of *believing* churches down through the centuries. There is evidence of ancient Waldensian manuscripts.[66] In the case of Beza, Calvin's successor, there is the possibility that he came into possession of ancient Waldensian manuscripts of the New Testament. (See appendix E for further details.) In short, these early publishers of the printed Received Text sought to conform their work to the usage of the *believing* churches through the centuries gone before. Their starting point was not complicated at all. They simply *believed* that the Word of God had been providentially preserved by God in the Received Text through the usage of churches. (To be sure, their convictions of church history may have varied, but nevertheless they looked to whatever view of the church they had as their pole of guiding light.) Their work therefore was based in belief.

Textual Criticism Based in Rationalism

The critical text, from which almost all modern translations of the Bible are translated, was developed and popularized by British text critics Westcott and Hort in the latter part of the nineteenth century. They were not the first to advance the idea. German Rationalist J. J. Griesbach certainly predated them with the concept of a critical text.[67] Furthermore, they merely adopted the method of Griesbach.[68] However, it was the work of Westcott and Hort which produced the essence of the *modern* critical text. Though the critical text going into the twenty-first century has had continual refinements along the way, its essence remains the work of Westcott and Hort.

---

[66] Jean Leger, *Histoire de Piemont des Eglises Evangeliques des Vallees de Piemont*, trans. Lauri Stiles (Leyde: J. Le Carpentier, 1669), 165-67.

[67] Hills, *The King James Version Defended*, 65.

[68] Letis, *The Ecclesiastical Text*, 17.

In fact, the preface of the United Bible Societies' Greek New Testament (critical text) third edition of 1966 states, "The Committee carried out its work . . . on the basis of Westcott and Hort's edition of the Greek New Testament."[69] The current edition of the United Bible Societies' critical text (the fourth edition) differs from the third edition only in its footnotes (apparatus). The influence of Westcott and Hort remains to this hour in the modern critical text.

Summary of Westcott and Hort's Theory

The work of these two textual critics is based in a complicated theory about which entire books have been written. A summary of it however might be made in the following statements. The original scriptural text was represented in what Westcott and Hort called the "neutral text." (There is no historical evidence that such a "neutral" text ever existed.) For Westcott and Hort, Vaticanus and Sinaiticus best represent this so-called neutral text and therefore were the preferred sources for textual criticism. The Received Text manuscripts are merely "copies" of a later "official church text" and hence have no critical value. This is circular reasoning at best. They allege that the (theoretical) neutral text is the closest to the originals.[70] Sinaiticus and Vaticanus are closest to the neutral text. Thus, Sinaiticus and Vaticanus are closest to the originals. And therefore, the modern Greek text should primarily follow these two Alexandrian texts. The "rules" for textual criticism mentioned earlier in this chapter also derived from the work of Westcott and Hort.[71]

---

[69]Kurt Aland and others, eds., *The Greek New Testament*, 3d ed. (London: United Bible Societies, 1966), v.

[70]Ironically, all textual critics today reject the phrase "neutral text."

[71]Jack Moorman, in his work *Forever Settled*, lists nine principles of the Westcott and Hort theory of textual criticism. They are as follows. (1) In textual criticism the N. T. is to be treated like any other book. (2) There are no signs of deliberate falsification

Westcott and Hort's View of the Bible as Any Other Book

One telling aspect of the rationalistic-based form of modern text criticism (from Griesbach onward) has been the view of treating the biblical manuscripts as one might treat any other book. Hort wrote in 1881, "For ourselves, we dare not introduce considerations which could not reasonably be applied to other ancient texts, supposing them to have documentary attestation of equal amount, variety, and antiquity."[72]

In plain English, this simply means that Hort believed the Bible should be treated no differently than any other book. He and most text critics since have viewed the Bible in a neutral fashion as any other piece of literature might be viewed. Hort also wrote, "The principles of criticism explained in the foregoing section hold good for all ancient texts preserved in a plurality of documents. In dealing with the text of the New Testament no new principle whatever is needed or legitimate."[73]

---

of the text. (3) The numerical preponderance of the Received Text can be explained through genealogy. Basically this means frequent copying of the same kind of "defective" manuscripts. (4) Despite its numerical advantage, the Received Text is merely one of several competing text types. (5) The fact that the Received Text is fuller is because it is a conflated text. It was combined with the shorter readings of the other competing text types. This conflation was done with the official sanction of the Byzantine Church during the fourth century. (6) There are no distinctive Received Text readings in the writings of the church fathers before A.D. 350. (7) Where there are several variant readings, the right one can be determined by two kinds of internal evidence. The first is intrinsic probability (i.e., which reading best fits the context and conforms to the author's style and purpose.) The second is transcriptional probability. (8) Whereas the first has to do with the author, the second concerns the copyist. What kind of error did he make deliberately or through carelessness? (9) Under transcriptional probability, two basic norms were established: one, the shorter reading is to be preferred (on the assumption that a scribe would be more likely to add material); and two, the harder reading is to be preferred (on the assumption that the scribe has attempted to simplify). Moorman, *Forever Settled*, 198.

[72]Fenton John Anthony Hort, *The New Testament in the Original Greek*, 2d ed. (New York: Harper, 1882), 277.

[73]Ibid., 73.

However, the Bible is not like any other book. It has been inspired and preserved by God through the ages. Moreover, such a "neutral" view of the Scripture reveals the rationalistic approach modern textual criticism has toward the Bible. To them, it is no different than any other book.

Summary

Thus to summarize this chapter, (1) there has indeed been a *double stream of Bibles* down through the centuries. (A) There are the few English translations which are based upon the Received Text. (The major modern manifestation of that is the King James Version.) (B) There are also those translations which are based upon the modern critical text. (Almost all modern translations derive therefrom.)

(2) There are thus *two textual bases*. (A) The first is the historic Received Text. (B) The other is the Alexandrian-based critical text.

(3) There are *two undergirding philosophies*. (A) The first is the Received Text position which is based in belief. (B) The other is the modern critical text position which is based in the rationalism of reconstructing the text by scientific means.

(4) Finally, there are *two types of textual criticism*. (A) The Received-Text method is based in belief following the usage of the church through the centuries. (B) The modern critical-text method is based in rationalism.

The Double Stream of Biblical Texts

Review Questions for Further Study

1. What are the two basic types of Bibles?

2. What are the two basic types of textual bases?

3. In what ancient type of textual family is the critical text rooted?

4. What is the goal textual critics have regarding the text?

5. The Received Text position begins with the premise that God has not only inspired His Word, but also has done what with it?

6. The Received Text position looks to whom for guidance in textual questions?

7. What agency has the Holy Spirit worked through to preserve God's Word?

8. The critical text position comes close to the position that the Bible _____ the Word of God.

9. The critical text position seeks to reconstruct the text by _____ means.

10. Most modern textual critics are of what theological persuasion?

11. The Received Text position holds the view that proper textual criticism must be based in what?

12. Upon what is the critical text position of textual criticism based?

CHAPTER FIVE

EARLY HISTORY OF THE RECEIVED TEXT

Some of the material to be presented in this chapter has already been touched upon briefly in earlier chapters. Let us, however, delve more deeply into the early history of the Received Text.

The Historic Received Text

A prevailing chorus of the critical text position is that there is no historical record of the Byzantine Text (i.e., Received Text) to be found prior to the last half of the fourth century. Though Hort conceded that there might be some evidence of the Syrian text (i.e., Received Text) as early as middle of the third century;[1] as far as he was concerned and for all practical purposes, there were no characteristic readings of the Received Text before the middle of the fourth century (A.D. 350).[2] In other words, their allegation is that there is no history of the Received Text being used by anybody prior to the last half of the fourth century. Therefore, the Received Text could not reflect the original, autographic writings of the New Testament. (Westcott and Hort, of course, alleged rather that the Alexandrian text [or neutral text as they imagined it] was that which most closely followed the originals.) This allegation is still repeated by recent Fundamentalists such as Edward Glenny, formerly

---

[1] Brooke Foss Westcott and Fenton John Anthony Hort, *Introduction to the New Testament in the Original Greek with Notes on Selected Readings*, (London: Macmillan & Co.,1882; reprint, Peabody, Mass.: Hendrickson, 1988), 115 (page citations are to reprint edition).

[2] Frederic Kenyon, *Recent Developments in the Textual Criticism of the Greek Bible: Schwieich Lectures of the British Academy* (London: Oxford University Press, 1932), 7-8.

of Central Baptist Theological Seminary.³ However, they are simply wrong.

Edward Miller was an accomplished textual historian living at the end of the nineteenth century. His exhaustive research showed that portions of Scripture distinctive to the Received Text were quoted extensively by notable church leaders as early as the second century and onward.⁴ Frederic Kenyon, a textual critic who advocated the critical text position, has attempted to dismiss Miller's research.⁵ Though he criticized Miller, he did not answer his evidence and he therefore did not refute Miller's research. It stands to this day. It has never been answered.⁶ (Miller's research is routinely ignored by advocates of the critical text position, but that does not dislodge his research as historical evidence which demolishes the central pillar of the critical text position.)

For the most part, advocates of the critical text have confined themselves to debating over existing Greek manuscripts of the New Testament. However, they have largely ignored ancient translations of the New Testament which support the Received Text. The logic at this point is simple. If these early translations of the New Testament reflect the Received Text, they must have been translated from it. The manuscripts underlying these translations therefore must be very early copies of the Received Text—maybe even the autographs themselves. Do such translations exist? Indeed they do. Notwithstanding, they either are ig-

---

³Edward Glenny, since writing for Central Baptist Theological Seminary, has left the Fundamentalist movement and now teaches at Northwestern College, a New-Evangelical institution. W. Edward Glenny, "The Preservation of Scripture," in *The Bible Version Debate*, ed. Michael Grisanti, (Minneapolis: Central Baptist Theological Seminary, 1997), 74.

⁴John Burgon and Edward Miller, *The Causes of the Corruption of the Traditional Text of the Holy Gospels* (London: MacMillan Co., 1897), 64.

⁵Frederic Kenyon, *Handbook to the Textual Criticism of the New Testament*, 2d ed. (Grand Rapids: Eerdmans Publishing Co., 1951), 67-68.

⁶Ibid., 68.

nored by advocates of the critical text or are dismissed as being of later dates.

Translations of the Earliest Church

Let us consider several of these translations. They point clearly to the use of the Received Text as early as A D. 150.

The Itala Version

A mistake which is often made is the assumption that anything Latin or pertaining to Italy is to be associated with the Roman Catholic Church. However, in northern Italy as early as the second century, there existed what was known as the Italic Church. Because it was located in the region of the sub-Alpine Italian Alps, its geographic remoteness and topographical ruggedness kept it from significant interaction with the Church of Rome. The Italic Church was the forerunner of churches in this same region which would later be called the Vaudois, or, alternatively, the Waldenses. Both of these names simply refer to "peoples of the valleys."[7] The Italic or pre-Waldensian Church produced a version of the New Testament which was translated from the Received Text by the year A.D. 157.[8] Theodore Beza, the associate and successor of John Calvin and the great Swiss reformer, credits the Italic Church to have begun in A.D. 120.[9] The Bible translation of the Italic Church came to be known as the Itala translation (also known as the Italic). The point of

---

[7] *Vaudois* is a French language derivative for "valleys" as *waldenses* is an Alpine word for "valleys."

[8] Frederick Henry Scrivener, *A Plain Introduction to the Criticism of the New Testament*, 2d ed. (Cambridge, Deighton, Bell, & Co., 1874), 2:43.

[9] McClintock and Strong, *Encyclopedia*, s.v. "Waldenses."

all of this is that the Itala Bible was translated from the Received Text![10] It has existed since A.D. 157. Noted church historian Frederic Nolan confirms the same.[11] This date is less than one hundred years after most of the books of the New Testament were written. The greater point is that the Itala (or Old Latin) was translated from the Received Text, indicating its existence to the earliest days of the New Testament church. Therefore, the Received Text clearly existed and was used by churches in early church history.

The Peshitta

Another ancient translation of the New Testament is the Syrian Peshitta Version. It should be recalled that it was in Antioch of Syria that the disciples were first called Christians.[12] Moreover, the church at Antioch was the sending church as well as the home church of the apostle Paul. In the mid and latter portion of the first century, the church at Antioch arguably was one of the pre-eminent churches in the Christian world. This church undoubtedly was the mother church for numerous other churches of Syria during that early period of church history. Accordingly, a translation of the New Testament into Syrian was made in A.D. 150.[13] This translation was called the Peshitta Ver-

---

[10]Kenyon, *Our Bible and the Ancient Manuscripts* (New York: Harper Brothers, 1895, 1951), 169-71. Kenyon here refers to the Itala as the Old Latin which is another name for it. It should also be noted that Kenyon, though acknowledging that the Itala (Old Latin) was based upon the Received Text, rather sought to date it much later.

[11]Frederick Nolan, *An Inquiry into the Integrity of the Greek Vulgate: or, Received Text of the New Testament* (London: F. C. & J. Rivington, 1815), xvii, xviii.

[12]Acts 11:26.

[13]Westcott and Hort, *Introduction to the New Testament*, 143.

sion. Even Hort acknowledged that this translation paralleled the Received Text.[14]

Of interest is that the word *peshitta* is a Syrian word which means "common."[15] It thus was analogous to the later Latin term *vulgate* which essentially meant the same thing. It would also approximate the later sense of the term *Received Text*. In each case, the idea was that of the commonly "received text" (or in this case, "version") of the Bible for a given language. There is little question, even by proponents of the critical text, that the Peshitta Version was translated from a Greek text rooted in the Received Text.[16] Liberal historians, however, have tried to place the date of the Peshitta Version into the fifth century. For example, this date was alleged by the liberal text critic F. C. Burkitt. His purpose in so alleging a later date was to eliminate any early historic usage of the Received Text. (He of course claimed that the Received Text was not invented until at least the fifth century and therefore had no true ancient basis.) However, historians have fairly well discounted

---

[14]Hort, however, went on to allege in his notorious theory that the Greek text used by the Syrians was an official church "recension" or revision. That is, he claimed that a church council had officially revised the Greek New Testament into the form which became later known as the Received Text. Westcott and Hort claimed that because the Syrian text was therefore a revision, it had no value in seeking the original text of the New Testament. There is absolutely no historic evidence, however, that any of that ever happened. Moreover, there have been more than one hundred years for proponents of their position to produce documentation for the alleged church council and its "official recension" (revision). Search though they have, nothing has ever been found to substantiate their claim. The upshot of all of this is that though Hort agreed that the Peshitta was an early translation, he discounted it of having any worth because of his theory of an official church revision of its underlying text. Hills, *The King James Version Defended*, 170-176.

[15]"Our Authorized Bible Vindicated," in *Which Bible?* ed. David Otis Fuller (Grand Rapids: Grand Rapids International Publications, 1970), 198.

[16]Hills, *The King James Version Defended*, 172.

Burkitt's claim that the Peshitta was produced in the fifth century.[17] John Burgon noted that the churches of the region of Syria have *always* used the Peshitta. There has never been a time when these churches did not use the Received-Text-based Peshitta.[18] The greater point, however, is that one of the earliest churches of the Christian era used a translation of the New Testament based upon the Received Text. That is a clear indication that the Received Text was the true text of the New Testament with roots leading back to autographa.

The Gothic Version

Another early translation of the New Testament in a European language was what has come to be known as the Gothic Version. The Gothic language was that used by Germanic tribes in central Europe in the fourth century. In about A.D. 350, a missionary to the Goths by the

---

[17]Hills, *The King James Version Defended*, 172-74. Hills explains that Burkitt claimed the Peshitta was produced by one Rabbula, the bishop of Edessa, which was the capital city of Syria. Burkitt therefore claimed that Rabbula's authorization of the Peshitta was somewhere between A.D. 411 and 435. However, Burkitt's claim does not stand. There were two sects within the Syrian Church at that time and the Received Text was used by both sects. As Hills notes, "Since this division took place in Rabbula's time and since Rabbula was the leader of one of these sects, it is impossible to suppose that the Peshitta was his handiwork, for if it had been produced under his auspices, his opponents would never have adopted it as their received New Testament text" (172). Hills also quotes another historian who contends that Rabbula did not even use the Peshitta (174, n. 1). Hills continues, "If this is true and if Burkitt's contention is also true, namely, that the Syrian ecclesiastical leaders who lived before Rabbula also did not use the Peshitta, then why *was* it that the Peshitta was received by all the mutually opposing groups in the Syrian Church as their common, authoritative Bible? It must have been that the Peshitta was a very ancient version and that because it was so old the common people within the Syrian Church continued to be loyal to it regardless of the factions into which they came to be divided and the preferences of their leaders. It made little difference to them whether these leaders quoted the Peshitta or not. They persevered in their usage of it, and because of their steadfast devotion this old translation retained its place as the Received Text of the Syrian-speaking churches" (174).

[18]John Burgon and Edward Miller, *The Causes of the Corruption*, 128.

name of Ulfilas translated the New Testament into the Gothic language.[19] Textual critic Frederic Kenyon wrote in 1912 that the Gothic Version "is for the most part that which is found in the majority of Greek manuscripts.[20] Or, in other words, Kenyon conceded that the Gothic Version was based upon the Received Text. Recall that the vast "majority of manuscripts" are that which support the Received Text. The point of logic here again is simple. When the missionary Ulfilas translated the Gothic Version from the Received Text in about A.D. 350, it must have been in existence long before that date. When a missionary on the field had the Received Text with him, it certainly implied that it was the well-established, common text.

The clear historic indication is that the Received Text was the common text of the New Testament used throughout the civilized world from the earliest times of Christianity. Though we live in an age of relatively-rapid editing, publishing, and distribution of new Bible translations, that was not the case in the first millennium of Christianity. For translations of the Bible to exist in the second to fourth centuries based upon what is distinctively the Received Text is *prima facie*, historic evidence that the Received Text was the commonly used, commonly translated, and commonly copied text of the New Testament. This is apparent. (The critical-text-position view that there is no record of any historic usage of the Received Text prior to the fifth century is simply wrong. There is a substantial historic record to the contrary.) The text used by the churches of Jesus Christ in the first five centuries was primarily the Received Text. To be sure, there were localities which used the Alexandrian text, but they were limited largely to Alexandria and Rome.

---

[19]Hills, *The King James Version Defended*, 174.

[20]Frederic Kenyon, *Handbook to the Textual Criticism of the New Testament*, 2d ed. (Grand Rapids: Eerdmans Publishing Co., 1951), 240.

Manifold Translations

As history has unfolded, many groups of believers down through the ages have either used the Received Text or have translated the New Testament therefrom. In addition to the three examples noted in detail above, D. A. Waite lists additional groups bearing historical witness to the Received Text underlying the King James Bible.

Early European Translations

These various groups include the Gallic Church of southern France (A.D. 177); the Celtic Church of Great Britain; the Church of Scotland and Ireland; Codex W of Matthew in the fourth or fifth century; Codex A in the Gospels in the fifth century; the vast majority of extant New Testament manuscripts; the early Greek church (A.D. 312-1453); all the churches of the Reformation; Erasmus's Greek New Testament of 1516 as well as his later editions thereof; the Complutensian Polyglot of 1522; Luther's German Bible; the French Version of Olivetan of 1535; the Coverdale Bible of 1535; the Matthew's Bible of 1537; the Taverner's Bible of 1539; Stephanus' Greek New Testament (1546-51); the Geneva Bible of 1557-60; the Bishops' Bible of 1568; the Spanish Version of 1569; Beza's Greek New Testament of 1598 as well as his other editions thereof; the King James Bible of 1611; and the Elzivers' Greek New Testament of 1624.[21]

If the Received Text is an inferior text, why would the Holy Spirit allow it to *completely* dominate the propagation of God's Word over the first 1500 years of Christianity? If the critical text is really the best record of the New Testament, why did the Holy Spirit allow it to be suppressed for all these centuries? Are we to believe that the Holy Spirit was on vacation while all the manuscripts of the Received Text or translations thereof were being produced? Or, is it reasonable to pre-

---

[21]D. A. Waite, *Defending the King James Bible* (Collingswood, N.J.: Bible for Today, 1992), 45-48.

sume that the Holy Spirit had no interest in the propagation of the Word of God throughout the church age? The contention of this writer is that the Holy Spirit indeed providentially superintended the preservation, transmission, translation, and propagation of the Word of God through the centuries. To assume anything less is to presume that He did not care.

Modern-Era European Translations

But there is more. As the gospel has gone to the uttermost parts of the earth through the centuries of the Christian era, multitudes of translations into indigenous languages have been based upon the Received Text. For example, the Swedish Uppsala Version was translated from the Received Text in 1514; the Danish Christian Version was translated from the Received Text in 1550; and the New Testament was translated into Icelandic from the Received Text in 1584. The Received Text became the basis for the following translations as well: the Slovenian Version of 1584, the Irish Version of 1685, the French Geneva Version of 1588, the Welsh Version of 1588, the Hungarian Version of 1590, the Italian Diodati Version of 1607, the Dutch Statenvertaling Version of 1637, the Finnish Version of 1642, the Syrian Version of 1645, the Armenian Version of 1666, the Romanian Version of 1688, the Latvian Version of 1689, the Lithuanian Version of 1735, the Estonian Version of 1739, the Georgian Version of 1743, the Portuguese Version of 1751, the Gaelic Version of 1801, the Serbo-Croatian Version of 1804, the Albanian Version of 1827, the Slovak Version of 1832, the Norwegian Version of 1834, the Russian Version of 1865, the Yiddish Version of 1821, the Turkish Version of 1827, and the Bulgarian Version of 1864.[22] These all are based upon the Received Text.

---

[22]David Cloud, *Myths about the Modern Bible Versions* (Oak Harbor, Wash.: Way of Life Literature, 1999), 21.

How can anyone claim that God's Spirit was not involved in such propagation and translation of God's Word for peoples the world around? Can we imagine that the Holy Spirit allowed so great a company of translators to use an inferior text laced with hundreds of spurious words? (Recall how that the critical text has deleted hundreds of words when compared to the historic Received Text.) The psalmist wrote, "The Lord gave the word: great *was* the company of those that published it" (Ps. 68:11). It is evident that a great company of scribes, translators, and then printers have indeed published the Word of God.

The fact that virtually all Bible translators and publishers prior to the twentieth century worked from the Received Text is *prima facie* evidence that the Holy Spirit indeed did providentially so direct them. The alternative is that this unanimous consent was just a quirk of history. Can we believe that the Holy Spirit cast off His written Word to drift across the oceans of time to fend for itself? The only *believing* alternative is that God through His Spirit has providentially guided not only the preservation of the text, but also its numerous translations and their propagation as well. The witness of the first eighteen centuries of Christianity is virtually unanimous in pointing to the translation and propagation of the Word of God based upon the Received Text. The notable exception thereof is the Latin Vulgate produced by the Roman Catholic Church.

American Indian Translations

The New Testament has been translated from the Received Text into the varying languages and dialects of these North American Indian tribes: the Pequot in 1663, the Mohawk in 1787, the Eskimo in 1810, the Delaware in 1818, the Seneca in 1829, the Cherokee in 1829, the Ojibway in 1833, the Dakota in 1839, the Ottawa in 1841, the Shawnee in 1842, the Pottawotomi in 1844, the Abenaqui in 1844, the Nez Perce in 1845, the Choctaw in 1848, the Yupik in 1848, the Micmac in 1853, the Plains Cree in 1861, and the Muskogee in 1886.[23] Why would God allow His Word to be propagated from an inferior text? If the critical text is superior, why then did God allow it to be kept from these peoples?

Asian and other Translations

The Received Text was the base for translating the New Testament into the Malay language in 1734. Each of the following nationalities had the New Testament translated into their native language from the Received Text: the Persian and Arabic in the early 1800s, Burmese in 1835, Bengali in 1809, Oriya in 1815, Marathi 1821, Kashmiri in 1821, Nepali in 1821, Sanskrit in 1822, Gujarati in 1823, Panjabi in 1825, Bihari in 1826, Kannada in 1831, Assamese in 1833, Hindi in 1835, Urdu in 1843, Telugu in 1854, and 35 other languages of India.[24]

Other of the world's languages had the New Testament or portions thereof translated from the Received Text as well including the Bullom translation of Sierra Leone in 1816, the Saraiki Version of Pakistan in 1819, the Faroe Translation of the Faroe Islands in 1823, the Stranam Version of Suriname in 1829, the Javanese Version of Indonesia of 1829, the Aymara Version of Bolivia in 1829, the Malay Version of Indonesia of 1835, the Manchu Version of China in 1835, the Malagasy Version of Madagascar 1835, the Mandinka Version of Gambia in 1837, the Hawaiian Version of 1838, the Mongolian Version of 1840, the Karaite Version of Crimea Mountains of 1842, the Azerbaijani Version of Russia in 1842, the Subu Version of Cameroon in 1843, the Mons Version of Burma in 1843, the Maltese Version of 1847, the Udmurt Version of Russia in 1847, the Garifuna Version of Belize-Nicaragua in 1847, the Ossete Version of Russia of 1848, the Bube Version of Equatorial Guinea in 1849, the Arwak Version of Guyana of

---

[23]Ibid., 21.

[24]Ibid., 22.

1850, the Maori Version of the Cook Islands of 1851, the Tontemboan Version of Indonesia of 1852, the Somoan Version of 1855, the Sesotho Version of Africa of 1855, the Setswana Version of South Africa of 1857, the Basque Version of Spain in 1857, the Hausa Version of Nigeria in 1857, the Nama Version of Africa in 1866, the Maori Version of New Zealand of 1858, the Dayak Version of Indonesia of 1858, the Isixhosa Version of South Africa of 1859, the Karan Version of Burma of 1860, the Nubian Version of Egypt of 1860, the Igbo Version of Nigeria of 1860, the Efik and Yoruba Versions of Nigeria in 1862, the Tibetan Version of 1862, the Ga Version of Ghana of 1866, the Tonga Version of Africa of 1862, the Twi Version of Ghana of 1863, the Isizulu Version of Africa of 1865, the Niuean of Tonga of 1866, the Dehu Version of New Caledonia in 1868, the Benga Version of Africa of 1871, the Ewe Version of Africa of 1877, the Batak Version of Ind-onesia in 1878, the Thai Version of 1883.[25] Each of these many versions was based upon the Received Text.[26] Moreover, this listing is by no means complete. Many of these versions have fallen into disuse and some of them have been *revised* into more modern versions based upon the critical text. However, as the Word of God has gone around the world through the centuries, its initial entrance has almost always been with translations based upon the Received Text.[27]

One cannot dismiss this massive evidence pointing to the Received Text unless he is willing to discount the providential leading of the Holy Spirit. Alas, many of the critical text position seem willing to do just that.

---

[25]Ibid.

[26]Some of these versions may have been translated from the King James Version and are thus translations of a translation. However, the King James Version is translated from the Received Text. The list of versions noted above is not intended to vouch for the quality of their translation. Rather, it is to establish the simple point that *all* of these translations are either directly or indirectly based upon the Received Text.

[27]That practice is certainly changing as modern Bible societies for the most part now base their work upon the critical text of the United Bible Societies.

The Eastern Church Copied the Received Text

The Roman Empire eventually developed into two divisions with the western portion having its capital at Rome and the eastern portion thereof having its capital at Constantinople. The latter came to be known as Byzantium, and that which pertains thereto came to be called "Byzantine." From the Byzantine era of church history eventually came the Greek Orthodox Church along with several divisions of it. Of interest is that the Greek Orthodox Church continues to use the Received Text to this day. Because of this, the Received Text in some quarters is routinely referred to as the Byzantine text. The Byzantine Empire along with the Byzantine Church ruled from Byzantium (Constantinople) from A.D. 452 until 1453. This region was conquered by Islamic Turks in 1453. However, during the approximately one thousand years of Byzantine influence, the Eastern Orthodox Church copied large quantities of New Testament manuscripts, many of which remain to this day.

Scriptoriums were places (usually associated with the Byzantine Church) where Scripture and other documents were officially copied. One locale with a large number of such scriptoriums was located on Mount Athos. This mountain actually rose out of the Aegean Sea close to Thessalonica of Macedonia and was connected to the mainland by a narrow isthmus.[28] Large quantities of New Testament manuscripts, it is thought, were copied in scriptoriums such as were located on Mount Athos. Certainly, a significant portion of extant manuscripts of the Byzantine text were copied in this region during the Byzantine era.

---

[28] James H. Sightler, *A Testimony Founded For Ever: the King James Bible Defended in Faith and History* (Greenville, S.C.: Sightler Publications, 1999), 125.

De Facto Canonical Status of the Received Text

When one refers to the canon of Scripture, the traditional sense refers to the recognition or decision as to which books are indeed Scripture and should be included in the Bible. The word *canon* essentially means a "standard" or a "ruler" by which a given document might be measured against. Thus, during the early centuries of Christianity, church councils wrestled over which books and epistles of the apostles should be considered as Scripture. By A.D. 400, several church councils had been convened and the books which presently compose the New Testament were by consensus agreed upon. These various church councils did not create the canon, but rather they recognized and ratified that which was already the common use of the churches.[29] Once again, the providential working of the Holy Spirit is apparent.

There is no record of any church council ever making a formal decision as to which textual base was deemed appropriate. However, church history does indicate that the "Byzantine" type of text was routinely used over and above the "Alexandrian" type of text.[30] As has been detailed above, significant bodies of churches in various parts of the civilized world used translations of the New Testament which follow the Received Text. They in effect gave *de facto* canonical status to it. The term *de facto* is a Latin phrase and essentially means "after the fact" or "in fact." Though the Received Text was never given *de jure* (official) canonical status, for all practical purposes it was used as such (*de facto*). Notwithstanding that the Alexandrian type of text was used in Egypt (around Alexandria), it never was widely used elsewhere. Moreover, Alexandria developed as a source of apostasy during early church history.

The simple fact that so many manuscripts of the Received Text (Byzantine Text) are extant today is quite simple. They were the form

---

[29]Paul W. Downey, "Canonization and Apocrypha" in *From the Mind of God to the Mind of Man,* ed. James B. Williams (Greenville, S.C.: Ambassador—Emerald International, 1999), 56.

[30]Cloud, *Myths,* 17.

of the New Testament which was used and adopted by the churches down through the centuries. It was a *de facto* canonization. There was common usage of it by most churches. Furthermore, implicit once again is the providential guidance of the Holy Spirit. Whether it was the early Syrian churches, the Italic churches, the Greek churches, the Waldenses, or *all* the Reformers (as well as other early European churches), they each had one thing in common: they gave credence to and used only the Received Textual base for translating the New Testament.

Erasmus and Vaticanus

The Received Text is closely connected to the Renaissance scholar Desiderius Erasmus. It was Erasmus who first published the Greek New Testament in printed form in 1516. This, of course, was the traditional Received Text. The text of the New Testament was thus for the first time in history essentially standardized in printed form. Accordingly, the King James Version of the New Testament finds much of its roots in the work of Erasmus.

However, those disinclined to favorably view either the King James Version or the Received Text have advanced a number of erroneous misconceptions about Erasmus and his work. One criticism is that Erasmus had only a handful of manuscripts from which to work. (The contention of the critics is that modern scholars have a far greater abundance of manuscripts available to them. They therefore can come to better textual judgments than did Erasmus.) However, Erasmus in fact had access to at least ten manuscripts, four of which he found in England, five at Basle, and a tenth one lent to him by a friend.[31] (Of further interest is that the *actual* core of the modern critical text is based upon not many more manuscripts than Erasmus used.) Moreover, in his extensive travels across Europe and always in search of biblical manu-

---

[31] Preserved Smith, *Erasmus: A Study of His Life, Ideals and Place in History* (New York: Dover Publications, 1923; reprint, 1962), 163 (page citation is the to the reprint edition).

scripts, there is little question that Erasmus had studied many more. Specifically, in preparing for printing his Greek New Testament, Erasmus had also consulted manuscripts at Cambridge and Brabant.[32] By the time that Erasmus began the editing for his printed Greek New Testament, he already had come to a firm conviction that the Received Text used by the church through history was the proper text.

Proponents of the modern critical text again advance the idea that the discovery of Sinaiticus and Vaticanus (along with the discovery of other ancient manuscripts) has necessitated revising the biblical text to take into account the textual differences found in them. The implication is that Erasmus and the other Renaissance textual editors and publishers were not aware of these later finds and therefore could not benefit from them. The assumption is that modern textual critics have an advantage over Erasmus because of the more recent textual discoveries. Their rationale is that since Sinaiticus and Vaticanus are earlier manuscripts than anything that Erasmus had, they must be used and Erasmus's work set aside. Sinaiticus (Aleph) and Vaticanus (B) therefore take precedence over the Received Text of Erasmus. That is the logical foundation and distilled essence of the modern critical text position.

However, that rationale is in error because of its faulty premises. **Erasmus was aware of Vaticanus and its major variant readings**. In preparing his later editions of his printed Greek New Testament, Erasmus had a friend in Rome who also was expert in Greek texts. His name was Bombasius. Erasmus therefore requested Bombasius to go to the Vatican library and research the various passages of Vaticanus which are distinctive to it; namely, the elimination of the last twelve verses of Mark, the elimination of 1 John 5:7, the deletion of John 7:53-8:11, and other readings characteristic to what later became the critical text. Bombasius did as requested and reported back to Erasmus. Based upon his voluminous research over the years, Erasmus concluded each and every one of the variant readings of Vaticanus to be defective and

---

[32]Ephraim Emerton, *Desiderius Erasmus of Rotterdam* (New York: G. P. Putnam's Sons, 1899), 200.

rejected them.³³ Furthermore, the discovery of Vaticanus by Tischendorf in the mid-nineteenth century was not so much of a discovery as has been portrayed. It had actually been printed by the Catholic Church in 1587 under the authority of Pope Sixtus and came to be known as the Sixtine edition. It was substantially the text of Vaticanus.³⁴ Tischendorf's enthusiasm of having "discovered" Vaticanus was thus not such a big deal after all. The Catholics had been aware of it for centuries and had even used it for the basis of a Greek text they had printed about 275 years earlier.

In addition, the other textual editors of the Received Text were aware of Vaticanus and its spurious readings. Erasmus had made significant notes which were available to Stephanus and Beza. It should be recalled that the King James Version was translated primarily from Theodore Beza's Greek New Testament, fifth edition of 1598.³⁵ Beza was well aware of Erasmus's notes about variant passages such as the last twelve verses of Mark which Vaticanus and the later critical text rejected. He wrote about the deletion of John 7:53-8:11 and the numerous other deletions of the Vaticanus. Beza accordingly had access to these notes.³⁶

Therefore, the contention of the critical text theory that modern scholarship has a distinct advantage over medieval textual editors simply is incorrect. They were completely aware of the major variants in Vaticanus (and similar texts) and rejected them because they did not follow the usage of the church down through the centuries. Moreover, modern scholarship is arrogant to think they have superior judgment

---

³³Hills, *The King James Version Defended*, 198-199. See also Preserved Smith, *Erasmus: A Study of His Life, Ideals and Place in History* (New York: Dover Publications, 1923, reprint, 1962), 165-168 (citations are to reprint edition).

³⁴Richard Ottley, *A Handbook to the Septuagint* (London: Methuen, 1920), 64.

³⁵Frederick Henry Scrivener, *The New Testament in Greek: According to the Text Followed in the Authorized Version Together with the Variations Adopted in the Revised Version* (London: Cambridge University Press, 1881), vii.

³⁶Hills, *The King James Version Defended*, 199.

compared to medieval scholars who were much closer to the time when many of these manuscripts were produced. Men such as Erasmus and Beza were masters of New Testament manuscripts (and their history) to a far greater degree than modern textual critics removed from their origins by an additional half millennium.

Why the Name of the Received Text

Though critics of the Received Text routinely refer to it as the Byzantine Text, almost as a pejorative term, the primary name it bears reflects its usage through the centuries. The text type from which the King James Version has been translated was received, accepted, used, and believed in by virtually all groups outside of the Catholic Church and Alexandria, Egypt. This widespread usage was so from the time of the church at Antioch through the end of the nineteenth century. The early Syrian churches planted from the church at Antioch used such a text. The Italic churches received it. Other believing churches across southern and central Europe received it. All the Reformers received it. In the great missionary movements of the eighteenth and nineteenth centuries *all* translations into other languages were based upon the text which had been used and accepted for almost two millennia. With the exception of the twentieth century, the Received Text was just that. It was received by all. Only as modernistic Rationalism permeated Christianity in the nineteenth and twentieth centuries did the critical text become prominent. To this day, these two (Rationalism and the critical text) reflect a symbiotic relationship.

Review Questions for Further Study

1. The critical text position asserts that there is no historical evidence of the received text prior to the last half of the fourth century. Is this true?

2. When was the Itala Version likely translated? What was its textual base?

3. What was the early Syrian translation of the New Testament called? When was it translated?

4. When was the Gothic Version translated? What was its textual base?

5. What has been the textual base of almost all New Testament translations made up through the nineteenth century?

6. Does the fact that virtually all translations of the New Testament prior to the twentieth century point to the providential working of the Holy Spirit?

7. Why is the Received Text sometimes called the Byzantine Text?

8. Why is the Received Text hold *de facto* canonical status?

9. Was Erasmus aware of Vaticanus and the readings distinct to the critical text?

10. Why is the Received Text so called?

CHAPTER SIX

ADDITIONAL HISTORY OF THE CRITICAL TEXT

The modern critical text was popularized in 1881 when B. F. Westcott and F. J. A. Hort released their Greek New Testament. However, the roots of it certainly predate that. Throughout the spectrum of textual critics, both recent and old, there is no dispute that the primary sources of the critical text originated in Alexandria, Egypt. As noted earlier, the two-load bearing columns of the modern critical text remain Codex Sinaiticus (Aleph) and Codex Vaticanus (B). Though other manuscripts are integrated with these, they remain the predominant essence of the modern critical text. Bruce Metzger, one of the committee members involved in producing the modern critical text indicated, "We took as our base at the beginning the text of Westcott and Hort (1881) and introduced changes as seemed necessary on the basis of MSS evidence."[1] The twin pillars of Westcott and Hort's text were Sinaiticus and Vaticanus. Therefore, let us move back in time and consider the seed bed of Alexandria, Egypt, where these two major Alexandrian manuscripts were derived.

---

[1] This information came from a personal letter sent by Bruce Metzger to Pastor Kirk DiVietro in 1990. Pastor Divietro had written to Metzger asking him how he and other members of the Nestle-Aland and the UBS committee began their work on their New Testament Greek texts. This information was faxed by Donald Waite to this author. It may be also found in *The Dean Burgon Society (1978-1994)*: "Messages from the 16th Annual Meeting, August 1994" (Collingswood, N.J.: Bible for Today, 1994), 272.

The Alexandrian Origin

Most textual critics agree that Vaticanus (B) and Sinaiticus (Aleph) were produced in the mid-fourth century in Alexandria, Egypt. Therefore, let us probe into the religious climate there of the day.

Alexandria, Egypt

Alexandria was unique in its religious and historical context. The city had long maintained a sizable population of Jews. It also was one of the major centers of higher learning in the Roman Empire. The city was founded by Alexander the Great during his visit to Egypt in 331 B.C. Throughout its illustrious history, Alexandria was always a city of Greek learning and culture, notwithstanding the fact it was in Egypt. This was particularly so during the Roman period of influence. Like Athens in Paul's day, Alexandria was a major center of academic elitism. It truly was an erudite city. The founding of the University of Alexandria was called the third great epoch in the history of civilization and it was modeled after the great school of Athens. The library at the University of Alexandria was reputed to hold up to 900,000 volumes.[2]

Because of its Greek origins and ongoing Greek culture, Alexandria became a magnet for both Greek philosophy and Greek philosophers. It was in Alexandria that other pagan philosophies arose. Plato was considered one of the prophets in Alexandria and from the Platonic influence in Alexandria developed the heresy of Gnosticism.[3]

---

[2]Camden M. Cobern, in James Orr, gen. ed., *International Standard Bible Encyclopedia* (Grand Rapids, Mich.: Wm. B. Eerdmans Publishing Co., 1939 ed.), s.v. "Alexandria."

[3]Complete volumes have been written describing the heresy of Gnosticism. However, in its distilled essence, Gnosticism believed that all matter was evil. Because Jesus of Nazareth possessed a human body, they alleged that He was not the Christ. It therefore denied the humanity of Christ as well as the personality of the Supreme God. It also advocated asceticism as a means of achieving communion with God. The Gnostics denied that the Old Testament Scriptures were from the true God. They attempted to

Additional History of the Critical Text

Because of the large Jewish community in Alexandria, the gospel also came there. Tradition holds that it was John Mark who brought Christianity to this city. However, even by the end of the *first* century, the Greek philosophical heresy of Gnosticism had infiltrated the early Alexandrian church.[4] This may have been what the apostle Paul had in mind, at least in principle, when he wrote, "Beware lest any man spoil you through philosophy and vain deceit, after the tradition of men, after the rudiments of the world, and not after Christ."[5] Platonism and Gnosticism certainly were philosophies prevalent in Paul's day and were already infecting early churches through their influence.

The Catechical School of Alexandria

In the second century, the first "Christian" theological school was founded in Alexandria and "was modeled after earlier Gnostic schools established for the study of religious philosophy."[6] This institution was called the "Catechical School of Alexandria." Its founder, one Pantaenus, was a Gnostic. In the early third century, Clement of Alexandria became the next head of the Catechical School. Clement likewise was heavily influenced by Pantaenus' Gnosticism and complimented him by calling him "the deepest gnostic." Thus, the prevailing religious climate of philosophically-oriented, official Alexandria was apostate by the end of the second century. Its principal school of theology was apostate. The Catechical School of Alexandria also became an educational center for Greek philosophy and science.

---

combine elements of Christianity with their philosophical base which was rooted in the teachings of Philo, Plato, and Buddhism. John Rutherfurd, in James Orr, gen. ed., *International Standard Bible Encyclopedia*, s.v., "Gnosticism."

[4]Ibid.

[5]Col. 2:8.

[6]*International Standard Bible Encyclopedia*, s.v. "Alexandria."

Clement's successor was Origen who became head of the Catechical School in A.D. 232. Under his leadership, the school reached its zenith. Though Origen was one of the greatest minds of the early church, he also was one of the greatest corrupting influences upon the early church as well as upon the copies of the Bible.[7] Origen practiced rigorous asceticism. He also "sought to gather the fragment of truth scattered throughout the pagan philosophies and unite them to Christian teaching" (68). Origen taught that infants were to be baptized for the forgiveness of sins. He did not believe in the resurrection of the body. He was a universalist believing that all, including demons, would be saved. Moreover, Origen took the position that "the Scriptures are of little use to those who understand them as written" (68). He thus strongly advocated allegorizing for the interpretation of the Bible. Origen was thought to be the first to teach purgatory. In the famous dispute between Arius and Athanasius a century later regarding the Deity of Christ, Origen's influence was considered the beginnings of Arianism. It was Origen who first included the Apocrypha with the Bible (69). Moreover, Origen freely acknowledged volitional alterations and corrections of the New Testament manuscripts in Alexandria (69). It also was in the Catechical School of Alexandria that Arius taught and later developed his heresy of denying the Deity of Christ. This was the theological and philosophical climate of Alexandria prior to the production of Vaticanus and Sinaiticus.

After the death of Origen, another notable leader arose in Alexandria by the name of Eusebius. Eusebius was a loyal follower of Origen who "worshipped at the altars of Origen's teachings" (69). Furthermore, it was Eusebius who sought to make reconciliation between the apostate Arius and the orthodox Athanasius at the Council of Nicea in A.D. 325. Again, the heretical, apostate character of Alexandria and its leadership is apparent by the fourth century. Moreover, it was from this apostate milieu that Vaticanus and Sinaiticus arose.

---

[7] Jack Moorman, ed., *Forever Settled: A Survey of the Documents and History of the Bible*. (Johannesburg, South Africa: privately printed, 1985; reprint, Collingswood, N.J.: Bible for Today, 1997), 68.

Additional History of the Critical Text

During the time of Eusebius, Constantine the Great came to power as the emperor of the Roman empire. Though Constantine would eventually profess Christianity, ordering his army to be baptized and finally declaring Christianity to be the official religion of the empire, there is little question that he was never truly born again. His "conversion" to Christianity was more likely that of convenience and political expediency. As Constantine made himself aware of the details of Christianity, he learned that the Bible was the holy book of Christians. Moreover, he also learned that there were two major competing forms of the New Testament even in that day. One was the modest text used by the more common people. This is what would eventually come to be called the Received Text. The other was that of Eusebius and Origen, which was favored by the more philosophically-oriented, upper-class "Christians." This was the Alexandrian text type of which Vaticanus and Sinaiticus are extant examples (100).

Fifty Manuscripts for the Churches of Constantinople

In A.D. 331, the emperor Constantine ordered Eusebius (who had by now moved to Caesarea in Palestine) to provide fifty manuscripts for the churches of Constantinople.[8] Tischendorf suggested that Sinaiticus was one of these fifty manuscripts. There is no evidence to prove that. However, the text type used by Eusebius for the official copies for Constantine is likely that which was quite similar if not identical to Vaticanus and Sinaiticus. This was the text of Alexandria of which Eusebius was familiar and accustomed. Furthermore, the scribal quality of both Vaticanus and Sinaiticus (as well as the quality of the vellum used) suggest that their original copying was by well-paid, professional scribes producing work suitable for the upper class. Modern textual criticism claims that these two famous manuscripts were probably produced in the middle of the fourth century.

---

[8]Ibid.

The greater point in all of this is that Vaticanus (B) and Sinaiticus (Aleph) had their origins from a source already given to apostasy, pagan Greek philosophy, confirmed heresy, and upper-class elitism. Is this consonant with the tenor of how God has typically worked through the ages? Would God use such a setting for the transmission and propagation of His Word? Does God work in concert with apostates and apostasy? (What fellowship hath righteousness with unrighteousness?[9]) Moreover, if Sinaiticus and Vaticanus represent a strain of the New Testament text closest to the originals, why did God then allow them to be hidden for many centuries. None of this is consistent with the biblical principles of holiness, righteousness, or separation from apostasy. Yet, each of these biblical principles must be compromised if we accept that God allowed the transmission of His Word to flow through Eusebius and Alexandrian ecclesiastical academia.

These two manuscripts (though well known today) eventually passed on into oblivion. The manuscript called Sinaiticus wound up in a Greek Orthodox convent at Mount Sinai where it sat gathering dust for untold centuries. Vaticanus wound up in the bowels of the Vatican library. In the intervening centuries, the Alexandrian text type was used primarily in Egypt. It was rejected as defective elsewhere. After many centuries, Tischendorf "discovered" both of these manuscripts in the middle of the nineteenth century. Thus, let us look at the story of his "discoveries" more closely.

Tischendorf's Discoveries

Friederich Constantine Von Tischendorf was a German textual critic who lived in the middle of the nineteenth century. He had been trained in German Higher Rationalism (i.e., Liberalism) and fully accepted the rationalistic theories of text criticism of men such as Karl Lachmann and Johann Jakob Griesbach, both German Rationalists. Like most rationalistic textual critics of the nineteenth century, Tischendorf

---

[9] 2 Cor. 6:14.

began with the premise that the original form of the New Testament had been lost. He therefore viewed his mission as trying to regain the original text of the New Testament.[10] Like his other Rationalist colleagues, Tischendorf erred in not believing God's promise of preservation. However, the New Testament has never been lost. It therefore did not need to be recovered!

Codex Sinaiticus

Notwithstanding, Tischendorf traveled extensively across Europe and the Mediterranean world searching for ancient manuscripts. In 1844, he arrived at the Greek Orthodox Convent of St. Catherine located at Mount Sinai. While there, he noticed what appeared to be leaves of an ancient document in a waste paper basket used for kindling a heating stove. Upon inspection, he found these to be forty-three parchment pages of the Septuagint version of the Old Testament which were part of a greater manuscript including the New Testament. In his excitement he sought permission to copy it, but the monks became suspicious that they had something of value. He therefore was only allowed to copy one other page of that manuscript. He returned nine years later in 1853 to further examine this ancient manuscript, but was not allowed to take it. This of course is what came to be known as Sinaiticus.

Tischendorf returned again in 1856. Once again, perceiving from Tischendorf's interest that they had something of value, the monks were not inclined to part with it. Tischendorf finally prevailed upon the Superior Abbot over the monastery to be allowed to bring the prized manuscript to Cairo where he was allowed to copy it in its entirety. In 1862, after much negotiation, he was allowed to take the manuscript to St. Petersburg, Russia, upon the promise of a large sum of money and the pledge of honors for the monastery. He subsequently had it published

---

[10]Bruce M. Metzger, *The Text of the New Testament: Its Transmission, Corruption, and Restoration* (New York: Oxford University Press, 1964), 126.

from Leipzig, Germany.[11] Thus, from an old document found in a wastebasket, ready to be burned, came a manuscript which modern textual critics claim to reflect the true New Testament. Modern textual critics date Sinaiticus to the mid-fourth century and acknowledge that its original source was from Alexandria, Egypt.

However, as other textual experts examined this newly-found manuscript, it became apparent that it was not such a prize as was first thought. In 1864, F. H. A. Scrivener found that "the codex is covered with alterations of an obviously correctional character—brought in by at least ten different revisers, some of them systematically spread over every page, others occasional, or limited to separate portions of the Ms., many of these being contemporaneous with the first writer, but for the greater part belonging to the sixth or seventh century."[12]

The significance of this analysis is that Sinaiticus is not a reliable manuscript. It had been "doctored" by at least ten revisers over the centuries. Some of the changes were made shortly after its original copying by someone who obviously intended to alter it. Others were done later. These alterations and changes were made throughout the manuscript. In short, the very character of Sinaiticus was such that it certainly had no internal integrity. It therefore can only be viewed as marginal in its reliability. Conservative British textual expert John Burgon characterized Sinaiticus (Aleph) as the second "most untrustworthy codex" to exist.[13] It simply is a bad manuscript as to its textual integrity and its historical reliability. Nevertheless, modern textual critics have held it up as an example of the true and superior text of the New Testament.

---

[11]Metzger, *The Text of the New Testament*, 44-45.

[12]Frederick Henry Scrivener, *A Full Collation of the Codex Sinaiticus*, (Original publisher unknown, 1864); quoted in David Cloud, *Myths about the Modern Bible Versions* (Oak Harbor, Wash.: Way of Life Literature, 1999), 192.

[13]John Burgon, *The Revision Revised*, (Original publisher unknown, 1883); reprint, (Collingswood, N.J.: Dean Burgon Society, n.d.), 13 (page citation is to reprint edition).

Additional History of the Critical Text

Codex Vaticanus

During the mid-nineteenth century, the young Tischendorf became aware of what was purported to be an ancient manuscript of the New Testament in the Vatican library. This old manuscript was not really a secret. Erasmus at one time had specific readings sent to him for his analysis and rejected them. He published his findings regarding these and other Reformation textual editors were quite aware of them. Vaticanus had actually been printed by the Catholic Church in 1587 under the authority of Pope Sixtus and came to be known as the Sixtine edition. It was substantially the text of Vaticanus.[14] Napoleon had even taken this manuscript to Paris as a prize. It was returned to the Vatican library in 1815. In 1843, when he was but twenty-eight years old, Tischendorf was allowed by the Catholic authorities of the Vatican to see this manuscript for a total of six hours. In 1845, the British scholar Tregelles was allowed to see this manuscript, but forbidden to copy even one word thereof. In fact, the Catholic authorities searched his person for any writing materials before allowing him access. While he viewed the manuscript, two Catholic clerics stood beside him and took it from him if he looked too long at any one passage.

Finally, twenty-three years later in 1866, Tischendorf was allowed to not only view the manuscript which came to be known as Codex Vaticanus, but also to make editorial notes. After much negotiating with the Vatican authorities, he was allowed access to Vaticanus for a total of fourteen days for three hours each day.[15] Frederic Kenyon goes on in this context to say, "By making the most of his time Tischendorf was able in 1867 to publish the most perfect edition of the manuscript which had yet appeared."[16] How one could make a "perfect edition" with only forty-two hours of access time seems to be an oxymoron. Evidently, this

---

[14]Richard Ottley, *A Handbook to the Septuagint* (London: Methuen, 1920), 64.

[15]Frederic Kenyon, *Our Bible and the Ancient Manuscripts,* 4th ed. (New York: Harper Bros., 1895), 138-9.

[16]Ibid., 139.

first edition of Vaticanus was not so perfect, for in 1881 an improved Roman Catholic edition was published.

The Primary Pillars of the Critical Text

As the modern critical text would shortly develop, it was composed almost entirely of Sinaiticus and Vaticanus. That fact remains unchanged to this day. Burgon noted that Sinaiticus and Vaticanus very likely were derived from the same source, which is to be expected inasmuch as they both were copied at Alexandria, Egypt.[17] When Burgon compared Vaticanus (B) to the Received Text, he found that Vaticanus omitted at least 2,877 words; added 536 words; substituted 935 words; transposed 2,098 words; and modified 1,132 words for a grand total of 7,578 changes. In comparing Sinaiticus to the Received Text, he found 3,455 words omitted; 839 words added; 1,114 words substituted; 2,299 words transposed; and 1,265 words modified for a grand total of 8,972 changes.[18]

However, Burgon added, "Be it remembered that the omissions, additions, substitutions, transpositions, and modifications, *are by no means the same* in both. It is in fact *easier to find two consecutive verses in which these two MSS. differ the one from the other, than two consecutive verses in which they entirely agree*"[19] (italic emphasis retained from the original quote). In other words, though Sinaiticus and Vaticanus are of the same textual origin, they are utterly inconsistent with each other. They do not agree with each other. They reflect confusion rather than harmony. Yet, from these two manuscripts comes the overwhelming majority from which modern critical text has been cobbled together. Philip Mauro went so far as to suggest that the Sinaiticus

---

[17]Burgon, *The Revision Revised*, 12.

[18]Ibid.

[19]Ibid.

was originally copied from the Received Text and that the voluminous modifications noted above were actually intentionally done to modify it to suit the theological disposition of the correctors.[20]

Westcott and Hort's Collation

In 1851, the well-known British textual critics Westcott and Hort began their task of collating Sinaiticus (Aleph) and Vaticanus (B) into one unified text. It became known as the Westcott and Hort Greek Text. What they produced was not a revision of the time-honored Received Text. Rather, what they created was an entirely new Greek text which had never before existed. From their new Greek text, the English Revised Version was published in 1888. That began the string of literally hundreds of modern English translations, almost all of which have been based upon the direct descendent of Westcott and Hort's Greek text—the modern critical text. That modern critical text has changed only slightly from the work of Westcott and Hort near the end of nineteenth century.

The Men behind the Critical Text

Those who view reconstruction of the New Testament text as a science, like any other form of historical research, bristle when the character or the theology of those involved in modern text criticism is examined. The charge of *argumentum ad hominem* is immediately raised. (*Argumentum ad hominem* is a Latin phrase which means arguing one's case by attacking the *man* representing your opposition rather than the issues.) Lawyers regularly use this device in court when the facts do not favor their case. In the arena of scientific research therefore, *argumentum ad hominem* is considered to be an invalid argument.

---

[20]Philip Mauro, *Which Version? Authorized or Revised?* (Boston: Scripture Truth Depot, 1924), 36.

It therefore is usually dismissed indicating a weak case on the part of the one bringing it up. In a court of law, guilt by association is not a valid argument. But, *influence by association* certainly is a valid premise, especially in things spiritual.

However, Fundamentalists do not view the Bible as just another book. Its history is not just ordinary history. There is a great, ongoing spiritual battle. When individuals in the battle can be identified as being sympathetic to or actually advocating apostasy, that is a valid charge for consideration. Such leanings and associations indicate their true colors in the greater battle. They either are wittingly or unwittingly cooperating with God's archenemy, the evil one.

Westcott and Hort

In the ongoing controversy, some Fundamentalists have sought to portray Westcott and Hort as orthodox, Fundamentalist brethren. One such writer has gone on record regarding the above-mentioned editors as saying, "I challenge anyone to find one sentence that would be a departure from Fundamentalist doctrine."[21] That we shall.

The Broad Church Party

Westcott and Hort were both clergymen in the Anglican Church of England during the mid and latter portion of the nineteenth century. Both of these scholars graduated from Cambridge University. However, by the middle of the nineteenth century, Cambridge University had become completely infected by German Higher Rationalism (Liberalism) through men such as the Unitarian Samuel Coleridge. The utter apostasy and theological Liberalism of Coleridge and other members of

---

[21] James B. Williams, "Introduction," in *From the Mind of God to the Mind of Man*, ed. James B. Williams (Greenville, S.C.: Ambassador—Emerald International, 1999), 4.

the Cambridge faculty have been well documented by James Sightler.[22] Another Liberal theological professor at Cambridge was a man by the name of J. F. D. Maurice who along with Coleridge founded the Broad Church Party of the Anglican Church. Maurice grew up in a Unitarian home (12-13). When later in life, Westcott read Maurice's biography, he commented, "I never knew before how deep my sympathy is with most of his characteristic thoughts" (14). The Broad Church Party of the Anglican Church would be analogous to the American National Council of Churches in its theology and apostasy. It was utterly liberal. Yet, Westcott and Hort voluntarily belonged to the Broad Church Party (15).

Westcott and Hort were typical Liberals of their day. Because the grass-roots level of the Church of England was still relatively orthodox along with the official position of the Church, they had to be careful in what they published or publicly said. Therefore, they did not outrightly deny the fundamental doctrines of the Word of God. Rather, they undermined them with subtle questions and theological doublespeak. They were masters of using orthodox terminology but importing unscriptural meaning to those terms.[23] This has been a standard Liberal tactic for more than two hundred years.

Mentors of Westcott and Hort

To better understand where Westcott and Hort are coming from, it is insightful to know something of their mentors. Johann Salomo Semler (1725-91) has been called the father of German Higher Rationalism (i.e., Liberalism).[24] Theodore Letis describes Semler as "one of the dec-

---

[22]James Sightler, *Tabernacle Essays on Bible Translations* (Greenville, S.C.: Tabernacle Baptist Church, 1993), 11-14.

[23]Examples of this will be presented later in this chapter and also again in chapter 9.

[24]Metzger, *The Text of the New Testament*, 11-12.

isive architects of the higher-critical method.[25] Semler profoundly influenced Johann Jakob Griesbach (1745-1812) who was one of the fathers of Modernism.[26] Moreover, Semler viewed the Bible as a man-made book.[27] From these two German Rationalists sprang the ugly stream of modern apostasy which afflicts the church of Jesus Christ to this hour. In America, theological Liberal Joseph Steven Buckminster "persuaded the officials at Harvard College in 1809 to publish an American edition of the Griesbach's critical Greek New Testament, because he saw its value in promoting text criticism, in his opinion, '*a most powerful weapon to be used against the supporters of verbal inspiration*'"[28] (emphasis mine). Perhaps Fundamentalists who support the critical text should pause and reread that last statement. Contained therein is damning evidence of the origins of rationalistic textual criticism. Westcott and Hort were deeply influenced by both Semler and Griesbach and adopted their theories of textual criticism.[29] Letis notes that Westcott and Hort adopted the method of Griesbach "whose name they venerated" above all other textual critics.[30] Hort himself wrote that he and Westcott revered the name of Griesbach "above that of every

---

[25]Theodore Letis, *The Ecclesiastical Text* (Philadelphia: Institute for Renaissance & Reformation Biblical Studies, 1997), 11.

[26]D. A. Thompson, "The Controversy Concerning the Last Twelve Verses of the Gospel according to Mark." Surrey: Bible Christian Unity Fellowship, 39-40; reprint of an article which appeared in *Bible League Quarterly*, London, 1973.

[27]Ibid.

[28]Letis, *The Ecclesiastical Text*, 2.

[29]Brooke Foss Westcott and Fenton John Anthony Hort, *Introduction to the New Testament in the Original Greek with Notes on Selected Readings* (1882; reprint, Peabody, Mass.: Hendrickson, 1988), 185 (page citation is to the reprint edition).

[30]Letis, *The Ecclesiastical Text*, 17.

other textual critic of the New Testament."[31] They went on to note that they felt there was no valid objection which could be made of Griesbach's views.[32] The mentors and guides by which Westcott and Hort worked were the very fathers of German Higher Rationalism (i.e., Liberalism).

The Theological Liberalism of Westcott and Hort

In a doctoral thesis presented to Dallas Theological Seminary in 1951, Alfred Martin, former vice president of Moody Bible Institute wrote, "At precisely the time when Liberalism was carrying the field in the English churches the theory of Westcott and Hort received wide acclaim. These are not isolated facts. Recent contributions on the subject—that is, in the present century—following mainly the Westcott-Hort principles and methods, have been made largely by men who deny the inspiration of the Bible."[33] Let us therefore consider documentation of the positions which Westcott and Hort took on major biblical doctrines.

Inspiration and Inerrancy

Regarding inspiration and inerrancy of the Bible, never did either Westcott or Hort once make positive statements thereto in their voluminous writings. Rather, they either ignored the subject altogether or made light of it. For example, in a letter to J. B. Lightfoot in 1860,

---

[31]Fenton John Anthony Hort, *The New Testament in the Original Greek*, 2d ed. (New York: Harper, 1882), 185.

[32]Letis, *The Ecclesiastical Text*, 17.

[33]Alfred Martin, "A Critical Examination of the Westcott-Hort Textual Theory" (Th.D. thesis, Dallas Theological Seminary, 1951), 70.

Hort wrote sarcastically, "I am convinced that any view of the Gospels which distinctly and consistently recognizes for them a *natural and historical origin* . . . and assumes that they did not drop down ready-made from Heaven must and will be startling to an immense proportion of educated English people"[34] (emphasis mine).

Notice how that Hort refers to the Gospels as having "a natural and historic origin" rather than a heavenly one. Though a great many of the English people of his day believed in inspiration, he mocked it in this letter. James Sightler, in analyzing Westcott and Hort's introductory comments to their Greek New Testament, has written, "Westcott and Hort . . . stated in the introduction to their Greek text that they did not accept inerrancy, even of the autographs."[35] There is worth in stating again that nowhere in the writings of Westcott and Hort is any statement made that they believed in the verbal inspiration of the Bible or of its inerrancy. They *always* either were silent on the issue or wrote in such a way that their leanings against it were quite clear.

Theology Proper

Let us look at the stated views of Westcott and Hort regarding theology proper.[36] Wescott and Hort advocated the universal fatherhood of God. This is standard Liberal theology which alleges that God is the spiritual Father of all and that all men are His children. Westcott, in commenting on John 1:29, wrote that "the thought, which is concrete in v. 28, is here traced back to its most absolute form as resting on the

---

[34]Arthur Fenton Hort, *Life and Letters of Fenton John Anthony Hort*, (London: MacMillan & Co., 1896), 2:411.

[35]Sightler, *Tabernacle Essays*, 51.

[36]It is noteworthy, as early as 1908, that historians discerned how Westcott had a unique brand of theology. It was described as a modern "incarnation" of and in general sympathy to the Alexandrian teachings of Clement and Origen. W. R. Inge in James Hastings ed., *Encyclopedia of Religion and Ethics* (New York: Charles Scribner's Sons, 1908), s.v. "Alexandrian Theology."

essential power of God in His relation of *universal fatherhood*"³⁷ (emphasis has been added). Westcott also denied that God had to be propitiated. In his commentary on 1 John 2:2, he wrote, "They show that the scriptural conception is *not* of appeasing one who is angry, with a personal feeling, against the offender; but of altering the character of that which from without occasions a necessary alienation, and interposes an inevitable obstacle to fellowship. Such phrases as *'propitiating God' . . .* are *foreign to the language of the NT'"*³⁸ (emphasis mine).

This sounds like theological mumbo-jumbo, which it is. However, what is significant is that Westcott is quite clear in noting that propitiation is not propitiation. In other words, the righteous demand of a holy God did not need to be met by Christ's work on the cross. That, however, is the clear meaning of 1 John 2:2.

Creation and Evolution

Both Westcott and Hort were evolutionists. In his commentary of Heb. 1:2, Westcott wrote, "The universe may be regarded either in its actual constitution as a whole . . . or as an order which exists through time *developed in successive stages.* There are obvious reasons why the *latter mode* of representation should be adopted here³⁹ (emphasis mine).

In his commentary on Heb. 7:10, Westcott wrote, "Each man is at once an individual of a race and a new power in the *evolution of the race*"⁴⁰ (emphasis mine). Westcott believed in evolution even before

---

[37] B. F. Westcott, *The Epistles of St. John: The Greek Text with Notes and Essays*, 2d ed. (Cambridge: Macmillan, 1886), 159.

[38] Ibid.

[39] B. F. Westcott, *The Epistle of Paul the Apostle to the Hebrews: The Greek Text with Notes and Essays*, 3d ed. (London: Macmillan, 1920), 8.

[40] Ibid., 179.

Darwin's book popularized the idea.[41] He later wrote, "If we feel that the balance of *evidence favours the belief in the evolution of life*, or more truly of the organisms through which the life reveals itself, according to the action of uniform laws, we do not lose but gain by the conclusion."[42] (emphasis mine).

In a personal letter written in 1890, Westcott wrote, "No one now, I suppose, holds that the first three chapters of Genesis, for example, give a literal history—I could never understand how any one reading them with open eyes could think they did."[43] In another letter, Westcott wrote, "I am inclined to think that no such state as 'Eden' (I mean the popular notion) ever existed, and that Adam's fall in no degree differed from the fall of each of his descendants, as Coleridge justly argues."[44]

In 1860, Hort wrote a personal letter to one John Ellerton in which he wrote, "But the book which has most engaged me is Darwin. Whatever maybe thought of it, it is a book that one is proud to be contemporary with. . . . My feeling is strong that the theory [of evolution] is unanswerable."[45] Though some Fundamentalists have sought to deny that Westcott and Hort were evolutionists, their own words speak for themselves.

The Resurrection of Christ

Regarding Westcott and Hort's view of the resurrection of Christ, there is considerable evidence that they believed in a *nonliteral*, spiritual

---

[41] Sightler, *Tabernacle Essays*, 112.

[42] B. F. Westcott, *The Gospel of Life* (London: Macmillan & Co., 1888), 245-246.

[43] Arthur Westcott, *Life and Letters of Brooke Foss Westcott* (London: MacMillan & Co., 1903), 1:69.

[44] Ibid., 78.

[45] Arthur Hort, *Life and Letters*, 2:416.

resurrection. This has been a longstanding way that Liberal theologians refer to the resurrection. However, it imports into it an unbelieving nuance alien to Scripture. Let us look briefly at this matter.[46]

Westcott grudgingly acknowledged the *physical* resurrection of Lazarus. However, he was unwilling to ascribe the same *physical* resurrection to Jesus. In that regard, he wrote the following: "In doing this I have been led to emphasize *two facts* which are, I believe, of the highest importance and clearly established by the documents . . . that the Lord was *not raised again* to the *natural human life*, as Lazarus was raised. . . . The *first fact* seems to me to involve the *essence* of the whole *revelation of the risen*. No *material*, no *physiological test* could have established the fulness of the Truth which is required. . . . In other words the *physiological test would establish failure* just at the point where revelation is needed"[47] (emphasis mine). Notice Westcott's comment that the Lord was "*not* raised again to the natural human life." He went on to explain that, in essence, Christ's resurrection was not physiological (i.e, physical). That, dear reader, is unadulterated Liberalism.

Though Westcott claimed to believe in the resurrection of Jesus Christ, he viewed it rather as a "spiritual" resurrection. He went on to write, "Or to put the thought in another form, in our earthly life the spirit is manifested through the body; in the life of the risen Christ, the body is manifested (may we not say so?) through the spirit."[48]

What he is saying here is that the manifestation of Christ's resurrection was through His spirit. That may sound pious, but it

---

[46]Donald Waite has written a 50-page booklet documenting in considerable detail Westcott's denial of Christ's bodily resurrection *Westcott's Denial of Christ's Bodily Resurrection* (Collingswood: N.J.: Bible for Today 1983).

[47]B. F. Westcott, *The Revelation of the Risen Lord* (New York: Macmillan & Co., 1891), xxxiii.

[48]Ibid., 8.

directly contradicts the New Testament record. Jesus said to His disciples on the first evening after the resurrection, "Behold my hands and my feet, that it is I myself: handle me, and see; for a spirit hath not flesh and bones, as ye see me have" (Luke 24:39). Westcott's position comes perilously close to that of the Gnostics which denied that Christ had a physical body. Westcott essentially advanced the idea that Jesus did not rise again physically, only spiritually. That once again is old-fashioned Liberalism. Moreover, as he had opportunity, Westcott sneered at those who believed in a bodily, physical resurrection of our Lord.[48] Numerous other quotes could be added to further establish this point. However, the simple fact is that Westcott did not believe in a literal, bodily resurrection of Jesus Christ. He advanced that Jesus only arose spiritually.

Salvation

In other areas, Westcott espoused standard theological Liberalism. For example, regarding salvation, he advocated the idea of universal salvation. In his commentary on Heb. 2:9 regarding Christ Jesus, he wrote, "The glory which followed the death (of Christ) marked its *universal efficacy*. Thus Christ was made lower than angels that He might accomplish this complete redemption"[49] (emphasis mine). This implies that Christ's death was automatically efficacious for all.

Or, to put it another way, because Jesus died, all will be saved. This notion is further reenforced in Westcott's commentary of I John 2:12 where he wrote,"Forgiveness is granted to men because Christ is what He is revealed to be and what His 'name' expresses."[50] To the contrary, forgiveness is not automatically granted to men just because of who Christ is or what He did. It requires repentance and faith on the part of

---

[48]Ibid., 39.

[49]B. F. Westcott, *Hebrews*, 46.

[50]B. F. Westcott, *I John*, 59.

the sinner coming to Christ. Once again, his views reflect the Liberalism prevalent in his day which was rooted in German Rationalism.

Christology

One of the worst aspects of Westcott's position was his view of Christology. In his commentary on John 1:1, he wrote, "The 'being' of the Word is thus necessarily carried beyond the limits of time, *though the pre-existence of the Word is not definitely stated*. The simple affirmation of existence in this connexion suggests a loftier conception than that of *pre-existence*; which is embarrassed by the idea of time"[51] (emphasis mine).

Though Westcott was notorious for his doublespeak and mumbo-jumbo style of theological writing evident above; at this juncture, he clearly questions the pre-existence of Jesus Christ. He similarly wrote in his commentary for John 1:15 ("He that cometh after me is preferred before me") that "the *supposed reference to the pre-existence of the Word . . . seems to be inconsistent* with the argument which points to a present consequence"[52] (emphasis mine). Again, Westcott questions the pre-existence of our Lord. In his comments on John 4:1, Westcott wrote, "Nothing implies that the knowledge of the Lord was supernatural."[53] He clearly undermines the omniscience of our Lord.

In his commentary of John 1:1, he wrote further, "Because the Word was personally distinct from 'God' and yet *essentially* 'God,' he could make Him known."[54] As D. A. Waite notes at this point, "If the Lord Jesus was *distinct from God*," then he could not have been 'God'

---

[51]B. F. Westcott, *The Gospel according to St. John: The Authorized Version with Introduction and Notes* (London: John Murray, 1892), 2.

[52]Ibid., 13.

[53]Ibid., 66.

[54]Ibid., 2.

... yet Westcott wants merely to say that He was 'essentially God' without *actually being* God"[55] (emphasis has been added). In this same context, Westcott went on to say, "Thus we are led to conceive that the *divine nature is **essentially** in the Son*"[56] (emphasis has been added). Jesus was not *essentially* divine. He *is* Deity! Though Westcott stops short of outright denial of the Deity of Christ, he certainly does not affirm it either. To the contrary, he openly sows the seeds that Jesus Christ was something less than altogether God. This is classic Liberalism. To avoid the political heat of being called a heretic, many Liberals (then and now) stop short of outright denial of clear biblical truth. However, they clearly sow the seeds of doubt to let their readers jump to the intended conclusion.

There is much more which could be noted regarding the theological Liberalism of Westcott and Hort. We will not take the time and space to further document their theology. However, from the quotations cited above, it should be clear to any impartial reader that Westcott and Hort were theological Liberals. Their avowed mentors were the same. The Broad Church Party of the Anglican Church of which they chose to be a part was the same. Notwithstanding, these rationalistic Liberals were responsible for the initial production of the modern critical text. Their work remains the standard and basis thereof going into the twenty-first century.

Text Critics of the Twentieth Century

As the twentieth century dawned and Westcott and Hort passed from the scene, a new generation of modern textual critics arose. The modern critical text is presently manifested in the United Bible Societies' Greek Text and the Nestlé-Aland Greek Text. They are quite

---

[55]D. A. Waite, *Heresies of Westcott and Hort* (Collingswood, N.J.: Bible for Today, 1998), 24.

[56]B. F. Westcott, *The Gospel According to St. John*, 3.

Additional History of the Critical Text

similar though the textual apparatus (footnotes) of the two will differ. These more recently have been combined into what is now called the N/U text with the "*N*" referring to the Nestlé-Aland text and the "*U*" referring to the United Bible Societies text.

More specifically, shortly after the turn of the twentieth century, the British and Foreign Bible Society published a Greek text of the New Testament based upon the work of Eberhard Nestlé. Nestlé's text, in turn, was based upon (1) Tischendorf's eighth edition of 1869-72, (2) Westcott and Hort's Greek New Testament of 1881, and (3) the Weiss edition of 1902. Since then, the Nestlé text has undergone twenty-six revisions and is presently in its twenty-seventh edition. Later in the twentieth century, Kurt Aland became co-editor and this Greek text is now called the Nestlé-Aland Text.[57]

In 1965, the United Bible Societies published their first edition of the Greek New Testament which is presently in its fourth edition. The title page to the Third Edition of the United Bible Societies's Greek New Testament lists the following editors: Kurt Aland, Matthew Black, Carlo M. Martini, Bruce Metzger, and Allen Wikgren. Who are these men and what do they believe? Regarding these five editors, David Cloud has written, "Not one of these men believes the Bible is the infallible Word of God."[58]

Kurt Aland

Kurt Aland has served as a co-editor of the Nestlé-Aland Text since World War II. He also is one of the contributing editors for the United Bible Societies Greek Text. He is a German, educated by the notorious rationalistic institutions of pre-war Germany. His wife, Barbara, has

---

[57]Kurt Aland and Barbara Aland, *The Text of the New Testament: An Introduction to the Critical Editions to the Theory and Practice of Modern Textual Criticism,* 2d ed. (Grand Rapids: W. B. Eerdmans, 1989), 20.

[58]David Cloud, *Myths about the Modern Bible Versions* (Oak Harbor, Wash.: Way of   Life Literature, 1999), 34.

directed the Institute for New Testament Textual Research in Munster, Germany, for many years.[59] However, Kurt Aland rejects the doctrine of the verbal inspiration of the Scriptures. He wrote in 1962, "This idea of verbal inspiration (i.e., of the literal and inerrant inspiration of the text), which the orthodoxy of both Protestant traditions maintained so vigorously, was applied to the Textus Receptus with all of its errors, including textual modifications of an obviously secondary character (as we recognize them today)."[60]

Though written in the somewhat obtuse style of academia, it is clear that Aland mocks the concept of inerrancy as well as verbal inspiration of the Bible. He, of course, had followed the principles of modern textual criticism to their logical conclusion. Considering the bottomless pit of critical text variants, Aland *rationally* concluded that there could be no such thing as either inerrancy or verbal inspiration.

Aland went on to write about his belief that the canon of the New Testament text is not established. Continuing, he wrote, "The first thing to be done, then, would be to examine critically one's own selection from the formal Canon and its principles of interpretation, but all the time remaining completely alive to the selection and principles of others. . . . This road will be long and laborious and painful. . . . If we succeed in arriving at a Canon which is common and actual, this means the achievement of the unity of the faith, the unity of the Church."[61]

To any observer, it should be apparent that Aland does not view the New Testament text as settled. He, like so many modern text critics, has been seeking to reconstruct the text. Everything is open to challenge. He is willing to cooperate with whoever in an ecumenical spirit. This is one of the men through which the modern critical text has been greatly shaped.

---

[59]Ibid., 228.

[60]Kurt Aland, *The Problem of the New Testament Canon* (London: A. R. Mowbray, 1962), 6-7.

[61]Ibid.

Additional History of the Critical Text

Bruce Metzger

Another editor of the United Bible Societies' Greek New Testament is Bruce Metzger. He is the George L. Collord Professor of New Testament Language and Literature at Princeton Theological Seminary. That seminary has long been modernistic. He also is on the board of the American Bible Society. Metzger was part of the committee which produced the Revised Standard Version. He also is the head of the continuing translation committee of the National Council of Churches. It was Metzger who was chairman for the Reader's Digest (RSV) condensed Bible which chopped out 40 percent of the Bible, ignoring the warning of Rev. 22:18-19. The pre-face to that abridged perversion of the Bible noted that Metzger was actively involved with every stage of it including his approval of the finished condensation.[62]

From his writings, Bruce Metzger clearly fits the profile of a classic theological Modernist. He questions the authorship, traditional dates, and supernatural inspiration of various books of the Bible. Let us briefly look at some examples of these. In his comments on Genesis, Metzger writes, "Nearly all modern Scholars agree that, like the other books of the Pentateuch, (Genesis) is a composite of several sources, embodying traditions that go back in some cases to Moses" (1). In introductory comments about Exodus, Metzger writes, "As with Genesis, several strands of literary tradition, some very ancient, some as late as the sixth century B.C., were combined in the makeup of the books" (30). In comments about Daniel, Metzger wrote, "Most scholars hold that the book was compiled during the persecutions (168-165 B.C.) of the Jewish people by Antiochus Epiphanes (465). This is the standard, Liberal theological party line. Metzger questions whether the Gospel of John was written by John. He questions whether the pastoral epistles were written by Paul. He also denies that Peter wrote 2 Peter. In his "Introduction to the Old Testament," he refers to the times of David and

---

[62]Bruce Metzger, ed., *The Reader's Digest Bible: Condensed from the Revised Standard Version, Old and New Testaments* (Pleasantville, N. Y.: The Reader's Digest Association, 1982) ix-xi.

Solomon as myth, legend, and history. He denies a universal flood. He refers to the book of Job as ancient folklore. He claims that there were two or three separate authors of Isaiah. He calls the book of Jonah a "legend" (xiv). These are only a sampling of his apostasy. Notes throughout the Reader's Digest Revised Standard Version (RSV) condensed Bible provide numerous other examples of classical, apostate, liberal theology. Moreover, the copyright page of this truncated Bible notes that Metzger's work was with the express permission of the National Council of Churches (NCC). Notwithstanding, Bruce Metzger is considered, even by many Fundamentalists, to be the preeminent authority today on the modern critical text of the New Testament.

Carlo Maria Martini

Cardinal Carlo Maria Martini has been the Jesuit Roman Catholic Archbishop of Milan. He became a part of the editorial committee of the United Bible Societies' Greek New Testament in 1967. He heads the largest Roman Catholic diocese in Europe with more than five million laity and two thousand priests. He has been a professor at the Pontifical Biblical Institute in Rome. This same institution promotes evolution as well as heretical views of biblical inspiration. He once was listed as a possible candidate for the papacy. He has been an advocate of a new-age and of a universal, one-world religion.[63] That sounds very much like the Antichrist. Nevertheless, Cardinal Martini has helped shape the current United Bible Societies' critical text of the New Testament.

Eugene Nida

Finally, Eugene Nida has been associated with the American Bible Society and the United Bible Societies since 1946. He no longer is

---

[63]Cloud, *Myths*, 220.

active in either, but during his tenure was involved in virtually every part of these organizations. He was instrumental in the development of the first edition of the United Bible Society Greek Text. He was the Translation Research Coordinator of the United Bible Societies from 1970 to 1980. It was Eugene Nida who widely popularized the notion of "dynamic equivalency." Regarding his views on religion and communication, Nida has made the following statements:

- "God's revelation involved limitations."[64]

- "Biblical revelation is not absolute and all divine revelation is essentially incarnational" (225).

- "Even if a truth is given only in words, it has no real validity until it has been translated into life" (226).

- "The words are in a sense nothing in and of themselves" (226).

- "The word is void unless related to experience" (226).

These quotations reflect a direct repudiation of the doctrine of verbal, plenary inspiration of the Scriptures.

These men have been the chief architects and editors of the modern critical text of the twentieth century. Yet, many a Fundamentalist still tenaciously clings to the work of these apostates.

---

[64]Eugene Nida, *Message and Mission: The Communication of the Christian Faith* (New York: Harper, 1960), 222. It is further noteworthy that Nida used terminology unique to Neoorthodoxy to describe his views in the book mentioned above (e.g., "Gestalt psychology" [226] and "encounters with God" [224] et al.).

The Apostate Character of the United Bible Societies

Though the issue at hand is the history of the critical text, its modern manifestation is produced primarily by the United Bible Societies (UBS). In the preceding section, we looked at some of the major players thereof insofar as their Greek text is concerned. Most Fundamentalists are unaware of the history or character of the United Bible Societies and its roots in England. It began as the British and Foreign Bible Society in 1804 in London, England. In 1946, a number of national Bible societies including the American Bible Society joined together with it to form an international organization called the United Bible Societies. However, the flagship society of the several nations with Bible societies, especially through the nineteenth century, was the British and Foreign Bible Society.

The British and Foreign Bible Society and the Trinitarian Bible Society

Amazingly, the British and Foreign Bible Society (BFBS) was apostate from its inception in 1804. From its beginning, the British and Foreign Bible Society cooperated with Roman Catholic groups. At the urging of the British and Foreign Bible Society, Roman Catholic clerics were invited to participate in the organization of the American Bible Society in 1816.[65] Even worse, the British and Foreign Bible Society voluntarily allowed Unitarians into their society in those early years.[66] (Unitarians deny the Deity of Christ and scoff at the idea of the Trinity. They were the original, modern, theological Liberals in England.) In fact, Unitarians gained substantial influence in the British and Foreign Bible Society not only in Britain but in other European Bible societies.

---

[65]"The Bible Societies," *Trinitarian Bible Society Quarterly Record*, Jan. - Mar. 1979, 13-14.

[66]Andrew Brown, *The Word of God among All Nations* (London: Trinitarian Bible Society, 1981), 12.

Additional History of the Critical Text

In some cases, Bible societies were run almost exclusively by those holding Unitarian convictions.[67] Public prayer and even public reading of Scripture were not allowed in British and Foreign Bible Society meetings lest Unitarian members be offended by someone praying in Jesus' name or by the Scripture read.[68] When more conservative members of the British and Foreign Bible Society sought to prevent membership to Unitarians, the motion was rejected by a majority vote of six to one.[69]

This prompted the creation of the Trinitarian Bible Society in 1831.[70] From its inception, the Trinitarian Bible Society has, as a condition of membership, maintained a firm conviction in the Trinity and other orthodox doctrine. From its beginning, the Trinitarian Bible Society has always advocated use of the Received Text and the King James Version. The British and Foreign Bible Society and its later partner, the United Bible Societies, has, since the arrival of the Westcott and Hort Greek text, promoted the latter and its closely related twentieth-century cousins. The British and Foreign Bible Society and its related Unitarian-oriented European Bible Societies have since their earliest days worked closely with Rome in helping to produce and distribute Roman Catholic Versions.[71]

---

[67] "The Bible Societies," *Trinitarian Record*, 13-14.

[68] Brown, *The Word of God*, 12-16.

[69] Ibid.

[70] The Trinitarian Bible Society continues to this day. Its address is Tyndale House, Dorset Road, London, SW19 3NN, England. Its e-mail address is *trinitarian.bible.society@ukonline.uk*.

[71] Brown, *The Word of God*, 20-21.

Catholics and the World Council of Churches

In the twentieth century, the United Bible Societies have worked to a greater degree with the Vatican than any other one group with perhaps the exception of the World Council of Churches. Members of major committees of the United Bible Societies routinely include Roman Catholic Bishops such as the Right Reverend Monsignor Alberto Ablondi, Bishop of Livorno in Italy.[72] One Catholic group participating with the United Bible Societies is the World Catholic Federation for the Biblical Apostolate. A former Vice-President of the United Bible Societies was Cardinal Francis Arinze. A word which accurately defines the United Bible Societies in the last part of the twentieth century is "ecumenical." The honorary president of the United Bible Societies in the 1980s was the Archbishop of Canterbury, Lord Coggan. Another member of its executive committee at that time was the Very Reverend Gunnar Stalsett who was also a member of the executive committee of the World Council of Churches.[73] In most nations of the Third World, participating societies of the United Bible Societies are dominated by Roman Catholics.[74] One of the major editors of the United Bible Societies Greek New Testament was Cardinal Carlo M. Martini, Archbishop of Milan, Italy. The United Bible Societies has either been responsible for or has gladly participated in such Bible versions as the Revised Standard Version, Today's English Version, and the New English Bible. Of course the United Bible Societies critical text was used for all of these translations.

Almost all modern English translations have been based upon the modern critical texts produced by the United Bible Societies or Nestlé-Aland. These include the New American Standard Bible and the New International Version. Yet, as this chapter has documented, the critical

---

[72]*Ecumenism and the United Bible Societies* (London: Tyndale House, 1985), 8.

[73]Ibid., 9.

[74]Ibid., 9-25.

text from its ancient roots in Alexandria to the current United Bible Societies Greek Text is associated with apostasy at *every* step of its history.

Summary

Origen and Eusebius were apostates in the early church, but there remains uncertainty whether Eusebius had any direct contact with the production of Vaticanus or Sinaiticus. However, there is little question that his *influence* was directly involved. When these two Alexandrian manuscripts were brought out of darkness in the middle of the nineteenth century, they were done so by a German Rationalist. Westcott and Hort (who collated, published, and popularized Sinaiticus and Vaticanus) were not only closet Liberals themselves, but their whole background and circles of associations were with apostates. In the twentieth century, the modern critical text has changed only slightly from the Westcott and Hort Greek text.

Moreover, most of the major editors of the modern critical text are demonstrative theological Liberals and apostates. The organization which has published the critical text (the UBS) for the past fifty years has been Liberal and apostate from its historical roots in the British Foreign Bible Society. Furthermore, the leadership of the United Bible Societies is largely connected to the Vatican or the World Council of Churches. Throughout the world, the United Bible Societies is ecumenical often working directly with Roman Catholic officials.

This is the lineage and associations of the modern critical text. Fundamentalists who cling to it will have to answer to themselves, their constituencies, and to God for their compromise in so supporting such apostasy. Its direct manifestations are in the United Bible Societies, Nestlé-Aland, or the N/U Greek New Testaments and thence in their resultant translations. There is no coincidence that the Trinitarian Bible Society (founded upon orthodox convictions) has always used the Textus Receptus and the King James Version. The United Bible Societies, with its ecumenicalism and apostasy, has always used and promoted the critical text with its modernist translations. As the translation and textual debate continues, Fundamentalists are going to have to decide which side they are on!

Additional History of the Critical Text

Review Questions for Further Study

1. From where did the ancient origins of the critical text come?

2. Who were two early church leaders from Alexandria which helped shape the theological and philosophical climate in the third and fourth centuries?

3. What were the two ancient pillars of the Alexandrian text?

4. Where did these two manuscripts spend many centuries?

5. Who was the German Rationalist who traveled extensively in search of manuscripts during the nineteenth century?

6. Who were the two British scholars who collated the Alexandrian manuscripts together?

7. What are the two main components of the Westcott and Hort text?

8. Were Westcott and Hort Fundamental in their doctrine?

9. Today, who is the primary publisher of the modern critical text?

10. Who are some of the editors of the United Bible Societies Greek text?

11. Can it be shown that any of these men are theological Liberals?

12. Is the United Bible Societies a Fundamentalist organization?

CHAPTER SEVEN

DATING, WEIGHTING, AND COUNTING

In the last chapter, we looked at additional details of the history of the critical text, showing its long associations and connections to apostasy both ancient and modern. Now, let us consider the logic and some of the logical fallacies of the critical text.

The Primary Logic of the Critical Text Position

As we have reviewed the essence of the critical text position in earlier chapters, it is evident that it is complex and confusing in its tenets. Most proponents thereof do not dispute that it is complex and best left to the experts. However, the distilled essence of it is actually quite simple. From the time of Westcott and Hort and onwards, the byword of the modern critical text has been that the earliest manuscripts are the best (older is better).

The logic is simple. The presumption is that the earliest New Testament manuscripts are the closest to the originals and therefore should take precedence over manuscripts which are later in their dating. Scribal errors would have accumulated less in the earliest manuscripts and therefore the earliest manuscripts are to be preferred over more recent ones. It sounds quite reasonable. Presumably, in manuscripts which date to later centuries, scribal errors would be compounded by the passage of time. Successive copyists would have recopied earlier errors and inadvertently introduced errors of their own. Therefore, later manuscripts being farther removed from the originals undoubtedly contain more errors—or so the theory goes. (However, in this theory there is no allowance made for the providential guidance of the Holy Spirit in the transmission of the text. Moreover, it rests completely upon what is logical, reasonable, and *rational*. The foundation therefore lies in human reason.)

According to the theory, because Vaticanus and Sinaiticus are probably the earliest largely intact copies of the New Testament, they therefore should be elevated above all other manuscripts—especially those which are later in their production. Most *existing* copies of manuscripts supporting the Received Text were produced between the tenth and fifteenth centuries. Most text critics estimate that Vaticanus and Sinaiticus were produced in the middle of the fourth century. Notwithstanding the fact that there are thousands of existing manuscripts favoring the Received Text, because Vaticanus, Sinaiticus, and several other manuscripts are earlier; the *rational* conclusion is evident. The critical text theory demands that we must view these several early manuscripts as the closest representatives to the original documents of the New Testament. Therefore, the critical text advocates tell us that Vaticanus, Sinaiticus, and their ancient allies must become the principal sources for *reconstructing* the text of the New Testament text. (Recall that critical text theory begins with the *assumption* that the text of the New Testament has been lost.)

From this point flows the entire theory of modern textual criticism. It makes little difference that there are more than five thousand manuscripts which favor the Received Text and only dozens supporting the primary essence of the critical text. We are told that those manuscripts supporting the Received Text are to be discounted because the earliest manuscripts are *assumed* to more closely reflect the autographa.

Weighting

Modern textual critics thus consciously "weight" texts; that is, they purposefully designate some manuscripts as being more important than others. When asked why there are so many copies of the Received Text, proponents of the critical text theory have a standard answer. In their complex theory, the *assumption* is made that the numerous manuscripts of the Received Text came from an official revision of the text. (They refer to this as a "recension." The latter word simply means "revision.") The *assumption* is that this was done by some unknown church council or decree. (However, there is positively no historical evidence to support this *assumption*. Notwithstanding, it remains part of the stock and trade of the ongoing theory of modern textual criticism.)

Because the many existing copies of the Received Text are *assumed* to be copies of an official "ecclesiastical text," they are therefore considered (by advocates of the critical text) to be secondary copies, much like a translation of the Bible. According to advocates of the critical text, the value of the thousands of Received Text manuscripts for determining the "real" text of the Bible is thus thought to be negligible. Therefore, most modern textual critics ignore these thousands of manuscripts of the Received Text.

The lynchpin of the dismissal of the Received Text is once again the *presumption* that its source was some unknown, official, ecclesiastical copy. However, there is absolutely no historical support for this *assumption*—nothing. It is like the nonexistent missing link in the theory of evolution.

Scientists allegedly are to be open-minded, approaching their research without prejudice or bias. However, before ever beginning their textual work in earnest, Westcott and Hort referred to the Textus Receptus as "vile."[1] A more recent critic wrote how that the Textus Receptus was a "tyrant" and therefore deservedly "died a slow death."[2] Philip Schaff (the mover and shaker behind the American Standard Version) said, "The Textus Receptus does not deserve that superstitious

---

[1] Arthur Fenton Hort, *Life and Letters of Fenton John Anthony Hort*, (London: MacMillan & Co., 1896), 2:211.

[2] Frederic Kenyon, *Recent Developments in the Textual Criticism of the Greek Bible: Schwieich Lectures of the British Academy* (London: Oxford University Press, 1932), 8, 10.

veneration in which it was held for nearly three-hundred years."[3] It should be apparent from such comments that these textual critics *do* have a prejudice and therefore are likely to be biased in their conclusions. The matter of weighting of biblical manuscripts is therefore by its very nature subjective. Textual editors must make "value judgments" regarding what they consider will be included in the text and what will not. Conservative Dutch textual historian Jakob Van Bruggen, in commenting on the critical text and its editors wrote, "One can even say that the modern textual criticism of the New Testament is at least *not* found in the great majority of the manuscripts. The text which the Greek Church has read for more than 1000 years, and which the churches of the Reformation have followed for centuries in their Bible translations, is now with certainty regarded as defective and deficient: a text to be rejected."[4]

Van Bruggen goes on to say that the rejection of the Received Text is a *fait accompli* (i.e., a thing accomplished) by most modern text critics today.[5] His point is that most modern textual critics approach the textual issue not only with subjectivity, but a distinct bias and foregone conclusion against the Received Text. Though they pride themselves on treating the issue scientifically, they surely are unscientific in their prejudice. Yet, this is the bias which undergirds the weighting process of determining which manuscripts reflect the Word of God. The weighted judgment of virtually all proponents of the critical text begins with a predetermined rejection of the Received Text. Then they proceed to determine which manuscripts, primarily of Alexandrian origins, are more important.

---

[3]Philip Schaff, *Theological Propaedeutic: A General Introduction to the Study of Theology, Exegetical, Historical, Systematic, and Practical, including Encyclopaedia, Methodology, and Bibliography; a Manual for Students,* 8th ed. (New York: Charles Scribner's Sons, 1909), 167.

[4]Jakob Van Bruggen, *The Ancient Text of the New Testament* (Winnipeg: Premier Printing, 1976), 11.

[5]Ibid.

Counting

Of interest are some basic statistics regarding New Testament manuscripts. At the end of the nineteenth century, conservative textual historian John Burgon estimated that 995 out of every 1,000 manuscripts supported the Received Text.[6] That proportion has not changed substantially in the intervening century. The specific numbers cited below will change with time as other manuscripts are occasionally found. However, their essential proportions do not change appreciably. Estimates have been made regarding the number of existing manuscripts supporting or favoring the Received Text. Various textual experts *estimate* that from 80 to 90 percent of extant manuscripts support the Received Text.[7] However specific counting shows this number to be higher.

As of 1994 Kurt and Barbara Aland produced their latest combined statistics of extant manuscripts of the New Testament and estimated there to be 5,656 Greek manuscripts of the New Testament in varying form.[8] However, in 1967, Kurt Aland presented additional analysis of existing manuscripts. At that time, he noted a total of 5,255 New Testament manuscripts of varying form. Of that number, 5,210 manuscripts supported the Received Text. In his twenty-sixth edition of the Nestlé-Aland Greek text, Aland considered 5,210 manuscripts to belong to the Received Textual group. Or to put it another way, he determined that only forty-five of those 5,255 manuscripts were something other than the Received Text. It was from those forty-five manuscripts that the twenty-sixth edition of the Nestlé-Aland Greek text was produced. Therefore, in 1967, 99 percent of all existing manuscripts favored the

---

[6]John Burgon, *The Revision Revised* (original publisher unknown, 1883; reprint, Collingswood, N.J.: Dean Burgon Society, n.d.), 134.

[7]Wilbur Pickering, *The Identity of the New Testament Text* (Nashville, Tenn.: Thomas Nelson, 1977; reprint, Collingswood, N. J.: Bible for Today. n.d.), 118.

[8]Kurt Aland and Barbara Aland, eds., *Kurzgefasste Liste der grieschen Handscriften des Neuen Testaments* (Hawthorne, N. Y.: Walter de Gruyter, 1994), 72-84.

Received Text and only 1 percent supported the critical text.[9] That proportion has changed only slightly in the intervening years as other manuscripts have been discovered.[10]

The proponents of the modern critical text defend this relatively small number of manuscripts contending that the weighting of these texts, largely by their early dates, makes them far more important than the large number of later manuscripts which support the Received Text. Thus, to them, the numbers are not important. According to them, the weighting (not the counting) is what should be considered.

The precise percentage of manuscripts supporting the Received Text is not what is significant. That number will vary over time. However, what is important is that the *overwhelming majority* of existing manuscripts of the New Testament are of the Received Text group. Whether that number is 90 percent, 95 percent, or 99 percent is beside the point. The point is that the *overwhelming majority* of existing manuscripts of the New Testament support the Received Text. (That is the reason the Received Text is also called the Majority Text.) Proponents of the critical text would have us to believe that this large number is merely a coincidence of history.[11] The alternative (which they steadfastly seek to ignore) is the distinct possibility that such a large percentage points to the Holy Spirit's providential preservation of God's Word therein.

Van Bruggen, in commenting about this large majority of manuscripts supporting the Received Text, notes the following. "This striking number . . . cannot be put aside as meaningless, as though it is to be traced back to one archetype in the fourth century. On the contrary, the

---

[9]D. A. Waite, *Defending the King James Bible* (Collingswood, N.J.: Bible for Today, 1992), 52-56.

[10]It should be noted, however, that most recent discoveries of New Testament manuscripts continued to be those which support the Received Text.

[11]Proponents of the critical text allege that because most of these manuscripts supporting the Received Text are of later dating, they are of no critical value and therefore can be discounted.

large number deserves attention, since, in the midst of all sorts of variation, it confronts us with a growing uniformity. This can hardly be described as spontaneous converging deviation. It rather points in the direction of a simultaneous turning-back in various centuries to the same central point of the original text."[12]

Factors Overlooked by the Critical Text Theory

Notwithstanding the basic premise of the critical text position in giving heavy weight to the earliest manuscripts, there are several major problems which are ignored or overlooked by advocates thereof. These pesky facts neutralize the logic and rationale of weighting manuscripts primarily by date. Let us consider three major problems with the premise that "earlier is better."

Destroyed Exemplars

The term *exemplar* refers to the previous copy from which a new manuscript was produced. It was the "example" or "master" from which new ones were made. Opponents of the Received Text ask, "If the Received Text is the true text, then why are there hardly any copies thereof dating before the tenth century?" and "If this was the primary text of the church in the first millennium, then where is the *textual* evidence of it?"[13] The answer to this question is relatively simple. It was customary in ancient times to destroy worn out copies of Scripture after having recopied it. This, without a question, was practiced by Jewish scribes as they copied manuscripts of the Old Testament. This practice was also practiced by copyists of New Testament manuscripts. Kirsopp

---

[12] Van Bruggen, *The Ancient Text*, 21.

[13] It should be noted that there is considerable ancient *translational* evidence of the Received Text as noted in chapter 5. At this point, we are dealing with *textual* evidence.

Lake was a Liberal textual critic favoring the critical text in the early twentieth century. However, Lake acknowledged that old exemplars were routinely destroyed after having been reproduced by copying.[14] Textual historian Jack Moorman makes the same assertion.[15]

In the lifetime of this writer, approximately four Bibles have been personally worn out by him. Though they still remain on the shelf, they eventually will be thrown out. One such Bible has fallen apart at the binding and sections of it lie "loose leaf" inside. When that Bible has fallen on the floor (which it has), whole sections have come out. (Could this not be one reason why some old manuscripts are incomplete?) That old Bible will pass into oblivion. Worn out copies of the Scriptures are not usually kept in perpetuity. Is it reasonable to believe that copies of the New Testament should exist for 1,500 years if they were used by believers? To the contrary, the fact that Sinaiticus and Vaticanus (and other extant ancient manuscripts) still exist is clear evidence that they were not used. Moreover, let us ask the proponents of the critical text why there are only a very small number of manuscripts supporting the critical text if it was the true text of the New Testament used by churches down through the ages? The logic cuts both ways. Documents which are unused wind up in dusty libraries and monasteries. Documents which are regularly used wear out relatively soon.

Wilbur Pickering writes, "Is it unreasonable to suppose that once an old MS became tattered and almost illegible in spots that the faithful would make an exact copy of it and then destroy it, rather than allowing it to suffer the indignity of literally rotting away? . . . Anyone who objects to this conclusion must still account for the fact that in three an-

---

[14] Kirsopp Lake, "The New Testament in the Original Greek," *Harvard Theological Review* 21 (1928): 345-46.

[15] Jack Moorman, ed., *Forever Settled: A Survey of the Documents and History of the Bible* (Johannesburg, South Africa: privately printed, 1985; reprint, Collingswood, N.J.: Bible for Today, 1997), 57 (page citation is to the reprint edition).

cient monastic libraries, equipped with scritoria (rooms designed to facilitate the faithful copying of mss), there are only 'orphan children.' "[16]

The author quoted uses the analogy of parents and children. The "orphan children" mentioned above refers to manuscripts in the scriptoriums which have no exemplars. His point is that as such places have been discovered, no exemplars were found with the later copies. In the ancient libraries found largely intact, this has been the case. This evidence clearly points to the practice of the destruction of exemplars. Ancient libraries should have both the exemplar and its copies. They do not. The conclusion which must be drawn is that exemplars were routinely destroyed.

During the tenth century and onward, manuscripts of the New Testament were "upgraded" from the uncial style of writing to the minuscule style.[17] This was a style which was easier to read. It took less space on costly writing materials, and it was easier for copyists to write. However, there is every reason to believe that as scriptoriums recopied very old uncials into the newer and better writing style of minuscules that the old uncial exemplars were summarily destroyed. This undoubtedly is why there are not many copies of the Received Text in existence which date earlier than the tenth century.[18]

Edward Hills suggests that the survival of the old uncial manuscripts such as Sinaiticus and Vaticanus was due to the rejection of these by the churches. They were set aside, forgotten, and wound up on library shelves or in ancient monasteries. Hills also notes Burgon as making the same assertion.[19]

---

[16]Pickering, *Identity of the New Testament Text*, 130.

[17]Recall from chapter 3 that *uncials* were upper case (or, "capital" letters). *Miniscules* were lower case letters written in a more cursive style.

[18]Van Bruggen, *The Ancient Text*, 27-28.

[19]Edward Hills, *The King James Version Defended* (Des Moines: Christian Research Press, 1956), 186.

If exemplars were routinely destroyed, which seems likely, the logic of the critical text theory is clearly in error. Early manuscripts therefore mean little. The working texts of the church were destroyed as they became worn and tattered. The earliest manuscripts of the churches (prior to advent of printing) were recopied in multiple copies and then destroyed. The whole business of weighting based upon antiquity therefore is rendered moot. It means nothing. The best manuscripts were those which were destroyed. The ones which wound up gathering dust in libraries and wastebaskets were those rejected or forgotten by the early churches. How ironic it is that those manuscripts rejected in ages past are the very ones which have been exalted to preeminence in more recent times.

Intentional Corruption

A second major flaw of the critical text theory is the intentional corruptions made in many early manuscripts. Scribes with a theological axe to grind intentionally changed manuscripts to suit their particular theological bias. In 1874, F. H. A. Scrivener wrote, "It is no less true to fact than paradoxical in sound that the worst corruptions to which the New Testament has ever been subjected, originated within a hundred years after it was composed: that Irenaeus (A.D. 150), and the African Fathers, and the whole Western, with a portion of the Syrian Church, used far inferior manuscripts to those employed by Stunica, or Erasmus, or Stephens thirteen centuries later, when moulding the Textus Receptus."[20]

We shall consider this charge in more detail momentarily. However, let us pause and consider the implications this accusation makes against the logic of the critical text theory. Recall that the major premise of the critical text is that the earliest manuscripts are the closest to the originals. Yet, as we shall see (and as Scrivener and Burgon have noted),

---

[20] Frederick Henry Scrivener, *A Plain Introduction to the Criticism of the New Testament*, 2d ed. (Cambridge, Deighton, Bell, & Co., 1874), 2:30.

the worst corruptions to New Testament manuscripts took place not long after the writing of the originals. And, as we shall see, much of it was *intentional*. Relying therefore on the earliest manuscripts, to the contrary, is risky. The earliest may be the worst. Moreover, as we shall soon note, much of this textual corruption took place in Egypt. Do you recall where Sinaiticus and Vaticanus were produced?

The apostle Paul wrote, "For we are not as many, which corrupt the word of God."[21] As early as approximately A.D. 60, the great apostle warned about those who would corrupt the Scriptures (possibly by selling them). Wilbur Pickering notes that the early church was focused on combating the error of heretics. This certainly was true in the first century as Paul, Peter, John and other inspired writers continually warned the early church to try the spirits whether they were of God.[22] In the second century, it is clear that heretics produced numerous copies of Scripture incorporating their own peculiar alterations. Moreover, some of these aberrant manuscripts were widely circulated.[23]

Several of the more famous manuscripts discovered in the twentieth century were the Chester Beatty Papyrus and the Bodmer Papyrus.[24] These were named after the men who found them and made them public. (Recall how that papyrus was crude paper type of manuscript used in Egypt.) Both of these manuscripts date to about A.D. 200 (or the end of the second century). The modern textual critic Kilpatrick admits that these several very early manuscripts were *intentionally* altered in numerous places.[25] Another critic notes that prior to about A.D. 200 there were "unbounded liberties" taken with manuscripts of the New

---

[21] 2 Cor. 2:17.

[22] 1 John 4:1.

[23] Pickering, *Identity of the New Testament Text*, 114.

[24] These two manuscripts together contained only about seventy verses.

[25] G. D. Kilpatrick, "The Transmission of the New Testament and its Reliability," *The Bible Translator* IX (July 1958): 128-129; quoted in Pickering, *Identity of the New Testament Text*, 114.

Testament.[26] An orthodox church father by the name of Gaius, who lived near the end of the second century, named four heretics by name (Theodotus, Asclepiades, Hermophilus, Apollonides) "who not only altered the text but had disciples who multiplied copies of their efforts."[27] Liberal text critic, Bruce Metzger, freely admits that early church fathers accused heretics of intentionally corrupting New Testament manuscripts to support their special views.[28]

Though the train of thought here has been a bit complex, the condensed reasoning is rather simple. The primary logic of the critical text theory is that the earliest (oldest) manuscripts are the best. However, as we have seen in this short section, many early manuscripts were intentionally altered by known heretics or scribes who had a theological axe to grind. Recall the documentation that Sinaiticus (Aleph) was intentionally altered in numerous places. "The codex is covered with alterations of an obviously correctional character—brought in by at least ten different revisers, some of them systematically spread over every page, others occasional, or limited to separate portions of the Ms., many of these being contemporaneous with the first writer, but for the greater part belonging to the sixth or seventh century."[29]

The testimony is clear that there were *intentional* alterations of Sinaiticus. How are we to know that this renowned manuscript was not altered by a scribe or heretic trying to advance his own peculiar doctrine?[30] (Appendices A, B, and D will document how the doctrine of

---

[26] Pickering, *Identity of the New Testament Text*, 115.

[27] Ibid., 116.

[28] Bruce Metzger, *The Text of the New Testament* (London: Oxford University Press, 1964), 201.

[29] Frederick Henry Scrivener, *A Full Collation of the Codex Sinaiticus* (original publisher unknown, 1864), n.p.; quoted in David Cloud, *Myths about the Modern Bible Versions* (Oak Harbor, Wash.: Way of Life Literature, 1999), 193.

[30] To the rejoinder that there is really no doctrinal difference between the Alexandrian manuscripts and the Received Text, see appendix D.

Christ for example has been seriously eroded in the critical text and translations based thereupon.) The whole logic of giving weight and preference to the earliest manuscripts is a vessel which has several large holes in its bottom. It would immediately sink if it were not kept afloat by the naturalistic prejudice and bias of modern textual critics. However, the latter have invested too much academic capital in this theory. Professional pride either blinds them or prevents them from admitting the holes in their theory.

Use of the Churches

There is a final flaw in the theory of giving greatest weight to the earliest manuscripts. The simple fact is that the majority of churches through the centuries of Christianity, little by little, set aside manuscripts of the Alexandrian variety or those which had been obviously corrected. The latter wound up gathering dust on forgotten shelves. The Received Text was that which was accepted, used, copied, and worn out. Through a combination of wise discernment along with the leading of the Holy Spirit, early churches used and accepted those copies of Scripture which followed the Received Text. That is why it came to be so called. It was gradually received or accepted by all orthodox, believing churches and groups. Notwithstanding claims by proponents of the critical text that church usage of the Received Text was by some ecclesiastical decree, there is no history of such an event ever taking place. To the contrary, even if such an event took place, it would only lend credence to the evidence that the church of Jesus Christ placed its stamp of approval upon the Received Text.

Prima Facie Evidence

The term *prima facie* is a Latin word still used in the legal profession. The term literally means "on its face," or by extension, "at first glance," or "obvious." In the courtroom, it has the idea of "not requiring further support to establish credibility or validity."[31] The fact that the overwhelming number of extant manuscripts support the Received Text is *prima facie* evidence that it is the proper text.[32] Moreover, implicit in this evidence is the providential preservation of the text by the Holy Spirit. It is He who led churches down through the ages to use and copy the Received Text. And it is He in His providence who has preserved it. The vast number of manuscripts supporting the Received Text is *prima facie* evidence thereof. The alternative is that the Holy Spirit allowed the essence of the true text of the New Testament to lay forgotten in the Vatican and in an obscure monastery in the Egyptian desert for 1,500 years missing the Reformation and some of the greatest events in Christian history. Let the reader be the judge thereof!

Summary

To summarize, the collective historical evidence mitigates against the critical text theory that the earlier is better. (1) The early church routinely destroyed their exemplars which renders the very concept of "earlier is better" as meaningless. (2) The fact of documented, intentional changes and corruption of *early* manuscripts including Sinaiticus again renders the theory of "earlier is better" as having little worth. (3) Use of the Received Text by *believing* churches through the centuries shows that they placed their stamp of approval upon what they accepted and received as the Word of God. Churches in the second and third centuries knew what the originals said. They likely had seen them. Churches thereafter were providentially led by the Holy Spirit to the proper text of the New Testament. (4) Finally, the overwhelming num-

---

[31]Steven H. Gifis, *Law Dictionary*, 2d ed. (New York: Barrons, 1984), s.v. *"prima facie."*

[32]Whether the number of manuscripts supporting the Received Text is 90 percent or 99 percent is irrelevant. It is indisputable that the *overwhelming* majority support the Received Text.

ber of manuscripts supporting the Received Text is *prima facie* evidence that God has preserved His Word therein.

Review Questions for Further Study

1. What is the primary logic of the critical text position?

2. Why are Vaticanus and Sinaiticus weighted as more important than many other manuscripts?

3. What is an example of bias in proponents of the critical text?

4. What is the range of estimates of the percentage of manuscripts representing the Received Text and what is the actual figure?

5. If exemplars were destroyed, what does that matter to the critical text theory?

6. What is another major flaw of the critical text theory?

7. Why did the Received Text come to be called thus?

8. What is *prima facie* evidence suggesting that the Received Text is the proper text?

CHAPTER EIGHT

THE SCRIPTURAL PRINCIPLE OF SEPARATION FROM APOSTASY

In the next chapter, the apostasy of the primary textual critics of the past 250 years will be linked with the principle of separation. However, before considering that, let us first consider what the Bible has to say about the matter of theological and ecclesiastical separation. This chapter will also pause briefly to review the history of theological Liberalism, Fundamentalism, and New Evangelicalism in the past century. Let us therefore begin by examining a number of scriptural convictions found the in the Word of God regarding the principle of separation.

Scriptural Principles

Significant portions of Scripture pertaining to the principle of separation will be considered here. In each case, the biblical principle is that an obedient Christian should separate from apostasy, especially as it relates to deviation from biblical truth. (Apostasy, it should be recalled, is a departure from the faith once delivered unto the saints. It refers to systematic unbelief characterized by theological Liberalism.)

2 Corinthians 6:14-18

The apostle Paul set forth a clear principle regarding the principle of separation in 2 Cor. 6:14-18. There, he wrote,

Be ye not unequally yoked together with unbelievers: for what fellowship hath righteousness with unrighteousness? and what communion hath light with darkness? And what concord hath Christ with Belial? or what part hath he that believeth with an infidel? And what agreement hath the temple of God with idols? for ye are the temple of the living God; as God hath said, I will dwell in them, and walk in *them*; and I will be their God, and they shall be my people. Wherefore come out from among them, and be ye separate, saith the Lord, and touch not the unclean *thing*; and I will receive you, And will be a Father unto you, and ye shall be my sons and daughters, saith the Lord Almighty.

Verse 17 summarizes, in concise form, the principle of separation found throughout the Bible. "Wherefore come out from among them, and be ye separate, saith the Lord, and touch not the unclean *thing*; and I will receive you." Lest there is any question from what we are to be separated, the apostle makes that clear in the greater context. For example, in verse 14 he enjoins, "Be ye not unequally yoked together with **unbelievers**." He follows that with the rhetorical questions, "For what fellowship hath righteousness with unrighteousness? And what communion hath light with darkness? And what concord hath Christ with Belial? Or what part hath he that believeth with an infidel? And what agreement hath the temple of God with idols?" The answers to these questions are apparent. There ought not be fellowship between righteousness and unrighteousness. There ought not be communion between light and darkness. The apostle clearly is referring to spiritual light versus spiritual darkness. Implicit is the holiness of God versus the spiritual darkness of the devil. There can be no communion between the two.

Lest there is further question whether this is what the apostle is driving at, verse 15 makes the application clear. "And what concord hath Christ with Belial?" The name *Belial* is another name for Satan. (Of interest is that Belial can also be pronounced "Beliar" signifying

Satan's character.[1] See John 8:44.) There can be no concord between our Lord and the devil. Of further interest is the word translated as "concord" (συμφωνησις or "symphonesis"). It is the word whence the English word "symphony" derives.[2] There is no symphony or harmony between Christ and the evil one!

In that immediate context, the apostle adds another rhetorical question, "Or what part hath he that believeth with an infidel?" The answer once again, especially in the context, is apparent. There ought not be close fellowship between a believer and an unbeliever. The word translated as "infidel" (απιστος or "apistos") essentially means an "unbeliever."[3]

Over the past two hundred years, theological Liberalism has been a system of unbelief. It has questioned, denied, and directly attacked the foundational tenets of New Testament Christianity. The miraculous is either questioned or denied. Science is elevated above Scripture. Major doctrines such as the verbal inspiration of the Bible, the Deity of Christ, the bodily resurrection of Christ, His second coming, and many other truths have been undercut, questioned, scoffed at, or simply ignored by modern theological Liberals. The roots of Liberalism were in German Rationalism which flourished especially during the nineteenth century.

2 Cor. 6:14-18 clearly directs obedient believers to separate from the *influence, association,* and *fellowship* of those who are unbelievers. That never has been a popular position. As it pertains to the textual issue, separation is even less popular amongst many Fundamentalists. Nevertheless, the issue is clear. There is definitive unbelief and apostasy in the primary textual editors and proponents of the critical text.

---

[1] *Thayer's Greek-English Lexicon of the New Testament* (1969), s.v. "βελιαλ" and "βελιαρ."

[2] *Thayer's*, s.v. "συμφωνησις."

[3] *Thayer's*, s.v. "απιστος."

Psalm 1:1

As an introduction to the magnificent Book of Psalms, David begins with the profound statement, "Blessed *is* the man that walketh not in the counsel of the ungodly, nor standeth in the way of sinners, nor sitteth in the seat of the scornful" (Ps. 1:1). Implicit is the principle of separation. The divinely inspired psalmist notes the blessedness of the man who does not walk in the *counsel* of the ungodly. If we agree that one who questions the Deity of Christ, the verbal inspiration of the Scriptures, the bodily resurrection of Christ, and other foundational doctrine is an unbeliever; it therefore follows that such an one is also ungodly. Such an unbeliever is unregenerate regardless of how many advanced degrees and technical expertise he might hold in textual criticism. Notice that David warns about walking in the *counsel* thereof. Such counsel is the instruction and philosophy of those who are not believers.

The psalmist also notes the blessedness of the man who does not sit in the seat of the scornful. This is clearly speaking of one who sits as a student under the influence of those who mock the truths of God. Most Rationalists and Modernists have routinely scoffed at such cardinal doctrines as verbal inspiration, creation, the Deity of Christ and other fundamentals of the faith.

The clear principle in Ps. 1:1 is that there is special blessing for those who will separate themselves from the *counsel* of the ungodly as well as those who *scoff* at the fundamental truths of the Word of God. The contention of this author is that the principle at hand applies to the textual debate.

Genesis 3:1

When Satan proceeded to tempt Eve in the garden of Eden, his approach was subtle. He approached her with the suggestive question, "Yea, hath God said?" (Gen. 3:1). The devil, the author of doubt, began his cunning work by questioning what God had said. (This tactic is noteworthy because Satan more often than not subtly undermines the Word of God rather than making an outright denial thereof.) The very essence of modern text criticism—transcriptonal probabilities, conjectural emendations, editorial recensions—begins with the premise of doubt. "Did God really say this?" The endless minutia of the modern critical apparatus begs the question of textual authority. In reading the writings of proponents of the critical text and their discussions over textual variants, the net result is question and doubt and never certainty. Even some evangelical sympathizers of the critical text readily admit there is uncertainty in the critical text. They even scoff at those who seek certainty in the biblical text.[4]

Furthermore, major participants in the formation of the modern critical text have openly questioned the stated authorship of biblical books as was noted in chapter 6. These same textual editors have routinely expounded standard positions of liberal, modernistic theology. When Bruce Metzger, for example, questions the Mosaic authorship of the Pentateuch, or if Isaiah wrote Isaiah, or if Daniel wrote Daniel, or if John wrote John, or if Peter wrote 2 Peter; is he not in effect saying, "Yeah, hath God said?"[5] The contention of this author is that he is so doing. Doubt has been the standard stock and trade of the devil since day one. Theological Liberals to this day still use this tactic with skill and alacrity.

2 Thessalonians 3:6 and 14

In 2 Thess. 3:6, the apostle is dealing with problems in the church at Thessalonica. Some there had stopped working and were sponging off other brethren for their living. In that context, the apostle wrote, "Now we command you, brethren, in the name of our Lord Jesus Christ, that ye withdraw yourselves from every brother that walketh disorderly, and not after the tradition which he received of us." The immediate application was to separate from *brethren* who were dis-

---

[4] James R. White, *The King James Only Controversy* (Minneapolis: Bethany House Publishers, 1995), 187.

[5] See comments about Metzger in chapter 6.

orderly by not working with their own hands. Such an one was in violation of the doctrine which Paul had taught the church when present with them.

However, the greater principle in this verse is that obedient Christians ought to separate from any *brother* who walks disorderly. This is especially so when the Bible has clearly dealt with an issue. The broader subject at hand is the principle of separation from unbelief and disobedience. Unfortunately, there are Fundamental *brethren* who insist upon sitting in the seat of the scornful of the rationalistic editors of the critical text. At the very least, it would seem that the New Testament principle at hand is to touch not the unclean thing—the apostasy associated with the critical text.

In verse 14 of 2 Thessalonians, the apostle essentially reiterated himself. "And if any man obey not our word by this epistle, note that man, and have no company with him, that he may be ashamed." It would seem that Fundamentalists who hold dear the principle of separation from apostasy ought to separate from those who "obey not the word of this epistle." The unbelief of the principal textual editors over the past two centuries is definitive and documented. The greater biblical principle is to separate therefrom.

Romans 16:17

Let us look at one final portion of Scripture in this regard. In Rom. 16:17, the apostle Paul wrote, " Now I beseech you, brethren, mark them which cause divisions and offences contrary to the doctrine which ye have learned; and avoid them."

Paul wrote here about two types of problems in the Roman church. (1) There were those who caused divisions in that church and (2) those who caused offences contrary to the doctrine which they had already learned. The doctrine taught by Paul was what might otherwise be called biblical or orthodox teaching. There apparently were some who were advancing teaching which was contrary to the doctrinal truth which Paul in his epistle had instructed them. He enjoined them to note those involved in such doctrinal deviation or apostasy and *avoid* them.

The clear New Testament principle is to avoid those who are apostate. The matter of separation once again presents itself.

In this generation, that principle is still true. We are enjoined by the Word of God to avoid those who are apostate or advance teaching contrary to the Word of God. As major text critics have demonstrated themselves to be apostate or at odds with orthodox Bible truths, the principle set forth in Rom. 16:17 is clear. Avoid them. By extension, that surely applies to the use or appropriation of their instruction. When major textual editors of the critical text have identified themselves with the theory of evolution, German Rationalism, the World Council of Churches, Unitarians, and the Roman Catholic Church; in the view of this writer, they have caused offences contrary to the doctrine which we have learned. The Holy Spirit has thus directed us to avoid them. It would seem only reasonable that this includes their textual work as well.

The Word of God is clear in that those obedient thereto must separate themselves from apostasy. It has never been a popular position. Separation and the willingness to practice it is the line of demarcation between the Evangelical movement and the Fundamentalist movement. Evangelicals make light of the principle of separation. Fundamentalists have generally sought to uphold the principle. However, few have applied the principle of separation to the textual issue. Nevertheless, the essence is the same. Only the application is different. As has been demonstrated throughout the earlier portions of this volume, the critical text is associated with apostasy at every stage of its long history. If Fundamentalists are going to be consistent to their principles, they are going to have to ask themselves this question: is using a textual base so tainted by apostasy not a breach of the principle of separation? The apostle wrote the Corinthian church to "touch not the unclean **thing**." The submission of this author is that the long association of the critical text with incipient apostasy, Liberalism, and Rationalism renders it unfit for use by a true Fundamentalist. Apart from intrinsic problems in the critical text, its extrinsic associations ought to be enough to cause a Fundamentalist, true to his convictions, to separate therefrom.

A Brief History of Fundamentalism and the Principle of Separation

Let us therefore consider the origins and history of Fundamentalism in summary fashion. As will be noted below, the essence of historic Fundamentalism has been the conviction to separate from apostasy.

Liberalism

In the twentieth century, several significant theological movements became clearly defined. Prior to the middle of the nineteenth century, with notable exceptions, Protestant Christianity in America essentially could be categorized as "orthodox." That is, most non-Catholic groups believed the cardinal doctrines of historic New Testament Christianity. A dictionary definition of the word *orthodox* is "sound in doctrine."[6] However, in the latter portion of the nineteenth century, a strain of "modern" theology began to become popular. It emerged particularly from the University of Tubingen located in Tubingen, Germany.[7] This was commonly known as German Higher Rationalism. European as well as American theologians flocked to this center for "higher" theological learning. Accordingly, they brought home what soon came to be known as "Modernism" or as it also came to be known, "theological Liberalism."

Though such theologians called themselves Christians, their entire system of Liberal theology was actually a system of unbelief. This noxious weed unfortunately blossomed in European and American seminaries. Within a generation, it had permeated even the grass-roots level of most denominations and churches. Liberalism remains the prevailing

---

[6]*Webster's New Collegiate Dictionary* (1953), s.v. "orthodox."

[7]Actually, the seeds of "modernism" were well established by the middle of the nineteenth century. Unitarianism, which denied the Trinity and Deity of Christ, was quite developed by the early nineteenth century. Deism and other forms of unorthodox theology were also prevalent.

form of theology in most major mainline denominations in North America and Britain.

Ernest Pickering in his excellent book *The Tragedy of Compromise* writes:

> Out of the matrix of this European mix of unbelief came the movement known in church history as modernism, now often referred to as theological liberalism. What are some hallmarks of liberalism?
>
> 1. A rejection of the historic Christian doctrine of biblical inspiration.
>
> 2. A tolerance of all views that come from within the religious community.
>
> 3. An emphasis upon the validity of human experience over the revealed truth of God.
>
> 4. A denial of the absolute and unique Deity of Christ.
>
> 5. An emphasis on the dignity and goodness of man.
>
> 6. A rejection of the total depravity of man and the resultant necessity of the new birth.
>
> 7. An evolutionary concept of the origin of all things as opposed to a creationist view.
>
> 8. A rejection of the supernatural interventions of God in human history.
>
> 9. An emphasis upon the social gospel, that is, that the main

mission of the church is to correct societal ills. Sin is essentially social and thus salvation must involve the correction of these social problems.[8]

As Liberalism spread across the religious map, especially in America at the end of the nineteenth century, Bible believers rose up against it. Bible conferences were held in places like Niagara Falls and Chatauqua, New York. In these large conferences, the great orthodox truths of historic, New Testament Christianity were preached. Doctrinal themes such as the Deity of Christ, the blood atonement of Christ, the verbal inspiration of the Bible, the bodily resurrection of Christ, and the visible second coming of Christ were emphasized. As the controversy carried into the twentieth century, sermons of these great conferences were printed, circulated, and later were bound together in book form. The latter came to be known as the "Fundamentals." Thus, in the 1920s, the term *Fundamentalist* was coined referring to those who adhered to the fundamentals of the Christian faith.

Notwithstanding these *ad hoc*, unofficial Bible conferences, the major denominations in America were quickly being taken over by Modernists and theological Liberals. The Northern Baptist Convention (later to be called the American Baptist Convention) was completely permeated by Modernists at the denominational level by the early twentieth century. The Methodists faced the same situation. Liberalism had made major inroads into the Presbyterian denomination as well as the Congregational and Episcopal Churches. The University of Chicago, started as a Baptist school in large part through the largesse of John D. Rockefeller, was liberal from the start. Flagship churches such as the Riverside (Baptist) Church in New York City were pastored by famous Liberals such as Harry Emerson Fosdick. Similar churches held the prominent pulpits of the land.

---

[8]Ernest Pickering, *The Tragedy of Compromise* (Greenville, S.C.: Bob Jones University Press, 1994), 3.

Fundamentalism

As conservative, Bible-believing pastors of churches in denominations such as the Northern Baptist Convention realized what was happening, they began to fight back. Men such as William B. Riley fought with the liberal leadership of the Northern Baptist Convention. J. Frank Norris battled with denominational Liberalism in the Southern Baptist Convention. W. B. Riley organized his Northwestern Schools in Minneapolis to combat the Liberalism in the majority of the colleges and seminaries of the Northern Baptist Convention. He valiantly fought the Liberals through political maneuvering in national denominational meetings. Riley truly thought that he could turn the Convention around through political means. He knew the grass roots of the Northern Baptist Convention were Fundamentalists. However, he underestimated the political power concentrated in denominational high places. Little by little, the great Fundamentalist-Liberal political battles fought in the Northern Baptist Convention (and other denominations) were won by the Liberals.

As a result, groups began to break away from the major denominations and separate themselves from the apostasy so prevalent therein. In 1932, a substantial group of churches separated from the Northern Baptist Convention and eventually organized themselves as the General Association of Regular Baptist Churches. After World War II, another large group of churches withdrew from the Convention and formed themselves into the Conservative Baptist Association of America.[9] Similar groups of Presbyterian churches also separated from the liberal Presbyterian Church USA and formed small separatist groups. In the south, many Baptist churches withdrew from the Southern Baptist Convention, especially after World War II, and formed independent fellowships and associations. Of these, the Baptist Bible Fellowship, the

---

[9]Ironically, of these movements which originally began as "separatist" groups, the Conservative Baptist Association today is no longer very conservative and certainly not separatist. Moreover, the GARBC is rapidly moving away from its separatist heritage. Some of its major educational institutions do not care to be called "Fundamentalist" and really no longer are.

Southwide Baptist Fellowship, and the World Baptist Fellowship remain prominent as Fundamentalist groups.

Though the Fundamentalist movement began with the doctrinal emphasis of adhering to the foundational tenets of the Christian faith, as the twentieth century wore on, the term came to have additional significance. As groups, little by little, began to separate from the apostate denominations, **the term *fundamentalist* also came to have the distinction of being separated from apostasy and unbelief**. Therefore, as the definition of Fundamentalism has fully developed in the last half of the twentieth century, it has a double connotation. (1) Fundamentalism is an adherence to the orthodox, cardinal truths of the Bible, and (2) Fundamentalism demands separation from error or apostasy as it becomes necessary to do so. Thus, the principle of separation has come to be a touchstone of the Fundamentalist movement.

Separation from error certainly is a biblical principle as noted earlier in this chapter. During the fight over Liberalism in England, Charles Haddon Spurgeon declared in 1888, "I have preached God's truth, so far as I know it, and I have not been ashamed of its peculiarities. That I might not stultify my testimony, I have cut myself clear of those who err from the faith, and even from those who *associated* with them"[10] (emphasis mine).

In the mid-twentieth century, Evangelist Perry Rockwood also wrote, "If we believe exactly what the Bible teaches, there will be no problem with the matter of separation. God's people cannot have fellowship, Bible fellowship, spiritual fellowship, doctrinal fellowship, soul-winning fellowship, with those who deny the essentials of the Bible, or with those who are not saved, or with those who compromise the spiritual principles of the Bible."[11]

In 1975, John E. Ashbrook of the Ohio Bible Fellowship wrote, "We must have no fellowship with apostasy." He also wrote, "There are two possibilities which Scripture sets forth. Action No. 1—purge the

---

[10] This battle was called the Down-Grade Controversy. Perry Rockwood, *Bible Separation*, (Halifax, Canada: The Peoples Gospel Hour, n.d.), 8.

[11] Ibid., 17.

apostasy from the church. . . . Action No. 2—the believer must separate from apostasy."[12]

The Fundamental Baptist Fellowship issued a *Manifesto on Biblical Separation* some years ago. Therein, it adopted this resolution: "Resolved, that we proclaim to the world, religious or otherwise, that we will in the best way we know how, and in the spirit of Christ, to . . . avoid being identified in any way, directly or *indirectly*, with doctrinal infidelity or in any way compromise with infidelity in our affiliations, relationships, *associations*, and in obedience to the Scriptures to touch not the unclean thing"[13] (emphasis mine).

The Northern Baptist Convention (NBC) was officially organized as a denomination in 1907. Though its historic doctrinal roots had been orthodox, Liberalism was entrenched in the leadership when the convention was officially organized. (Several missions societies and associations had joined together to form the Northern Baptist Convention.) However, there had developed an attitude of "inclusivism" by many in the rank and file of the Northern Convention. Though the majority of the grass-roots of the Convention were conservative, many were willing to peacefully "coexist" with the modernists. There developed a sort of theological *laissez faire* attitude of allowing the modernists to continue unopposed in the Northern Convention. It amounted to a "live and let live" philosophy.

It was not until the 1920s that the conservatives gathered enough political momentum to try and force the Liberals out of the Convention. The Liberals were well aware of this and worked insidiously to prevent it. Their strategy was that of toleration and inclusivism. The famous Harry Emerson Fosdick, Liberal pastor of the Riverside Church in New York City, publicly posed this question in 1922: "Has anybody a right to deny the Christian name to those who differ with him on such points

---

[12]John Ashbrook, *Separation from Apostasy* (Columbus, Ohio: Ohio Bible Fellowship, 1975), 3-4.

[13]Rod Bell, *Manifesto on Biblical Separation* (Virginia Beach, Virginia: Fundamental Baptist Manifesto, n.d.).

and to shut up against them the doors of Christian fellowship."[14] In thus appealing for toleration, Fosdick was in fact seeking further support for the policy of inclusivism. Accordingly, many of the Conservatives in the Convention were influenced by this appeal to toleration. In the great political floor fights that soon followed, the policy of inclusivism prevailed. The Fundamentalists lost the battle and the Liberals continued to consolidate their power and influence in the Northen Baptist Convention.

A decade later after the great Fundamentalist-Liberal battles had largely been lost to the Liberals, denominational leaders, fearful of seeing their empires diminished as groups of churches talked about pulling out, came up with a new strategy. They adopted the "big-tent" philosophy. Though they were not about to move away from their liberal theology, they liked the money and influence of numbers which the conservative segments of their denominations brought in. Therefore, the philosophy of "inclusivism" also worked in reverse. It essentially was the idea that one can be a Conservative and remain in the denomination. Their thought was that they would include both Liberals and Conservatives. (Just keep sending your money.) Conservative pastors were enticed to stay in the convention with the carrot of pension funds and denominational positions. And, many conservative pastors did keep their churches in the liberal denominations for just those reasons. They did not want to lose either their denominational pension or their prominence in the denomination. Thus, the philosophy of inclusivism became an issue in the major denominations from both directions. They were willing to include conservatives and liberals in the denomination.

In discussing this tragedy of compromise, Ernest Pickering has made this pungent comment. "There are certain truths, convictions, and positions which cannot be compromised. Martin Luther, pressed by his political and ecclesiastical foes, rightly refused to renounce his writings and said to his opponents, 'Here I stand; I can do no other.' Athanasius, a champion of the complete Deity of Christ versus the Arians who de-

---

[14]Raymond Teachout, *Breaking Down the Walls and the Gospel: The Subversive Work of Evangelical Inclusivism* (Quebec: Études Bibliques pour Aujord' hui, 1999), 22.

nied it, was warned by a colleague, 'The whole world is against you.' Replied Athanasius, 'Then I am against the whole world.' There would be no compromise for him on a matter so crucial."[15] The defining criteria of Fundamentalism as we have entered the twenty-first century is separation from apostasy and compromise therewith.

New Evangelicalism

World War II seemed to suspend significant action in the struggle between Fundamentalists and Liberals in the American mainline denominations. Moreover, Europe was utterly devastated. However, a new phenomena arose in America following the war. In 1948 in a convocation speech made at the inauguration of Fuller Theological Seminary, Harold Ockenga, its new president, coined the term *New Evangelical*. This term is still applicable to the present, though most "New Evangelicals" today prefer to simply call themselves "Evangelicals." With Fundamentalism on the right and Liberalism on the left, New Evangelicalism sought to compromise between the two, seeking a middle path. New Evangelicalism originally professed to adhere to orthodox (even fundamental) doctrine.[16] However, they saw no problem in associating with Liberals. In short, the New-Evangelical position originally could be aptly characterized as Fundamentalism minus any form of separation.[17] The New-Evangelical movement from 1948 to this day has ignored virtually all forms of personal separation from the world. The churches and people in this movement have become so worldly that one

---

[15] Ernest Pickering, *Tragedy of Compromise*, vii.

[16] Sadly, as the broad New-Evangelical movement enters the twenty-first century, there is an ongoing erosion of orthodox doctrine within its ranks. Such biblical truths as the inerrancy of Scripture or the omniscience of God, for example, have been seriously eroded in New-Evangelical institutions such as Fuller Seminary.

[17] At the beginning of the twenty-first century, there is a blurring of distinction between New Evangelicalism and theological Liberalism to such a degree the term *evangelical* no longer holds great significance.

New-Evangelical author wrote a book entitled *The Worldly Evangelicals*.[18]

Moreover, the New-Evangelical movement has also shunned any form of ecclesiastical separation. One of its flagship leaders, Billy Graham, for almost half a century has willingly cooperated and closely worked with theological Liberals, the Roman Catholic Church, and even the Communist Party in Europe. He has justified such compromise with a pragmatism that essentially embraced the philosophy that the end justifies the means.

The New-Evangelical movement has fully embraced the philosophy of inclusivism. Just about anything or anyone is acceptable as long as it is done in the name of Christian love. Even those who in earlier decades would have preferred to be called Liberals have come to refer to themselves as "Evangelicals." The New-Evangelical big tent has embraced the Pentecostal-Charismatic orbit along with conservative Catholics, not to mention the broad way of "conservative" interdenominational groups.

Ernest Pickering has noted several characteristics of the New-Evangelical movement which are (in the view of this author) germane to the translational and textual debate. Among other things, Pickering has characterized the New-Evangelical movement as having "a desire to be accepted by the scholarly world."[19] He also noted the influence of philosophy from theologically liberal institutions.[20] As we have studied the textual issue in this book, these characteristics of New Evangelicalism are strikingly similar to the attitudes of the advocates of the critical text. Also, as was noted earlier in this volume, the near-unanimous choices of translations by the New-Evangelical movement are those based upon the critical text.

Fundamentalists must come to grips with the fact that the critical text has been produced almost entirely by Liberals and apostates. New

---

[18]Richard Quebedeaux, *The Worldly Evangelicals* (San Francisco: Harper & Row, 1978).

[19]Pickering, *Tragedy of Compromise*, 8.

[20]Ibid., 9.

Evangelicals are not encumbered by this fact. It seems many Fundamentalists are not either. A true Fundamentalist will repudiate apostate theologians and their institutions. However, most Evangelicals will not. In 1924, J. Gresham Machen said, "The worst sin today is to say that you agree with the Christian faith and believe in the Bible, but then make common cause with those who deny the basic facts of Christianity."[21] Machen was not speaking in the context of the textual issue.[22] However, the simple fact is that those who advocate the fundamentals of the faith but use and defend the critical text, to that degree, are making common cause with those who deny the basic tenets of biblical Christianity!

As New Evangelicalism has developed in the last half of the twentieth century, it has also produced a diminished view of the Scripture. The fountainhead seminary of the New-Evangelical movement, Fuller Theological Seminary, has from its earliest years been weak on the matter of the inerrancy of the Bible.[23] In 1966, Clarence Bass, then a professor at Bethel Theological Seminary in St. Paul, Minnesota (a New-Evangelical school), said, "I clearly distinguish between inspiration as a Biblical doctrine and inerrancy as a logical correlative."[24] As noted in chapter 6, most major editors of the critical text likewise discount inerrancy and even verbal inspiration as well. This dangerous heresy is already nibbling at the edges of Fundamentalism as Fundamentalist schools teach and preach from the critical text.

The very underpinning philosophy of the critical text position is that actual words of the Biblical text are up for negotiation. The Nestlé-Aland Greek text is in its twenty-seventh edition. In less than one century, this critical text of the New Testament has modified its text or its

---

[21]Ibid., 26.

[22]Ironically, Machen himself accepted the essence of the critical text position.

[23]George Marsden, *Reforming Fundamentalism: Fuller Seminary and the New Evangelicalism* (Grand Rapids: Wm. B. Eerdmans Publishing Co., 1987), 227.

[24]Pickering, *The Tragedy of Compromise*, 100.

apparatus (i.e., footnotes) twenty-seven different times. Sadly, even some Fundamentalist institutions of higher learning have gone on record suggesting there are errors in the Biblical text regarding historical details. Are they not falling into the same position as most New Evangelicals?

Concluding Thoughts

New-Evangelical church historian, George Marsden has made this assessment: "What chiefly distinguished fundamentalism from earlier evangelicalism was its militancy toward modernist theology and cultural change."[25] Sadly, many Fundamentalists have no militancy toward the modernist textual editors who have produced the critical text. They are more than willing to look the other way or stick their head in the sand and act as if they have no knowledge of the apostasy connected with the critical text. Yet, the documentation concerning the modernistic views of its textual editors is no secret.

In 1982, O. Talmadge Spence, on behalf of the International Committee for the Propagation and Defense of Biblical Fundamentalism, wrote: "The final battle of the twentieth-century Christian will be fought on the battlefield of biblical separation, rather than the credal lip service of biblical inerrancy, inspiration, and infallibility. A new breed of so-called Fundamentalists gives lip service to biblical inerrancy, inspiration, and infallibility, but does not believe or practice biblical separation. But historic Fundamentalism will die at the loss of biblical orthodoxy or biblical orthopraxy in maintaining biblical separation."[26]

With all due credit, Spence was not writing about the textual controversy. However, the principle and his warning remain the same.

---

[25]George Marsden, *Understanding Fundamentalism and Evangelicalism* (Grand Rapids: Wm. B. Eerdmans Publishing Co., 1991), 66.

[26]O. Talmadge Spence, *Scriptural Separation* (Greenville, S.C.: International Committee for Propagation & Defense of Biblical Fundamentalism, 1982), 23.

The Scriptural Principle of Separation from Apostasy

There are many fundamentalists who today give lip service to inerrancy, inspiration, and infallibility but refuse to separate from a text of the New Testament which is associated with apostasy from its origins to the present hour.

Review Questions for Further Study

1. 2 Cor. 6:14-18 clearly directs believers to separate from what?

2. In Ps. 1:1, the clear principle is that a special blessing is for those who will do what?

3. The endless minutia of the critical text apparatus begs the question of what?

4. In Rom. 16:17, we are enjoined by the Word of God to avoid who?

5. What are some of the hallmarks of Liberalism?

6. What are the two major defining principles of Fundamentalism?

7. What is a short description of the New-Evangelical movement?

8. Fundamentalist must come to grips with what facts regarding the critical text?

9. What major doctrine has been eroded by the New-Evangelical movement?

CHAPTER NINE

APPLYING THE PRINCIPLE OF SEPARATION TO THE TEXTUAL ISSUE

In the preceding chapters of this book, we have in several places touched upon the apostasy and Liberalism of the principal architects of the modern critical text. Let us look more carefully at these charges, for at the root of the modern critical text lies German Higher Rationalism.

The Liberalism and Apostasy Associated with Modern Textual Editors

In chapter 6 of this book, we touched upon the apostasy connected with the critical text from early church history to recent times. In this chapter, we will zoom in and look more closely at the lineage of the apostasy of the critical-text editors of the nineteenth century. The simple fact is that virtually all major textual editors of the nineteenth century were either directly or indirectly connected to German Higher Rationalism. Some were directly influenced by the University of Tubingen in Tubingen, Germany. For others, the influence was more indirect. But the influence was there nevertheless. The University of Tubingen, perhaps more than any other one place, was the seed plot for the theological Modernism and Liberalism of the nineteenth and twentieth centuries. Let us therefore track the lineage of the modern critical text and see what influence German Rationalism had upon it.

Johann Salomo Semler

Johann Salomo Semler has been called one of the fathers of theological Liberalism. He lived in Germany from 1725-91. Bruce Metzer has said that Semler is "often regarded as the father of German Rationalism" and that he "made noteworthy contributions to the science of textual criticism."[1] Semler was also noted as "the leader of the reaction in Germany against the traditional view of the canon of Scripture."[2]

Johann Jakob Griesbach

A devoted German student of Semler was Johann Jakob Griesbach. Griesbach was one of the founding fathers of modern textual criticism. He produced what probably was the first "critical text" of the New Testament in 1744. Though Griesbach was not a Unitarian as such, he was viewed warmly by the British founders of the Unitarian movement.[3] Recall that Unitarians deny the Trinity, the Deity of Christ, the fall of man, and the substitutionary atonement of Christ to name a few of their teachings. They were among the original apostates in modern Britain and America. They in turn produced an English translation of the Bible in 1790 based upon Griesbach's critical text.[4] (Westcott and Hort's work about eighty years later was a continuation of Griesbach's principles.) Both Semler and Griesbach rejected the Deity of Christ as

---

[1] Bruce Metzger, *The Text of the New Testament: Its Transmission, Corruption, and Restoration* (New York: Oxford University Press, 1964), 115.

[2] Marvin Vincent, *A History of the Textual Criticism of the New Testament* (New York: Macmillan Co., 1899), 92.

[3] James Sightler, *A Testimony Founded Forever: The King James Version Defended in Faith and History* (Greenville, S. C.: Sightler Publications, 1999), 61.

[4] James Sightler, *Tabernacle Essays on Bible Translations* (Greenville, S. C.: Tabernacle Baptist Church, 1993), 11.

well as the infallibility of the Scripture.[5] Another historian notes that Griesbach, "influenced from his undergraduate days by the rising tide of Rationalism sweeping over his country, was a foe of orthodox Christianity."[6] Much more could be added regarding the apostate history of Jakob Griesbach, but what is significant is that Westcott and Hort "venerated" the name of Griesbach "above that of every other textual critic of the New Testament."[7] Metzger also notes that Westcott and Hort did not collate any manuscripts (other than Sinaiticus and Vaticanus) nor did they provide a critical apparatus (footnotes). Rather, Metzger says, they "refined the critical methodology developed by Griesbach, Lachmann and others, and applied it rigorously."[8]

Karl Lachmann

The next major textual critic to come on the scene was Karl Lachmann (1793-1851) who was a professor of German philology at the University of Berlin. He was a German Rationalist in every sense of the word. Marvin Vincent wrote, "To Lachmann belongs the distinction of entirely casting aside the Textus Receptus."[9] Lachmann did not view the New Testament as the inspired Word of God, but rather as just another old book. His textual research of the New Testament was treated simply as scientific study as he would research any other book. He was not a theologian and was considered a profane man. Never-

---

[5]David Cloud, *Myths about the Modern Bible Versions* (Oak Harbor, Wash.: Way of Life Literature, 1999), 185.

[6]D. A. Thompson, "The Controversy Concerning the Last Twelve Verses of the Gospel according to Mark." Surrey: The Bible Christian Unity Fellowship, 39-40; reprint of an article which appeared in *Bible League Quarterly*, London 1973.

[7]Metzger, *Text of the New Testament*, 185.

[8]Ibid., 129.

[9]Vincent, *A History of the Textual Criticism of the New Testament*, 110.

theless, his work was taken seriously by other textual critics of the nineteenth century.[10] He applied the same secular principles he used to edit the Greek classics to the New Testament Greek text.[11] Once again, the lineage of the critical text flowed through the hands of an apostate.

Samuel Tregelles

Another nineteenth century textual critic was Samuel Tregelles (1813-1875). Unlike the majority of textual critics of his day, Tregelles was not apostate. However, he accepted the theories, philosophies, and views of Lachmann and Griesbach. It was Tregelles who said, "To Lachmann must be conceded this, that he led the way in casting aside the so-called Textus Receptus, and boldly placing the New Testament wholly and entirely on the basis of actual authority."[12] The "actual authority" to which Tregelles referred was none other than textual "science" and the scientific reconstruction of the New Testament text.

---

[10] Metzger, *The Text of the New Testament*, 124-25.

[11] Ibid.

[12] Edward Miller, *A Guide to the Textual Criticism of the New Testament* (original publisher unknown, 1886; reprint, Collingswood, N.J.: Dean Burgon Society, 1979), 22.

Friederich Constantine Von Tischendorf

A contemporary with Tregelles was Friederich Constantine Von Tischendorf (1815-1874). Tischendorf was another German who was certainly influenced by the Rationalism so prevalent in his native land. His view was that the New Testament had been lost to history. Therefore, he traveled throughout Europe and the Mediterranean world searching for ancient manuscripts to "scientifically reconstruct" the New Testament. He produced several critical-text editions of the Greek New Testament. However, after having "discovered" Sinaiticus, he altered his eighth edition of his Greek text in 3,572 places almost completely in accordance with Sinaiticus.[13]

It is from this lineage of Semler, Griesbach, Lachmann, Tregelles, and Tischendorf that Westcott and Hort produced their famous Greek New Testament first released in 1881. As noted earlier, Westcott and Hort "venerated" the apostate Griesbach and worked almost exclusively from Sinaiticus (Aleph) and Vaticanus (B) which had been made public by Tischendorf.

B. F. Westcott and F. J. A. Hort

Let us therefore look even more closely at the views, writings, and associations of **Brooke Foss Westcott** and **Fenton John Anthony Hort**. Both were graduates of Cambridge University in England and they were students during the time when the university was completely repudiating orthodox Christianity. B. F. Westcott went on to become the Bishop of Durham of the Church of England and F. J. A. Hort eventually became a professor at Cambridge.

In 1851, these two distinguished British scholars began a thirty-year project of creating a *new* Greek text of the New Testament. That project would be based almost entirely upon Vaticanus and Sinaiticus. They also developed and published a theory for textual criticism which

---

[13]Metzger, *The Text of the New Testament*, 127.

remains to this day. J. H. Greenlee notes in his *Introduction to New Testament Textual Criticism* that "the textual theories of W-H underlie virtually all subsequent work in NT textual criticism."[14] Wilbur Pickering notes that both the Nestlé-Aland as well as the United Bible Societies' Greek texts (the modern critical text) "really vary little from the W-H text."[15] Moreover, virtually all modern Bible translations are based upon either of these variations of the critical text. Thus, Westcott and Hort are key figures in the development of the modern critical text.

Theological Liberalism

We have described Westcott and Hort in some degree in earlier chapters. However, let us look a bit further into their beliefs, their private correspondence, and their personal associations. As divines in the Church of England in the mid-nineteenth century, they had to be careful what they said or publicly wrote. Though the Anglican Church (the Church of England) was in the process of becoming apostate during that time, it was risky for leadership in the church to openly contradict its official doctrinal position. The official position of the Church of England then, at least on paper, remained relatively orthodox. Liberal theologians therefore had to speak or write obliquely lest they get themselves in trouble for saying what they really believed.

There is every reason to believe that Westcott and Hort did the same. Their published works are often written in an obtuse style that was theological mumbo jumbo, to say the least. However, their real views were quite plain in private correspondence. After their deaths, their respective sons both published detailed biographies of their fathers including copies of much of their private correspondence. It is revealing.

---

[14] J. Harold Greenlee, *Introduction to New Testament Textual Criticism* (Grand Rapids: Eerdmans Publishing Co., 1964), 78.

[15] Wilbur Pickering, *The Identity of the New Testament Text* (Nashville: Thomas Nelson, 1977; reprint, Collingswood, N.J.: Bible for Today. n.d.), 42 (citation is to reprint edition).

We shall draw quotes from some of their writings in the pages to follow.

As was noted in chapter 6, Westcott and Hort questioned, denied, or were fuzzy about fundamental doctrines such as creation, the substitutionary atonement of Christ, the resurrection of Christ, and others. Because the focus of this volume pertains to the text of the New Testament, it is germane to note there is every reason to believe that Westcott and Hort did not believe in verbal inspiration, inerrancy, or the infallibility of the Word of God. They were astute enough not to publish a public statement saying in effect, "We do not believe in the inerrancy or verbal inspiration of the Bible." However, there is ample evidence in their writings to indicate this was exactly their position. To begin with, there is no written record in their voluminous writings where they professed to believe in inspiration.[16] To the contrary, they rather mocked the belief in verbal inspiration and belittled those who did. (See quotation for note 41 in chapter 6.)

In notes written by Westcott and Hort appended to their work *The New Testament in the Original Greek*, they make some revealing comments. They are veiled and at the end of the actual text, but they are there nevertheless. Referring to variants in the New Testament text, they make the comment, "But it is at least theoretically possible that the

---

[16]The declaration of John Burgon, by way of contrast, leaves no doubt as to his position on the matter of inspiration and infallibility. He wrote, "I believe that the Bible is the Word of God—and I believe that God's Word must be absolutely infallible. I shall therefore believe the Bible to be absolutely infallible." John Burgon, *Inspiration and Interpretation* (London: J. H. & Jas. Parker, 1861); reprint, Collingswood, N.J.: Bible for Today, 1984, 74 (citations are to reprint edition). Burgon continued, "But if . . . I am asked whether I believe the *words* of the Bible to be inspired,—I answer, To be sure I do,—every one of them: and every syllable likewise" (Ibid.). He also wrote regarding the scriptural writers, "They neither spoke nor wrote one word of their own: but uttered syllable by syllable as the Spirit put it into their mouths" (Ibid., 77). Contrast these forceful declarations of Burgon with the weasel words and mockery of inspiration by Westcott and Hort. The difference is as day and night. Moreover, it should noted that Burgon was the arch rival of Westcott and Hort on the revision committee. It is ironic that most modern Fundamentalists who espouse the critical text position lift up Westcott and Hort and belittle Burgon.

originality of the text thus attained is *relative* only"[17] (emphasis mine). Their reference to "the originality of the text" can only refer to its originals—the autographa. In referring to it, they subtly suggest that the origins thereof are "*relative*." Referring to texts "so near the autographs," they go on to say that "complete freedom from primitive corruption would not be antecedently improbable."[18] Once again, they write in an oblique, doublespeak fashion. Let us therefore render this in plain English. They refer to texts "so near the autographs." They then go on to speak of primitive corruption antecedent to (prior to) those texts as being probable. The manuscripts antecedent to those "so near the autographs" can only be the autographs themselves. They therefore refer to "primitive corruption" of the autographs as being probable. In other words, in their characteristic, theological mumbo-jumbo style of writing, they imply the autographs themselves to be corrupt. Can anyone find a hint of verbal inspiration or inerrancy here?

On another occasion, Hort's son quoted him as saying that "evangelicals seem to me perverted. . . . There are, I fear, still more serious differences between us on the subject of authority and especially the authority of the Bible."[19] His reference to "between us" was between himself and evangelicals. (It should be noted that the term *evangelical* in nineteenth-century England would be roughly analogous to the term *Fundamentalist* in twentieth-century America.) Notice how that Hort had differences with evangelicals (Fundamentalists) of his day over the *authority* of the Bible. He also referred to "evangelicals" as "perverted." Clearly, he seeks to undercut the authority of the Bible.

Once again, in that same context, they go on to note, "There are however some passages which one or both of us suspect to contain a primitive error of no great importance, and which are accordingly indi-

---

[17]Brooke Foss Westcott and Fenton John Anthony Hort, *The New Testament Text in the Original Greek*, 4th ed. (New York: Macmillan Co., 1940), 563.

[18]Ibid., 564.

[19]Arthur Fenton Hort, *Life and Letters of Fenton John Anthony Hort* (London: MacMillan & Co., 1896), 2:421.

cated as open to question."[20] Notice their comments about "primitive error" and passages "open to question." Again, can anyone find a hint of verbal inspiration, infallibility, or inerrancy here? The greater point is that Westcott and Hort never stated a belief in verbal inspiration. Rather, they regularly made remarks raising doubts concerning the infallibility and inerrancy of the New Testament text.

Liberal Associates

A fair indication of what one believes can be found in the company with which he chooses to associate. Though the Church of England in the nineteenth century was still "officially" orthodox in its doctrinal position, there were prominent, unofficial "parties" within the Church which were not. One of these groups was the Broad Church Party to which both Westcott and Hort associated.[21]

The Broad Church Party within the Church of England (1) denied the doctrine of original sin. (2) They denied the orthodox satisfaction theory of the atonement. (3) Most denied the eternal sonship of Christ and some denied his Deity altogether. (4) They denied the virgin birth of Christ. (4) They denied a literal eternal life. (5) They denied a literal heaven and hell. (6) They denied the literal, physical resurrection of Christ, replacing it with a spiritual resurrection. (7) They denied a literal second coming of Christ. (8) They denied verbal inspiration. (9) They denied a literal incarnation of Christ and substituted it with the idea of union of God with all men in the unfolding of history. (10) They denied the literal creation account and in its place accepted Darwin's theory of

---

[20]Ibid.

[21]Sightler, *Tabernacle Essays*, 15. James Sightler has also provided extensive research on the Broad Church Party in his excellent work, *A Testimony Founded For Ever*. On pages 15 and 65-67, there are substantial sources cited concerning the Broad Church Party of the Anglican Church.

evolution.[22] This is quintessential, conventional Liberalism. It is apostasy. It is unbelief! Yet, Westcott and Hort *voluntarily* chose to associate with this party! Their true colors are therein evident. Can anyone claim that these men were not apostate?

Over their long careers, Westcott and Hort also formed (or joined) a number of exclusive clubs. These organizations provide additional insights into the interests of these principal editors of the critical text.

Occult Activities

In 1994, a book authored by G. A. Riplinger appeared in the United States which among other things charged that Westcott and Hort were involved in the occult.[23] It was immediately dismissed by virtually all who were sympathetic to the critical text position.[24] However, other authors have established the same charge. Les Garrett, an Australian researcher, noted the same thing eleven years earlier in 1982.[25] In 1999,

---

[22]Ibid., 16-18.

[23]G. A. Riplinger, *New Age Bible Versions*, (Munroe Falls, Ohio: AV Publications, 1994).

[24]Obviously, if Riplinger was right, this was a serious charge. Most critics, it seemed, dismissed her because (1) she was a woman, (2) she was not formally trained in the area of textual criticism (though she held a graduate degree in another field), and (3) they alleged there were a few minor errors in her book. However, there has *never* been any rebuttal of her major charges, especially regarding Westcott and Hort being involved with the occult. Riplinger's sources have proved accurate. This author personally knows one credentialed historian who spent eighty hours checking out each and every one of Riplinger's citations. His conclusion was that her data is essentially correct. The unforgiving facts of history are that Westcott and Hort did indeed dabble in the occult!

[25]Les Garrett, ed., *Which Bible Can We Trust?* (Queensland, Australia: Christian Center Press, 1982), 238.

James Sightler independently made the same charge.[26] In the mouths of two or three witnesses, shall not a word be established?

The Ghostly Guild

The fact of the matter is that Hort himself freely admitted the same. In a private letter, F. J. A. Hort wrote, "Westcott, Gorham, C. B. Scott, Benson, Bradshaw, Laurd and I have started a society for the investigation of ghosts, and all supernatural appearances, and effects, being all disposed to believe that such things really exist, and ought to be discriminated from hoaxes and mere subjective delusions; we shall be happy to obtain any good accounts with well authenticated names. Our own temporary name is the Ghostly Guild."[27]

This club was organized by Westcott and Hort in 1851 at Cambridge University the same year in which they began their work on their Greek Text. They continued to participate in the Ghostly Guild until 1861, a period of ten years. However, they were clever enough to realize that being connected with such an organization could impair their greater goals in life—the publishing and acceptance of their new Greek Text. They thus determined that their involvement in the Ghostly Guild would lead to no good.

Hort therefore wrote to Westcott in 1861, "This may sound cowardice—I have a craving that our Text ('New' Greek New Testament) should be cast upon the world before we deal with matters likely to brand us with suspicion. I mean a text issued by men who are already known for what will undoubtedly be treated as dangerous heresy will have great difficulty in finding its way to regions which it might otherwise hope to reach and whence it would not be easily banished by

---

[26]Sightler, *A Testimony Founded For Ever*, 103-109.

[27]Arthur Hort, *Life and Letters*, 1:211.

subsequent alarms.... If only we speak our minds, we shall not be able to avoid giving grave offence to the miscalled orthodoxy of the day."[28]

It is clear that Westcott and Hort knew their involvement in an occult society would be viewed as "dangerous heresy" and would thus brand their work with "suspicion." After 140 years, it indeed has come back to cause "subsequent alarms." They knew what they were doing and they knew the potential damage it would cause to their greater goals if it should be made widely known.

Did not the apostle warn Timothy, "Now the Spirit speaketh expressly, that in the latter times some shall depart from the faith, giving heed to seducing spirits, and doctrines of devils?"[29] It should be evident both from what they wrote and whence they associated that Westcott and Hort had departed from the faith. Their doctrinal positions are a clear departure from historic New Testament Christianity. Therefore, should it be any surprise that they dabbled with seducing spirits and doctrines of devils?

Spin Control

Fundamentalists sympathetic to the critical text have desperately tried to "spin" the occult connection of Westcott and Hort as the sophomoric foolishness of immature college boys. However, it should be noted first that their initial involvement in spiritism lasted for ten years and well after they had graduated from college. In the January 1994 issue of *Target* magazine, Robert Sumner claimed that the Ghostly Guild was "merely a humorous name given to an innocent organiza-

---

[28]Ibid., 1:421, 445.

[29]1 Tim. 4:1.

tion by immature college boys."[30] This same refrain is repeated again in 1999 by J. B. Williams when he excused Westcott and Hort's involvement in the Ghostly Guild as an unfortunate incident in their youth, giving it "a name that created a false impression."[31] However, as we shall soon see, the involvement of Westcott and Hort in their Ghostly Guild was more than the folly of youth. Moreover, even if that is all it was, they still were involved in occult activities. It went on for even more years while they were in the process of creating their new Greek text.

In the biography of his father, Hort's son quotes him as noting that Westcott was one of the most active members of the Ghostly Guild at Cambridge.[32] Regarding the Ghostly Guild, Westcott's son wrote that his father "took a leading part in their proceedings and their inquiry circular was originally drawn up by him."[33] In that circular (i.e., promotional flyer), the senior Westcott wrote, "But there are many others who believe it possible that the beings of the unseen world may manifest themselves to us.... Many of the stories current in tradition or scattered up and down in books, may be exactly true."[34] Westcott clearly wrote of "beings of the unseen world" manifesting themselves to them in their meetings (seances). He goes on to note that the stories of occult traditions very well may be true. Deut. 18:10-11 says, "There shall not

---

[30]Robert Sumner, "Sumner's Incidents and Illustrations—Were Westcott and Hort Members of a Ghost Society?" *Target,* January 1994, vol. ix, #1, 7.

[31]J. B. Williams, general ed., "Introduction: The Issue We Face," *From the Mind of God to the Mind of Man* (Greenville, S.C.: Ambassador—Emerald International, 1999), 4.

[32]Arthur Hort, *Life and Letters,* 1:219, 220.

[33]Arthur Westcott, *Life and Letters of Brooke Foss Westcott* (London: MacMillan & Co., 1903), 1:117-118.

[34]Ibid.

be found among you *any one* that [is] . . . a consulter with familiar spirits."

Other Clubs

The Ghostly Guild, however, was not the first or only club to which Westcott and Hort associated themselves. As a Cambridge undergraduate, Westcott organized a club and chose for its name "Hermes."[35] The latter title was so named by Westcott because it derived from "the god of magic . . . and occult wisdom, the conductor of Souls to Hades . . . Lord of Death . . . cunning and trickery."[36] Hermes was considered to be the entry point of scholars and philosophers into the occult. Westcott's Hermes club met weekly.[37] It seems that the occult was not the only activity at the Hermes Club. A secular book tracing occult societies cited a letter between members of Westcott's club and refers to a homosexual relationship between members. That same source quoted a member of the club (Arthur Sidgwick to Frederic Meyers) admitting that homosexuality was not rare among them.[38] There is no evidence that Westcott and Hort themselves were homosexuals.

However, it appears that such activity took place amongst other members of a club in which they participated and which Westcott himself organized. Moreover, it also appears that such activities were no secret to other members of the club.

In 1851 (the same year in which they began work on their new Greek text), Hort joined a secret society called the Apostles, founded

---

[35]Les Garrett, *Westcott & Hort: The Occult Connection and New Greek Text* (Queensland, Australia: Voice of Thanksgiving, 1997), 38.

[36]Arthur Westcott, *Life and Letters*, 1:47.

[37]Ibid.

[38]Alan Gauld, *The Founders of Psychical Research* (New York: Schocken Books, 1968), 90-91.

some years earlier by the utterly apostate Samuel Coleridge. Hort's son wrote that in June of that year, his father joined the "mysterious company of the Apostles." He notes that it was his own father which was "mainly responsible for the oath which binds members to a *conspiracy of silence*[39] (emphasis mine).

Westcott evidently joined as well for he is mentioned in later records pertaining to the club. Because of the secretive nature of this society, there is little direct information as to their activities. However, other members such as Henry Sidgwick and F. D. Maurice were deeply involved in occult activities. During the 1870s, some members of the Apostle's club met for seances at Lord Balfour's house.[40] The Apostles club was credited as the cause of Sidgwick's rejection of his Christian upbringing.[41] It should be recalled that Westcott and Hort's involvement in these organizations was voluntary. Again, it was simultaneous with the development of their new Greek text.

In 1872, Westcott then organized the Eranus Club which included not only Hort, but also Sidgwick, J. B. Lightfoot (of the English Bible Revision Committee), Arthur Balfour (later prime minister of England), and others. The club met to conduct seances in the homes of its members, including the home of Hort.[42] In 1882, Sidgwick and Frederic Meyers formed the Society of Psychical Research (SPR).[43] Notice the person common to most of these secret societies was Henry Sidgwick. There is no evidence that Westcott and Hort ever were personally part of the Society of Psychical Research. However, they had been closely connected with its founders in other mutual associations.

---

[39] Arthur Hort, *Life and Letters*, 1:170-71, 198.

[40] Garrett, *Westcott & Hort: The Occult Connection*, 32.

[41] Gauld, *Founders of Psychical Research*, 48-9.

[42] Arthur Hort, *Life of Hort*, 2:184-185. See also Arthur Westcott, *Life of Westcott*, 1:385.

[43] Sightler, *A testimony Founded Forever*, 108.

Fundamentalists sympathetic to the critical text and hence to Westcott and Hort have tried to trivialize their occult activities as sophomoric actions of immature college boys. However, as has been noted above, these activities continued on for many years after college.[44] Moreover, secular historians who have specialized in research of the occult certainly do not take a trivial view of these organizations. *The Encyclopedia of Occultism and Parapsychology* lists the "Ghostly Guild Club" in its roster of occult organizations. This same encyclopedia describes the Ghostly Guild Club as one in which members related personal experiences with ghosts.[45]

The Society of Psychical Research

The Society of Psychical Research went on to become a full-fledged occult organization continuing in both Britain and America to the present day. There are numerous websites on the Internet which pertain to the Society of Psychical Research.[46] In 1948, the ruling council of the Society of Psychical Research authorized its president, W. H. Salter, to write an official history of their organization. That official history lists the Ghostly Guild as "the forerunner of the Society of Psychical Re-

---

[44]Westcott and Hort openly acknowledged that between 1871and 1876, they "privately" sent copies of various books of their developing Greek New Testament to several of the revisors of the English New Testament. The point is that they were working on their Greek text while they were still involved in organizations with occult activities. Brooke Foss Westcott and Fenton John Anthony Hort, *Introduction to the New Testament in the Original Greek with Notes on Selected Readings* (London: Macmillan & Co., 1882; reprint, Peabody, Mass.: Hendrickson, 1988), 18 (citation is to reprint edition).

[45]Encyclopedia of Occultism and Parapsychology, 162; quoted in Les Garrett, *Westcott and Hort: The Occult Connection*, 32.

[46]The URL for the official website of the SPR is http://moebius.psy.ed.ac.uk/~spr. There are many articles and much information there regarding the occult and advocating the practice thereof.

search.[47] Both Westcott and Hort are here mentioned as members of that club.[48] That book goes on to describe the interests and activities of the Society of Psychical Research (among other things) as "phantasms of the dead," the Theosophical Society, "poltergeists," "spiritism," "telepathy," "automatic writing," "trances," "mediums," and the "paranormal."[49] Sigmund Freud was also associated with the Society for Psychical Research.[50]

Madame Helena Petrovna Blavatsky is considered to be the mother of the modern occult movement. She was a Luciferian and founded the Theosophical Society.[51] She has also been called the midwife of the New-Age movement.[52] In 1884, Madame Blavatsky visited England and met with a committee from the Society for Psychical Research. Records show that the committee was "considerably impressed" with their contact with Madame Blavatsky.[53] There is no record that Westcott or Hort ever had direct contact with Madame Blavatsky. However, what is significant is that the Society for Psychical Research grew out of the occult club they had organized in 1851. The official history of the Society for Psychical Research documents this. To trivialize their involvement in the organizations which preceded the Society for Psychical Research and from which it descended is to ignore history.

---

[47]W. H. Salter, *The Society for Psychical Research: An Outline of its History* (London: Tavistock Square, 1948), 5-6.

[48]Ibid., 6.

[49]Ibid., 19, 21, 23, 28, 32, 43, 48.

[50]Gauld, *Founders of Psychical Research*, index.

[51]*Encyclopedia of Occultism and Parapsychology*, 162; quoted in Les Garrett, *Westcott and Hort: The Occult Connection*, 42.

[52]Les Garrett, *Westcott and Hort: The Occult Connection*, 31.

[53]Salter, *Society for Psychical Research*, 21.

Were Westcott and Hort full-fledged Satanists? The evidence does not indicate they were. However, there can be no question that they dabbled in the occult throughout the time they were producing their new Greek text of the New Testament.

Westcott, Hort, and Darwin

Both Westcott and Hort had a fondness for Charles Darwin. When his book, *The Origins of the Species,* appeared in 1859, Westcott and Hort immediately had nothing but praise for it. In 1860, Westcott enthusiastically wrote to Hort, "Have you read Darwin? How I should like to talk with you about it. In spite of difficulties I am inclined to think it unanswerable. In any case, it is a treat to read such a book."[54]

In 1888, Hort wrote to his youngest son, then a student at Cambridge, "The Life of Darwin, which I dare say you have seen on our living room table is a very interesting book. . . . Some day you may like to have a talk about it. I hope the *Inhabitants of a Pond* are not put off for good."[55] The *Inhabitants of a Pond* was another book which Darwin had written. Hort clearly recommended Darwin to his son. This was almost thirty years after *The Origins of the Species* had appeared. Hort thus had had ample time to digest the implications of Darwin's theory of evolution! Notwithstanding, he recommended Darwin to his son.

Australian researcher, Les Garrett, additionally asserts that Charles Darwin was a member of the Ghostly Guild.[56] There is no record that Westcott and Hort had direct contact with Charles Darwin, but they were enamored with his theory of evolution. Darwin's involvement in the guild and the Society of Psychical Research evidently was after Westcott and Hort had pulled out. But the fact remains that Westcott

---

[54] Arthur Hort, *Life and Letters,* 1:414.

[55] Ibid., 398.

[56] Garrett, *Westcott and Hort: The Occult Connection,* 140.

and Hort started the Ghostly Guild and the Society for Psychical Research was its direct descendant.

Defense of Unitarianism

As has been related in earlier sections, Westcott and Hort were quite sympathetic to theological Liberalism. Should it therefore be any surprise that they were sympathetic to Unitarianism? It should be recalled that Unitarians were the original Liberals in modern church history. They, from the eighteenth century, have denied the Deity of Christ, the Trinity (whence derives the name "Unitarian"), and the fallen sin nature in man to mention a few of their apostate views.

After having worked upon their new Greek text of the New Testament for almost twenty years, Westcott and Hort were instrumental in a decision made by the Church of England to produce a new English Revised Version of the Bible. (Its New Testament, of course, would be based upon Westcott and Hort's new Greek text.) A substantial committee of British theologians and scholars were enlisted to participate as the Revision Committee. It was through the influence and invitation of B. F. Westcott that a Unitarian theologian by the name of George Vance Smith was appointed to the Revision Committee.[57] Smith was minister of the St. Saviour's Gate Unitarian Chapel in York, England. He was given equal vote on the Revision Committee even though he openly denied the Deity of Christ. After Smith had participated in a communion service with other members of the Revision Committee in 1870, he published a letter in the *Times* (of London) July 11, 1870. In that letter, he proudly announced that though he had received communion, he had refused to recite the Apostles' Creed. To do so, he claimed, would violate his principles as one who denied the Deity of Christ.

---

[57]Sightler, *A Testimony Founded Forever*, 115.

This created a storm of controversy in England. Several thousand clergymen of the Church of England demanded that Smith be removed from the Revision Committee. Both legislative bodies of the Church of England passed resolutions demanding that no person should be allowed on the Revision Committee who denied the Deity of Christ.[58] However, what is most shocking is that Westcott and Hort, along with several other liberal members, refused to serve on the Revision Committee if Vance Smith was removed.

Smith was no insignificant clergyman. He had published several books in England advancing Unitarian theology. One such book by him was entitled *Texts and Margins of the Revised New Testament Affecting Theological Doctrine Briefly Reviewed*. In that book, he gloried in the fact that many of the changes in the English Revised Version supported his apostate views of Jesus Christ. Let us consider one such example found on page 47 of that book. "The only instance in the N.T. in which the religious worship or adoration of Christ was apparently implied, has been altered by the Revision: 'At the name of Jesus every knee shall bow' [Phil. 2:10] is now to be read 'in the name.' Moreover, *no alteration of the text or of translation will be found anywhere to make up for this loss; as indeed it is well understood that the N.T. contains neither precept nor example which really sanctions the religious worship of Jesus Christ*"[59] (emphasis mine).

Notice that Smith delighted in the fact that the English Revised Version (based upon Westcott and Hort's text) deleted the reference to every knee bowing before Jesus. He goes on to falsely claim that there was no other place in the New Testament which directed worship of Jesus Christ. That is utter blasphemy! Yet, Westcott and Hort *insisted* that Smith remain on their Revision Committee and threatened to resign if he was forced off the committee.

---

[58]Cloud, *Modern Myths*, 198.

[59]George Vance Smith, *Texts and Margins of the Revised New Testament Affecting Theological Doctrine Briefly Reviewed* (original publisher unknown), 47; quoted in David Cloud, *Modern Myths*, 198-199.

"What fellowship hath righteousness with unrighteousness? And what communion hath light with darkness? And what concord hath Christ with Belial?" Can there be any question that Westcott and Hort were theological Liberals? They clearly dabbled with the occult. They recommended Charles Darwin and what he wrote. They publicly stood with a blatant Unitarian when he denied the Deity of Christ. If the principle of separation is a cornerstone of Fundamentalism, how can any Fundamentalist have anything to do with them? How can a Fundamentalist support their major work, the Westcott and Hort Greek New Testament? To this day it remains the essence of the critical text whence most modern translations of the Bible are based. Therefore, how can a Fundamentalist have anything to do with the versions of the Bible translated therefrom. "Come out from among them and touch not the *unclean* thing."

Would God transmit and preserve the Old Testament through the prophets of Baal? Would He then transmit and preserve the New Testament through men who were demonstrably unbelievers, who dabbled in the occult, and defended blatant apostasy? You be the judge!

Let us therefore move on to the contemporary scene and the atmosphere of the current debate over Bible translations and the textual issue. There are remarkable similarities and parallels between the current controversy and great Fundamentalist-Modernist battles in the first half of the twentieth century.

Accommodation and Inclusivism to Maintain Unity

There is no question that the controversy over Bible translations and the textual issue is divisive. Fundamental Baptist associations and fellowships are dividing over this very issue. In some cases, churches or groups of churches have been pressured to leave a national fellowship because they took some sort of stand upon the King James Version. In other cases, churches and pastors have pulled out of associations and fellowships because the association or fellowship refused to take any sort of stand on the Bible translation issue. This author is aware of instances where churches or even entire fellowships have disassociated themselves from state or national bodies because the larger group in their view was "soft" on the issue.

However, there is also a movement afoot in a number of national and state Baptist associations (or fellowships) in which an attitude of *inclusivism* has been advanced regarding the translation and textual issue. The posture in some circles is that this is not an issue worth fighting over here. Therefore, the issue should be a nonissue.[60] Those who insist on making an issue of the text are simply divisive and therefore ought to be quiet. The chorus in some circles is that let us accept in our fellowship those who hold either position. Those favoring the Received Text will with condescension be allowed by their more enlightened brethren who believe the critical text is superior. They say, let us therefore ignore the issue to maintain unity of fellowship.

The parallel to the attitudes of accommodation and inclusivism which existed in the great Fundamentalist-Liberal battles of the past is striking. In examining the incipient apostasy and unbelief throughout the lineage of the critical text, can one not cry out, "Is there not a cause?" Unless one is completely ignorant of the history of the critical text (and many have been), how can a true Fundamentalist have anything to do with it? Are we not enjoined to "touch not the unclean thing?" Putting aside for the moment internal deletions, dilutions, and changes in the critical text weakening significant doctrines, its associations and lineage ought to be enough to cause a true Fundamentalist to separate therefrom.[61] When the critical text has been developed by such unholy hands, how can God have had anything to do with it?

---

[60]Rolland D. McCune, "Doctrinal Nonissues in Historic Fundamentalism," *Detroit Baptist Seminary Journal* 1, no. 2 (fall 1996): 177. McCune writes, "Controversy over text, text types, and translations of the Bible is one of fundamentalism's greatest distractions. Historically, this has been a nonissue and, in the interests of the integrity of the Bible and the future of the fundamentalist movement, should remain so."

[61]In appendices A, B, and D at the end of this book, documentation will be provided of the dilution and weakening of major New Testament doctrine, especially that which pertains to our Lord.

Ralph Colas is the Executive Secretary of the American Council of Christian Churches (ACCC), a Fundamentalist organization. In his column in the paper of the Independent Baptist Fellowship of North America, the *Review*, (February 2000), he wrote, "There are some new evangelicals who believe in many of the fundamentals of the Faith. What distinguishes them from us is separation. Fundamentalists believe, preach and practice separation. Those who say they are Fundamentalists, but who fail to preach and practice separation, should drop the Fundamentalist name and correctly identify themselves as new evangelicals."[62]

Colas likely was not writing in the context of the textual issue. However, the principle he proclaims certainly is applicable. The bottom line of Fundamentalism in the twenty-first century remains separation from apostasy and compromise. It is the contention of this author that use of the critical text is a breach of the principle of separation and hence is spiritual compromise!

Review Questions for Further Study

1. With kind of theology were most textual editors of the nineteenth century connected?

2. Name several nineteenth century textual critics which were German Rationalists.

3. From whence do the several modern critical texts directly derive?

4. What was the view of Westcott and Hort toward inspiration and inerrancy?

5. What were some of the distinctions of the Broad Church Party?

---

[62]Ralph Colas, "Perspectives," *Review*, February 2000 (Sellersville, Pa.: Independent Baptist Fellowship of North America), 2.

Applying the Principle of Separation to the Textual Issue

6. Name at least one occult club founded by Westcott and Hort.

7. What was the parent organization of the Society for Psychical Research?

8. What was Westcott and Hort's attitude toward Charles Darwin?

9. Who was G. Vance Smith and what did he believe?

10. Is use of the critical text a breach of the principle of separation?

CHAPTER TEN

WHAT ABOUT ERASMUS, KING JAMES, AND HIS TRANSLATORS?

Many Fundamentalist proponents of the critical text have already heard most of the charges of apostasy filed against various textual editors thereof. Their reaction more often than not is to ignore the evidence and rather respond by attacking key figures related to the Received Text. There are several, standard, diversionary tactics used by advocates of the critical text position when charged with irregularities in its lineage. The first option is to bring up Desiderius Erasmus. When faced with charges against various editors of the critical text, the retort often is, "Well, what about Erasmus? Was he not a Roman Catholic?" Another standard response is "Well, what about King James I? Was he not a bawdy fellow and even a homosexual?" And then, they ask, "What about the King James translators? Were not they a group of profane men? Moreover, were not King James and his translators all Anglicans?"

The rationale therefore is, if there are problems with those connected with the critical text, there (allegedly) are also problems with those connected with the Received Text and its famous translation, the King James Version. Their mutual problems therefore cancel each other out. Thus, the apostasy of the critical text is of no importance because the lineage of the Received Text is just as bad. However, that logic is faulty. First, as we will demonstrate, the charges against Erasmus, King James, and the King James translators are empty. Second, even if they had some merit, they do not begin to measure up to the utter apostasy connected with the critical text. Let us therefore examine each of the allegations against key figures of the Received Text.

Desiderius Erasmus

It should be recalled that Desiderius Erasmus was the Renaissance humanist who first published the Received Text in 1516.[1] This was prior to the beginning of the Reformation in 1517 when Luther nailed his ninety-five theses to the door of the church in Wittenberg, Germany. Regarding the origins of the Reformation, it has been said by Catholic enemies thereof that "Erasmus laid the eggs and Luther hatched the chickens." Other Catholic enemies of both Erasmus and Luther charged that "Erasmus is the father of Luther."[2] These charges were based upon the fact that Luther was influenced in no small measure by Erasmus's publication of his Greek New Testament in 1516. In that year, there was no Reformation nor were there yet any official Protestants.

From Erasmus's 1516 edition of his Greek New Testament came another four editions, all of the Received Text. After the death of Erasmus, Robert Stephanus continued to publish and edit the Received Text from Paris. After Stephanus's death, Theodore Beza published nine or ten editions of the Greek New Testament. And, the King James translators worked primarily from Beza's fifth edition of 1598. There is no question that Desiderius Erasmus played a key role in the transmission of the Received Text. Thus, he is the primary figure that critics seek to disparage by saying he was a Catholic.

Erasmus the Scholar

Let us therefore briefly examine the life of Erasmus. Desiderius Erasmus grew up in fifteenth-century central Europe. Apart from the Waldenses in the valleys of the Alps and other remote separatist groups,

---

[1] The term *humanist* in the context of the Renaissance had an entirely different sense from the modern use. Its Renaissance meaning was of one who was a scholar and learned in the humanities. That is, he was expert in classical literature and classical languages such as Greek and Latin.

[2] Preserved Smith, *Erasmus*, 209.

there were very few other forms of Christianity than the Roman Catholic Church in that part of the world. (Even Wycliffe and Tyndale had been nominal Catholics.) The Reformation had not yet begun. There were no Protestant churches in central Europe or England at this time. Therefore, to charge Erasmus with being a Catholic is somewhat of a hollow charge. Though he was a clergyman in the Catholic Church, there is no record that he ever presided over any parish. Rather, he traveled across Europe throughout most of his career as a scholar. He was more or less an "independent Catholic." In his day, he was considered the foremost scholar of classical Greek and Latin literature. The course of his travels took him from Holland to France, England, and Switzerland.

Over the years, Erasmus became intimately acquainted with biblical manuscripts available throughout Europe, particularly of the New Testament. Because the Word of God is quick and powerful and sharper than any two-edged sword, it is evident as Erasmus began to search the Scriptures, they had a profound effect upon his life. By the time of his death, the theology of Erasmus had shifted closer to that of the Anabaptists than that of Rome. This will shortly be documented.

As noted above, in 1516, Erasmus published from Basel, Switzerland, his Greek New Testament which he called the *Novum Instrumentum*. In English that means the "New Instrument.[3] Contrary to popular misconception, Erasmus had more than a handful of manuscripts at his disposal. Preserved Smith, the noted expert on the life of Erasmus, comments, "For the first edition Erasmus had before him ten manuscripts, four of which he found in England, and five at Basle. . . . The last codex was lent him by John Reuchlin . . . (and) appeared to Erasmus so old that it might have come from the apostolic age."[4] He was aware of Vaticanus in the Vatican Library and had a friend by the name of Bombasius research that for him (165). He, however, rejected the characteristic variants of Vaticanus which distinguishes itself from

---

[3] Ephraim Emerton, *Desiderius Erasmus of Rotterdam* (New York: G. P. Putnam's Sons, 1899), 200.

[4] Smith, *Erasmus: A Study of His Life*, 163.

the Received Text. (These variants are what would become the distinguishing characteristics of the critical text more than 350 years later.)

Erasmus's Shift in Theology

The more Erasmus became involved in the study and editing of the New Testament, the more his theology and convictions began to change. He came to reject the typical Roman Catholic interpretation of Matt. 16:18 establishing papal primacy. He began to vehemently attack the abuses and scandals of the Roman Catholic clergy, particularly as they violated their vows of celibacy. He even attacked celibacy as fallacious (171).

Critics of Erasmus have been quick to point out that he dedicated his first edition of his Greek New Testament to Pope Leo X. However, there is more to that than meets the eye. The long established Catholic position was that the Latin Vulgate was the official church Bible. There was a hostility toward anything that threatened that primacy. Erasmus knew that and he knew the opposition his Greek text would receive. Therefore, without the pope even knowing it, he dedicated it to him and at the same time had his friend in Rome, Bombasius, obtain formal approval of his publication because it had been dedicated to the pope. Thus, when the Catholic establishment in central Europe began to vehemently attack his work, Erasmus produced the approval of the pope. Erasmus was not a separatist, but he was shrewd.

After having done an end run around the Catholic establishment in central Europe, he was accused by powerful elements of the church of being even more dangerous than Luther (174). Contrary to conventional Catholic dogma of the day forbidding laymen from the reading of the Scriptures, Erasmus rather invited all men to read the Bible. This drew great wrath upon him from French Catholic authorities (180). It was such deviation from Rome's dogma which prompted Catholics across Europe to soon utter the proverb, "Erasmus laid the eggs and Luther hatched the chickens" (209). In other words, Erasmus was the root of the Protestant Reformation. Though Erasmus had no personal influence upon Luther, his writings certainly did, especially his Greek Testament and his commentaries. Ironically, because Erasmus never officially left the Catholic Church, he soon came to be attacked by Luther and other of the Reformers. The attacks accordingly developed into a war of words between Erasmus and the Reformers.

Erasmus thus became an enigma. He slowly but surely shifted away from Catholic theology, but stopped short of joining with Luther. He attacked the Roman Catholic Church, but never officially left it. Part of this confusion is to be found in the personal temperament of Erasmus. Whereas Luther had the temperament to stand and thunder, "Here I stand, I can do no other," Erasmus was more timorous. He was not an open fighter. His battling was through his pen. Whereas Luther eventually was excommunicated from the Catholic Church, Erasmus tried to reform it from within.[5] Whereas Luther became a "come-outer," Erasmus remained a "stay-inner." He would have been better served to follow Luther's example. However, he did not. He thus became a target from both sides. The establishment of the Catholic Church detested him. Most of the Reformers were suspicious of him as well.

Erasmus the Evangelical

Reading some of the quotations of Erasmus in his later years is insightful. They reveal a man who had shifted from conventional Roman Catholic theology to one much closer to a biblical position. For example, he wrote: "Therefore if you will dedicate yourself wholly to the study of the Scriptures, if you will meditate on the law of the Lord day and night,

---

[5] It should be noted that Luther as well hoped to stay within the Catholic Church and work reform from the inside. Events so conspired that he did not. However, Erasmus was able to get away with that.

you will not be afraid of the terror of the night or of the day, but you will be fortified and trained against every onslaught of enemies."[6]

Elsewhere, he wrote, "Christ Jesus . . . is the true light, alone shattering the night of earthly folly, the Splendor of paternal glory, who as he was made redemption and justification for us reborn in him, so also was made Wisdom (as Paul testifies): 'We preach Christ crucified, to the Jews a stumbling block, and to the Gentiles foolishness; but to them that are called, both Jews and Greeks, Christ is the power of God and the wisdom of God.' "[7] The question may therefore be asked, does that sound more like a Fundamentalist sermon or a Roman Catholic homily? The quotations illustrate the shift of the convictions of Erasmus.

Erasmus and the Anabaptists

However, what is most amazing is that in Erasmus's later years, he came very close to becoming an Anabaptist. Though he never joined with them, his theology became somewhat parallel with theirs. Friesen shows that by 1530, his name had come to be associated with the Anabaptists whom the Catholics and many Protestants considered to be the arch-heretics of the sixteenth century.[8] One church historian, Walter Koehler, has gone so far as to assert that Erasmus "was the spiritual father of the Anabaptists" (22). Another historian, Leonhard von Muralt, credits Erasmus with having "prepared the way for Anabaptism and provided material for the construction of their teachings" (22). Friends of Erasmus thus warned him that he was moving dangerously close to an Anabaptist position (36).

---

[6]Matthew Spinka, *Advocates of Reform: From Wyclif to Erasmus* (Philadelphia: Westminster Press, 1953), 304.

[7]Ibid., 309.

[8]Abraham Friesen, *Erasmus, the Anabaptists, and the Great Commission* (Grand Rapids: Eerdmans Publishing Co., 1998), 21.

Perhaps more than anything else, Erasmus began to advocate baptism by immersion after conversion. Though this was called an Anabaptist heresy by the Catholics *and* Protestants, it was simply Bible teaching. The third edition of his Greek New Testament of 1522 differed from the second only in its introductory notes. There, Erasmus advocated that Christian youth be taught biblical instruction first — *before* they were baptized. He even advocated re-baptism for those already sprinkled as infants (45). Moreover, he came to believe that baptism was to be by *immersion*. In his annotations (i.e., commentary or notes) on Matthew 28, Erasmus wrote, "After you have taught them these things, and they *believe* what you have taught them, have repented their previous lives, and are ready to embrace the doctrine of the gospel (in their life), then *immerse* them in water, in the name of the Father, the Son, and the Holy Ghost" (51, emphasis mine).

That teaching concerning baptism is perilously close to, if not synonymous with, Fundamental Baptist theology. It certainly was Anabaptist doctrine. Balthasar Hubmaier was an early Anabaptist leader. He essentially quoted Erasmus's statement above to establish his own point regarding baptism by immersion in his book of 1526 entitled *Old and New Believers on Baptism*. After having quoted the above-mentioned statement by Erasmus, Hubmaier noted, "Here Erasmus publicly points out that baptism was instituted by Christ for those instructed in the faith and not for young children" (53). In his annotations (i.e., commentary or notes) on Matt. 28:18-20, Erasmus also went on to write, "The Apostles are commanded that they teach first and baptize later."

Erasmus in Summary

Erasmus is a fascinating character in the lineage of the Received Text of the New Testament. His Greek New Testament, without doubt, was the catalyst which sparked the Reformation. He was a Catholic at the beginning of the Reformation. However, as he continued to search the Scriptures, he increasingly became less and less Catholic in his position. By the time he died in 1536, he had virtually become an

Anabaptist in his theology. To his demerit, he never officially left the Catholic Church. However, when he died, it was not in the arms of Rome. Rather, in 1534, he returned to Basel, Switzerland, and two years later died in the midst of his Protestant friends, "without relations of any sort, so far as known with the Roman Catholic Church."[9]

To try and deflect attention from the apostasy of the critical text by pointing out that Erasmus was a Catholic reveals a lack of knowledge of who he was, what he did, and what he believed. Like virtually all of the Reformers, Erasmus originally was a Catholic. However, unlike the rest of the Reformers, he never formally left the Catholic Church. His crusade was with his pen. Accordingly, his own writings show that he changed to a position that even the persecuted Anabaptists used to support their theology. The Catholic establishment became a fierce opponent to him by the time of his death. Though not a separatist, by the time he had published the third edition of his Greek New Testament, the charge of Roman Catholic apostasy can no longer be applied to Erasmus.

King James I of England

The charge then is advanced by adversaries of the King James Version that King James I of England was a bawdy fellow and even a homosexual. However, these charges as well collapse upon further investigation.

James Stuart of Scotland became King James VI of Scotland and eventually went on to become King James I of England. In 1604, shortly after becoming king of all of England, King James, as titular head of the Church of England, "authorized" a new version of the Bible. This of course has come to be known ever since as the King James Version. Thus, those unsympathetic to the King James Version have been quick to point out alleged character flaws associated with James Stuart. At the

---

[9] Edward Hills, *The King James Version Defended* (Des Moines, Iowa: Christian Research Press, 1956), 194.

outset, it should be noted that we are dealing with the King James Version and not the "Saint James Version." James Stuart was a *man* and certainly had idiosyncrasies and flaws as do all men. He at times did not conduct himself with all the social graces one might expect from a king. And, he like all men had his foibles. But as will be documented below, in the main, James was a godly man who loved the Lord and tried to set an example for his family and his nation.

James's Bitter Enemies

King James I of England reigned at a time when vicious winds of political strife were rampant. England was in the throes of casting out the last vestiges and influences of the Roman Catholic Church. There also were bitter internal politics of longstanding adversarial parties. King James therefore had bitter enemies, both religious as well as political. Some of these dedicated themselves to tarnishing the reputation of James Stuart in any fashion possible.

Several of his bitter enemies were quick to point out his personal quirks and *faux pas* of social graces. However, the most serious allegation brought forth (after he was dead) was that he was a homosexual. This allegation was picked up and published in the *Moody Monthly* in its July/August 1985 edition.[10] These charges have never been proved. As will be noted below, they originated from an embittered political enemy of James who vowed vengeance against him. His charges are analogous to the tactics of the modern political operatives in attacking their foes. Other more recent publications also have insinuated that King James was less than a godly person.[11] However, before refuting these

---

[10] Karen Ann Wojan, "The Real King James" and Leslie Keylock, "The Bible That Bears His Name," *Moody Monthly*, July/August 1985, 87-89.

[11] John C. Mincy, "The Making of the King James Version," in *From the Mind of God to the Mind of Man*, ed. J. B. Williams (Greenville, S.C.: Ambassador—Emerald International, 1999), 130.

charges, let us present a brief overview of the man James Stuart. Understanding something about him personally will in itself go a long way to negate such politically motivated allegations.

James the Bible Student

James Stuart grew up in Scotland of royal descent. Through the political intrigue of that era, he became an orphan, brought up by tutors. As a lad, he was personally tutored by Peter Young who had studied at Geneva under Theodore Beza, John Calvin's successor. Therefore, from an early age Young trained the youthful James in Calvinistic theology.[12] The young prince thus developed a love of theology and the things of God. Not surprisingly, he also developed a deep aversion to the Roman Catholic Church. He was described as having a "keen intelligence, and a very powerful memory, for he knows a great part of the Bible by heart. He cites not only chapters, but even the verses in a perfectly marvellous way" (25). He is recorded as attending sermons "almost daily, on Sunday both morning and afternoon, (and) on Wednesday and Friday in the morning" (72).

James the Married Man

After becoming King James VI of Scotland, James married Princess Anne of Denmark on Nov. 23, 1589. Though their marriage would later become distant, his courtship and early marriage were those of romance. He was deeply in love with his young bride (85, 91). (Strange affections are these for a homosexual.) Lest there be any doubt of his infatuation with his wife, he wrote poems and sonnets describing her. In the poem

---

[12]David Wilson, *King James VI & I* (New York: Oxford University Press, 1956), 24.

below written by James about Anne, he imagines that three goddesses joined hands at her birth to bestow their graces upon her.

> How oft you see me have an heavie hart,
> Remember then sweete doctour, on your art,
> That blessed houre when first was brought to light
> Our earthlie Juno and our gratious Queene.
>
> Three Goddesses how soone they hade her seene
> Contended who protect her shoulde by right,
> But being as Goddesses of equal might
> And as of female sexe like stiffe in will
>
> It was agreed by sacred Phoebus skill
> To joyne there powers to blesse that blessed wight.
> Then, happie Monarch sprung of Ferguse race [i.e., James]
> That talkes with wise Minerve when pleaseth thee
>
> And when thou list some Princlie sports to see
> Thy chaste Diana rides with thee in chase.
> *Then when to bed thou gladlie does repaire*
> *Clasps in thine arms thy Cytherea faire* [James's term for his bride][13] (emphasis mine).

The question thus begs, is this the poem of a homosexual? Another historian wrote, "He remained infatuated with his bride, whose praises he sang in sonnets and other verse. Her beauty, he wrote, has caused his love."[14]

---

[13] Ibid., 94.

[14] Stephen Coston, *King James Unjustly Accused?* (St. Petersburg, Fla.: Konigswort, 1996), 41.

James the Godly Father

The marriage union of James and Anne in time produced Prince Henry and Prince Charles. The latter would later succeed him upon the throne of England. When little Prince Henry (who died a premature death) was only four years of age, his father, King James, wrote a book to him entitled *Basilikon Doron*. The title is Greek and simply means "a king's gift." The intent was to be a gift of advice and instruction for his son. After the death of Prince Henry, James's advice was thence directed to Prince Charles. Let us therefore consider some excerpts from James's own pen to his sons.

- "But the principal blessing [is] in your marrying of a godly and virtuous wife . . . being flesh of your flesh and bone of your bone. . . . Marriage is the greatest earthly felicity. . . . Without the blessing of God you cannot look for a happy marriage."[15]

- "Keep your body clean and unpolluted while you give it to your wife whom to only it belongs for how can you justly crave to be joined with a Virgin if your body be polluted" (44)?

- "Marriage is one of the greatest actions that a man does all his time. . . . When you are married, keep inviolably your promise made to God in your marriage" (45).

- "Especially eschew to be effeminate" (46).

- "Therefore first of all things, learn to know and love that God whom to ye have a double obligation" (47).

- "The whole scripture is dictated by God's spirit" (47).

---

[15] Ibid., 43.

- "As ye are a good Christian, so ye may be a good king, . . . establishing good laws among your people: the other, by your behavior in your own person with your servants" (48).

- "There are some horrible crimes that ye are bound in conscience never to forgive: such as witchcraft, willful murder, incest, and *sodomy*" (48, emphasis mine).

- "Abstain from the filthy vice of adultery; remember only what solemn promise ye made to God at your marriage" (54).

- "Holiness being the first and most requisite quality of a Christian (as proceeding from true fear and knowledge of God)" (55).

In these quotations from James to his son, notice the emphasis upon moral purity, fidelity, and personal holiness. His loyalty to God is apparent. Notice also how that he described sodomy as a *horrible crime*. Is this consonant with one living a homosexual lifestyle?

In the *Basilikon Doron*, he also wrote this poem to his son, the heir apparent, regarding ruling as a king.

> God gives not Kings the style of gods in vain,
> For on his throne his scepter do they sway:
> And as their subjects ought them to obey,
> So Kings should fear and serve their God again.
>
> If then ye would enjoy a happy reign
> Observe the statutes of your heavenly King,
> And from his law, make all your Laws to spring,
> Since his Lieutenant here ye should remain.
>
> Reward the just, be steadfast and true, and plain
> Repress the proud, maintaining aye the right,
> Walk always so, as ever in his sight,

> Who guards the godly, plaguing the profane
> And so ye shall in princely virtues shine
> Resembling right your mighty king divine.[16]

On other occasions, James wrote his correspondence gracing it with godly comments. Listed below are examples of such.

- "I never with God's grace shall do anything in private which I may not without shame proclaim upon the tops of houses."[17]

- "I must needs say with our Savior" (28).

- Referring to the death of his wife, he wrote, "God hath called her to his mercy" (29).

- Writing to the Earl of Somerset, he wished that "God moves your heart to take the right course" (29).

The devout character of King James should be evident from his personal and familial writings.

Sir Henry Wotton was a contemporary of King James. In commenting upon James's reign in Scotland, Wotton makes this comment about James's moral character. "An admirable quality is his chastity which he has preserved without blemish, unlike his predecessors who disturbed the kingdom by leaving many bastards."[18]

---

[16] Wilson, *King James VI & I*, 134.

[17] Coston, *King James Unjustly Accused*, 28.

[18] Wilson, *King James VI & I*, 137.

James the Theologian

The clergy of the Church of England, however, were the most profuse in their praise of their new king. After ascending the throne of England in 1603, Wilson writes, "They cast a halo of holiness about him and discovered his celestial proximity to the Deity. Astounded by his knowledge and grasp of theology, they declared that he spoke through the inspiration of the Holy Spirit and that God had bestowed upon him far more than upon ordinary mortals the power to interpret Scripture."[19] There certainly is hyperbole and overstatement here. However, the point is that the clergy of the Church of England were profoundly impressed with the godly character of their new king. Wilson goes on to comment that there was no more "familiar sight at court than that of the King at dinner discussing theology with three or four of his churchmen, bishops, deans and royal chaplains."[20]

The godly interests of James Stuart are also evident in that he even made his own personal translations of the Book of Psalms as well as of the Book of Revelation. This had nothing to do with the King James Version, but it indicates the depth of education as well as the spiritual interests of this unusual ruler.

James's Political Enemies

The charge that King James was a homosexual emanated from an old political enemy of the king, Sir Anthony Weldon, Clerk of the Green Cloth in the royal court. Moreover, his family for generations had provided officers for the royal household. However, Weldon was expelled from the court by James in about 1625 for political reasons. Weldon

---

[19] Ibid., 170.

[20] Ibid., 197.

subsequently "swore he would have his day of vengeance."[21] Curiously, Weldon never confronted the king but waited twenty-five years later to *hint* that James had effeminate interest in men. Moreover, he also waited until James's son, Charles I, had been executed in 1649. As we will note in the next section, Weldon not only came to hate James, but also had a racial hatred of the Scottish race from which James sprang.

Another enemy of James was one Guy Fawkes. Under the direction of Jesuit operatives, Fawkes even tried to bomb James and the entire English parliament with thirty-six barrels of gunpowder. There should be no question that James had both political and religious enemies.

It was Weldon who, after the death of James and Charles, wrote about the Scottish race: "Fornication they hold but a pastime, wherein man's ability is approved.... At adultery, they shake their heads.... Murder they wink at; and blasphemy they laugh at." He also wrote, "Their flesh naturally abhors cleanness. Their breath commly [*sic*] stinks of pottage; their linen of p...; their hands of pigs t...... To be chained in marriage with one of them, were to be tied to a dead carcass, and cast into a stinking ditch.... I do wonder that... King James should be born in so stinking a town as Edinburgh in lousy Scotland" (218).

The bigotry and hatred of Weldon are self-evident. Lest there be any doubt about his objectivity, here is how Weldon described James's person: "His tongue [was] too large for his mouth, which ever made him speak full in the mouth, and made him drink very uncomely, as if eating his drink, which came out into the cup of each side of his mouth. ... That [weakness in his legs] made him ever leaning on other men's shoulders.... He would never change his clothes until worn out to very rags.... (He was) the wisest fool in Christendom" (219).

It should be apparent that Sir Weldon was no impartial observer. Though King James was never known for his social graces and was somewhat gangling in his appearance, it is evident that Weldon had a visceral hatred of him. Yet, Sir Anthony Weldon is the primary source of the allegation that James was a homosexual.

---

[21] Coston, *King James Unjustly Accused*, xxx.

James's Enemies Discredited

Maurice Lee, Jr., a historian published by the University of Illinois Press, says, "Historians can and should ignore the venomous caricature of the king's person and behavior drawn by Anthony Weldon."[22] Another historian, Christopher Durston, writes regarding Weldon's book: "This poisonous piece of literary revenge was to do profound and lasting damage to James's reputation, as it became the prime source for many subsequent historical assessments whose authors failed to make sufficient allowance for its obvious bias."[23]

There were several others who *hinted* that James was a homosexual. However, upon examination, in each case, they turn out to be avowed political enemies of James and likely fed upon each other's gossip. Much could and has been written on this matter. However, Stephen Coston quotes a historian who lived much closer to these charges as "despicable and libelous, . . . full of lies, mistakes, and nonsense."[24]

James in Summary

It should be noted that no one in the seventeenth century, not even his bitter enemies, ever *openly* accused James of buggery (the British term for homosexuality). Rather, they circulated *hints* through gossip. Even after he was dead and his son had been executed, the enemies of the Stuart dynasty did not directly make that charge. The reason is apparent. Those close enough to have known him knew better. When this gossip is traced to its source, a handful of disgruntled courtiers and political enemies are at the core, long after his death.

---

[22]Maurice Lee Jr., *Great Britain's Solomon: James VI & I In his Three Kingdoms* (Champaign, Ill.: University of Illinois Press, 1990), 309-310.

[23]Christopher Durston, *James I* (London: Routledge, 1993), 2.

[24]Coston, *King James Unjustly Accused*, 233.

To the contrary, there are numerous contemporaries of James who paint the opposite picture. However, to make a judgment based upon gossip (howbeit historical) emanating from bitter enemies is no case at all. Proving a negative is difficult. Because someone alleges another to have failed morally does not establish the fact. Though vengeful enemies did spread gossip about James, there has *never* been any hard evidence by either contemporary or by modern historians to *prove* him a homosexual.

Rather, all the evidence points in the opposite direction. He was a married man who had children. He has a voluminous record of others attesting to his moral character. His own writings reveal a man with a godly predisposition. Moreover, he explicitly warned his sons against the evils of homosexuality. The proven facts are that James Stuart was a devout man who loved the Lord and His Word.

Did James have foibles and idiosyncrasies? Indeed he did. Was he gifted with social graces? No. However, there have been few monarchs in the annals of history who were more versed in Scripture, devout in their worship, knowledgeable of biblical theology, and morally upright than James I of England. There likely is not coincidence that God providentially allowed the most famous English version of the Bible to have been authorized at his hand.[25]

---

[25]It is interesting to note that the translator of the Spanish Bible, Cassiodoro de Reina, was also accused of being a homosexual. Accordingly, he was forced to flee from England to Germany where he finished his translation work. The Reina Spanish Bible (based upon the Received Text) was first published in Basel, Switzerland, in 1569. This translation was later revised by Valera in 1602 and came to be known as the Reina Valera Version.

Some ten years after fleeing England, English courts exonerated him of the charge of homosexuality. In the early 1970s, researchers were going through records of the King of Spain in Simancas, Spain, for the years 1563 and 1564. There they found an entry for a sum of money to be paid to a Spanish spy (operating in England) named Francisco de Abrio. This payment was for Abrio's part in accusing Reina of being a homosexual. Although it is now obvious that the charge against Reina was false, the stigma is still attached to his name.

It would appear that the enemies of Cassiodoro de Reina and James Stuart used the same tactic to discredit their foe. What is ironic is that both of these men were instrumental (though in differing ways) in the translation of the Received Text into their

The King James Translators

Another charge filed against the King James Version is that the translators thereof were a group of profane men. However, this is a specious charge. To the contrary, the fifty-four translators appointed to produce the Authorized Version were godly men.[26] They were divided into three groups: seventeen were to work at Westminster Abbey, fifteen at Cambridge University, and fifteen at the University of Oxford. At each place, the groups were further divided by two so that there were six companies of translators.

There probably has never been assembled at one time a greater group of English-speaking scholars of biblical languages. These men were head and shoulders higher in their expertise of Greek and Hebrew than any other body of English translators before or since. God's providential preparation is thus apparent. All of the translators held divinity degrees and thirty-nine of the forty-seven held doctor of divinity degrees. They all were either pastors, preachers, or professors in theological colleges.

A number of books and articles have been written providing biographical sketches of these forty-seven men. However, the work of Alexander McClure, written in 1858, is the most comprehensive.[27] Let us look at a sampling of comments about a number of these men. All quotations will be taken from McClure's book.[28]

---

vernacular languages. Gordon Kinder, *Cassiodoro de Reina, Spanish Reformer of the Sixteenth Century* (London: Tamesis Books, 1975).

[26]Records indicate that there were fifty-four men appointed, but only forty-seven actually worked on the translation. Also, some died during the seven years of translational work.

[27]It should be noted that McClure's work was done long before there was any question regarding the character of the translators.

[28]Alexander McClure, *The Translators Revisited* (original publisher unknown, 1858; reprint, Litchfield, Mich.: Maranatha Bible Society, n.d. (page citations are to the reprint edition).

Dr. John Reynolds

Dr. John Reynolds originally was a Catholic until he was converted to Christ by his brother. He went on to become a leader of the Puritan movement within the Church of England. He became a "vigorous champion of the Reformation." From the time of his conversion, he was a "most able and successful preacher of God's Word." He also was described as being "the very treasury of erudition" and had the reputation of being "a living library, and a third university." It was Reynolds who appealed to King James at the Hampton Court Conference for a new English translation of the Bible which in turn became the King James Version (93-103).

Dr. Lancelot Andrews

Dr. Lancelot Andrews was the chaplain to Queen Elizabeth, the dean of Westminster, and eventually the bishop of Chichester. He was a powerful preacher. Under his preaching, many Roman Catholics were converted to Christ. He was called the "star of the preachers." Moreover, many a younger preacher sought to imitate his style of preaching and used his sermons. He is described as having spent many hours each day in private and family Bible study. He had the reputation of being a "right godly man" and a "prodigious student." It was said of him, "The world wanted learning to know how learned this man was." At his funeral, Dr. Buckeridge said that Dr. Andrews was conversant in fifteen languages (60-67).

Hadrian Saravia

Dr. Hadrian Saravia, though Belgian by birth, later came to England. During his long ministry, he was (1) a pastor in Flanders and Holland, (2) a missionary to the islands of Guernsey and Jersey, and (3) an evangelist. He was also appointed prebendary of Gloucester, Canterbury, and Westminster.[29] He was said to be educated in all kinds of literature and in several languages, particularly in Hebrew (71-74).

Dr. Richard Clarke

Dr. Richard Clarke was vicar of Minster and Monkton in Thanet. He was described as a "learned clergyman and eminent preacher" (74).

Professor Edward Lively

Professor Edward Lively was noted as "one of the best linguists in the world." He also was a fellow of Trinity College at Cambridge University and the King's Professor of Hebrew. He also was an author of a Latin exposition of five of the minor prophets. He was described as being a man of great respect and one of the greatest Hebraists of that era (79-80).

Dr. John Richardson

Dr. John Richardson, among other things, was the King's Professor of Divinity and a fellow of Emmanuel College. He was noted as "a most excellent linguist." He is remembered as a "wise and faithful, as well as learned, Translator of the Book of God" (80-82).

---

[29] A prebendary was a rank of an honorary canon (i.e., degree) in the Church of England.

Dr. Lawrence Chaderton

Dr. Lawrence Chaderton was described as a "staunch Puritan," godly, learned, and full of moderation. He also had a reputation of being a "pious Protestant," who after being converted from Catholicism turned his back on Rome. He was familiar in Latin, Greek, and Hebrew and was "thoroughly skilled in them." When appointed to the translation committee, he was described as being "the most grave, learned, and modest of the aggrieved sort" to represent the Puritan faction of the committee. He also was noted as an excellent preacher (82-89).

Rev. Francis Dillingham

Rev. Francis Dillingham was the parson of Dean in Bedfordshire. He was described as the great "Grecian" on the committee and was noted as an excellent linguist. He later published a *Manual of the Christian Faith* taken from early church fathers noting the errors of Rome (89-90).

Dr. Thomas Holland

Dr. Thomas Holland in time became the King's Professor of Divinity. He was described as "a solid preacher, a most noted disputant, and a most learned divine." He was noted as "another Apollos, mighty in the Scriptures." When his translation work on the King James Version was complete, it is recorded that he "spent most of his time in meditation and prayer." At the hour of his death, he exclaimed, "Come, oh come, Lord Jesus; I desire to be dissolved and be with thee" (103-105).

Dr. Miles Smith

Dr. Miles Smith eventually became bishop of Gloucester. He was reputed to have high attainments in both classical and Oriental learning. As a bishop, he is noted as behaving with the "utmost meekness and benevolence." He was expert in the Greek and Latin fathers, as well as in the Chaldee, Syria, and Arabic languages. He was reputed to be as familiar in these as in his native tongue. He was noted as a great scholar and a strict Calvinist (108-110).

Dr. Richard Brett

Dr. Richard Brett was rector of Quainton in Buckinghamshire. He was revered for his piety. He also was skilled in Latin, Greek, Hebrew, Chaldee, Arabic, and Ethiopian. He was noted as a "most vigilant pastor, a diligent preacher of God"s Word . . . a faithful friend, and a good neighbor" (110-11).

Dr. George Abbot

Dr. George Abbot was a Calvinist who eventually became bishop of Litchfield in Coventry. He was described as an excellent preacher. He was eulogized as a grave man and unimpeachable in his morals (116-123).

Dr. Richard Eedes

Dr. Richard Eedes was at one time chaplain to both Queen Elizabeth and King James and eventually became dean of Worcester. He was described as "a pious man and a grace to the pulpit" (124-25).

Dr. Giles Thomson

Dr. Giles Thomson was also a chaplain to Queen Elizabeth and eventually rector of Herefordshire and then bishop of Gloucester. He was described as a man of piety and learning (125-26).

Dr. William Brainthwaite

Dr. William Brainthwaite was an academic who spent most of his life at Cambridge University eventually becoming the Master of Gonvil and Caius College. He was noted as being "learned, reverend, and worshipful" (145).

Rev. John Bois

Rev. John Bois occupied a number of pastoral assignments in the Church of England as well as at Cambridge University. He was reputed to be able to read the Bible in Hebrew when he was five years old. When he was six, he could write Hebrew characters elegantly. He was a major contributor to the Cambridge company of translators. It was said that he was so familiar with the Greek Testament that he could at any time turn to any word it contained. He also wrote voluminous commentaries on the Gospels and Acts. When he died on the Lord's day, it was said, "He went unto his rest on the day of rest; a man of peace, to the God of peace" (153-160).

Dr. John Aglionby

Dr. John Aglionby was a chaplain to King James and eventually became the principal of St. Edmund's Hall at the University of Oxford. He is described as being deeply read in the early church fathers, an "excellent linguist," and an "elegant and instructive preacher" (160-61).

These are brief biographical sketches of *some* of the godly scholars appointed to translate the King James Version. It should be evident that the charge they were profane men is ridiculous. Nevertheless, such foolish reports continue to bounce around the land.[30] To the contrary, it is apparent for any who can read that the forty-seven men appointed to be translators of the King James Version were renowned not only as scholars but as men of God as well. Some were thorough-going Anglicans, some were Calvinists, some were Puritans, and one may have been Arminian in his theology. But they all were fervent Bible believers and stood squarely upon the cardinal, orthodox doctrines of historic New Testament Christianity.

King James and His Translators as Anglicans

Another foolish charge made by unlearned critics is, "Why be hard on Westcott and Hort? Were not they Anglicans like King James and his translators?" However, to compare the Anglican Church at the end of the sixteenth century with the Anglican Church at the end of the nineteenth century is no equation. Though the Church of England in 1600 may have been unscriptural in its episcopal form of church polity, views on baptism, and an incipient lack of evangelistic fervor, it was solid on the fundamentals of the faith. Its ministers in that day were Bible believers and preached the gospel.

The Church of England at the end of the nineteenth century still was wrong in its polity and views on baptism, but it had become completely apostate concerning the fundamentals of the faith. Though orthodox on paper, the Anglican Church by the twentieth century had loosed its moorings, effectively departing from the faith once delivered to the saints. It had become intoxicated with the liquor of German Rationalism

---

[30]In researching the various translators, this author found that only one of the forty-seven translators may have been guilty of occasional intemperance in his use of table wine. That is the closest this author has come to finding fault with this august body of men.

and therefore died spiritually. Westcott and Hort clearly exhibited this in their writings.

Summary

The charges that Erasmus was a Catholic are hollow. The more he studied the Scriptures, the farther he moved from Rome in his position. By life's end, though never officially breaking with Rome, his associations were with Protestants; and he even espoused Anabaptist principles. The charges that King James I of England was a bawdy man and even a homosexual are unfounded. To the contrary, James Stuart was in many ways a devout man, married with children, and deeply interested in the things of God. Though unpolished and often lacking in social graces, there is no evidence of moral failure in his life. Such allegations have their root in bitter political enemies who vowed vengeance against him. The translators of the King James Version were demonstrably godly men with a degree of erudition never seen since in a body of translators. Moreover, the Anglican Church of 1600 was orthodox in its working as well as official theology. These charges are specious and without foundation.

Review Questions for Further Study

1. How many manuscripts did Erasmus have at his disposal for his first edition of his Greek New Testament?

2. How did Erasmus become aware of the variants of Vaticanus?

3. Why did Erasmus dedicate his Greek New Testament to the pope?

4. In what way was young James Stuart trained as a boy?

5. What did King James write for his son?

6. Why did several men attack King James's character?

7. Through what basic means was King James accused of being a homosexual?

8. What was the basic background of all the King James translators?

9. Describe the general character of the theology of the Church of England in 1600.

CHAPTER ELEVEN

THE ISSUE TODAY

As we have touched upon a wide variety of thoughts ranging from early church history to problems in modern textual criticism, let us consider the issue as it stands today. These will hopefully help the reader to come to a definitive conclusion on this matter if he has not already.

Reasons Why Many Fundamentalists Cling to the Critical Text

Many of the leading Fundamental colleges and seminaries in America still support the critical text and are therefore open, in principle, to the various translations of the Bible which derive therefrom. The question thus arises, "Why?" To be sure, many would reply that they believe the critical text is the best representation of the New Testament text. However, in light of the evidence presented in this book, it would seem that there are a number of other reasons. Certainly, these are subjective conclusions on the part of this author, but they are based upon approximately thirty years of experience on both sides of this issue. Let us therefore consider eight reasons, in the view of this author, why many Fundamentalists still cling to the critical text.

Many Early Fundamentalists Used the Critical Text

The simple fact is that many early Fundamentalists bought into the idea that Vaticanus and Sinaiticus were the best manuscripts. There were a few voices in the wilderness in the late nineteenth century such as John Burgon and Edward Miller who were warning of the fallacy of this view. However, they were in England and were discounted as right-wing eccentrics. Few in America at the time had the credentials to dispute Westcott and Hort's theory and no one did. Vaticanus and Sinaiticus, as they manifested themselves together in Westcott and Hort's new Greek text, were widely and loudly proclaimed as the "earliest and best manuscripts." Westcott and Hort's new Greek text was acclaimed as the work of modern scholarship. Most conservatives and Fundamentalists simply accepted this "party line" as it was promoted throughout Christendom. Even great men such as Charles Haddon Spurgeon did not initially criticize the new text. However, after having had about ten years to digest it all, Spurgeon in his final year repudiated Westcott and Hort's Greek text and the English Revised Version.[1]

The Scofield Reference Bible, perhaps more than any other one edition, was the Bible of choice by Fundamentalists in America in the twentieth century. However, C. I. Scofield also taught that Vaticanus and Sinaiticus were the earliest and best manuscripts available. Accordingly, Scofield, in his notes, made annotations on that basis as the opportunity arose. For example, Scofield has this footnote for Mark 16:9: "The passage from verse 9 to the end is not found in the two most ancient manuscripts, the Sinaitic and Vatican, and others have it with partial omissions and variations. But it is quoted by Irenaeus and Hippolytus in the second or third century."[2]

In John 7:53, Scofield adds a similar footnote: "John 7:53-8:11 is not found in some of the most ancient manuscripts."[3] He goes on to give several reasons why this might be, but the basic one is that Vaticanus and Sinaiticus omitted it. Similarly, Scofield makes this marginal com-

---

[1] Les Garrett, *Westcott & Hort: The Occult Connection and New Greek Text* (Queensland, Australia: Voice of Thanksgiving, 1997), 1-3.

[2] C. I. Scofield, *The Scofield Reference Bible* (New York: Oxford University Press, 1909; reprint 1945), 1069 (citations are to the reprint edition).

[3] Ibid., 1125.

ment for 1 John 5:7, "It is generally agreed that verse 7 has no real authority, and has been inserted."[4]

These comments by Scofield are quintessential examples of the rationalistic, critical text philosophy which he and many other early Fundamentalists assumed to be correct. Most Fundamentalist leaders in the first part of the twentieth century did in fact *assume* the Westcott and Hort text to be the superior text. However, this conclusion likely was not from careful examination of the matter, but simply by accepting the judgment of others.

In about 1960, Richard V. Clearwaters wrote: "We know of no Fundamentalists . . . that claim the King James Version as the best English translation. Those in the main stream of Fundamentalism all claim the American Revised of 1901 as the best English translation."[5]

This writer was trained at the feet of Richard V. Clearwaters and has the greatest respect for him. However, with all due respect, Clearwaters was simply wrong at this point.[6] Edward Hills had already written his book *The King James Version Defended* in 1956. Other conservative authors such as Alfred Martin and Philip Mauro had also published their research by this time. Clearwaters apparently was unaware of the research of these men. In all fairness, however, there was a paucity of material written on the issue prior to Hills's work. The last major works in defense of the King James Version (before Hills) dated back to Burgon and Miller prior to the turn of the twentieth century and Herman Hoskier in the early twentieth century. All three of these were in England. It is unclear if Clearwaters was aware of any of them. However, what is clear is that there are many in the mainstream of Fundamentalism at the beginning of the twenty-first century who claim the King James Version is the best English translation.

---

[4]Ibid., 1325.

[5]Michael Grisanti, ed., *The Bible Version Debate* (Minneapolis: Central Baptist Theological Seminary, 1997), v.

[6]It should be noted nevertheless that Richard V. Clearwaters preached only from the King James Version.

Notwithstanding, because early Fundamentalists did use and support the critical text, some of its supporters try to make the claim that it is the historic position. However, their history is quite short in its perspective. They seem to forget that in the first 1900 years of Christianity, the Received Text was the overwhelming text used by Bible-believing groups for the translation of Scripture.

Few Fundamentalists Have Investigated the Issue

Notwithstanding men such as Scofield and Clearwaters and numerous other Fundamentalist leaders in between, it is doubtful if many of them ever did any serious research into the history and lineage of the critical text. Had they spent the time and effort that many in later years did in researching the origins of the critical text, it is doubtful they would have continued their support. It was only in the last half of the twentieth century that conservative scholars such as Edward Hills, David Otis Fuller, Theodore Letis, Donald Waite, Jakob Van Bruggen, Dell Johnson, and others began to publish their research into the problems clinging to the critical text. For the most part, these men have been ignored or dismissed as right-wing extremists. However, the evidence uncovered by them has not and will not go away. Fundamentalists are going to have to confront the extensive evidence of apostasy associated with the critical text from Origen to Metzger. If separation is an inviolable foundation of Fundamentalism, Fundamentalists are going to have to admit the apostasy connected with the critical text.

The Modernist-Fundamentalist Battles Diverted Attention

In the view of this author, another considerable reason why many Fundamentalists never investigated the critical text and its problems in the first half of the twentieth century is that their major attention was focused upon the great Modernist-Fundamentalist battles. As Liberalism took over the major denominations early in the twentieth century, the focal point of most Fundamentalists, yea the very birth of Fundamentalism, was the resulting battles. Great Fundamentalist leaders such as W. B. Riley in the North and J. Frank Norris in the South were engulfed in the major battles with Modernism in their respective denominations. Their battles were with outright denial of such cardinal truths as the inspiration of Scripture, the Deity of Christ, the bodily resurrection of Christ, the virgin birth, the substitutionary atonement of Christ, and others. However, the textual issue was not one of them.

Then, as the battles were won by the Modernists in the major denominations, Fundamentalists became consumed with starting new associations, new institutions of higher learning, and new missions groups. All the while, leaders of the Fundamentalist movement were licking their wounds over their losses to the Liberals. Because few if any had researched the critical text, most Fundamentalists accepted it since it did not immediately change anything. It did not seem to be an issue. They kept on preaching and teaching from the King James Version. There were no popular, modern-language translations in spite of occasional rhetoric voicing the glory of the American Standard Version of 1901.

World Wars I and II Further Diverted Attention

Though World Wars I and II did not directly impact most theological controversies in the twentieth century, they certainly otherwise consumed the Western world. Britain and Europe were ravaged by the wars. America's focus as a nation, especially in World War II, was turned to the war effort. Such an esoteric issue as the textual issue of the New Testament was something forgotten as the nation mobilized, rationed basic commodities, and sent its young men off to distant battlefields. Even the printing of books was restricted during the war. The last thing upon the minds of most Fundamentalists was worrying about the critical text of the New Testament.

New Evangelicalism Became a New Concern

Following World War II, a new problem demanded the concern of Fundamentalists. This was the development of New Evangelicalism, particularly in the United States. With the heady flush of victory and the prosperity brought to American shores after the war, a new mood of theological compromise was sweeping the nation. As New Evangelicalism gained momentum in the generation after World War II, leading Fundamentalists sounded the alarm and sought to counteract it. It was also at this time that a number of Fundamentalist scholars were beginning to expose the apostasy and deviation connected with the critical text. However, they were still few in number and largely ignored by most Fundamentalists. They were ignored altogether by the New Evangelical movement.

Nonetheless, with the rise of Billy Graham, *Christianity Today*, Fuller Seminary, and the compromise of many previously separatist schools and institutions, Fundamentalists were occupied with resisting the incipient compromise taking place all around them. Some early Fundamentalists had accepted critical-text footnotes in their Scofield Reference Bible while continuing to preach the King James Version as the Word of God. Therefore, the text was not an issue on the radar screens of their leading institutions. The few who raised questions about it were dismissed as radicals.

Ruckmanism Confused the Issue

In 1970, Peter Ruckman published his book *Manuscript Evidence* which did take a strong King James position. In fact, Ruckman established what has come to be known as the King James Only position. His view of "advanced revelation"[7] amounts to "double inspiration" by insisting that the King James Version as a *translation* is inspired. Because of the unscriptural nature of his view, his abrasive

---

[7]These are his words to describe his position.

style, and problems in his personal testimony, Ruckman's position has been dismissed by the vast majority of Fundamentalists.

Unfortunately, for years major Fundamentalist institutions of higher learning encouraged the view that any position other than the critical text position was essentially Ruckmanism and summarily dismissed it. Therefore, to defend the King James Version as the best English translation was just another form of Ruckmanism according to many influential Fundamentalists.

A clear illustration of this took place in 1998. After Pensacola Christian College had sent several videotapes across the country stating its position in support of the Received Text and the King James Version, they were immediately accused of belonging to the King James Only position. One pastor in California, who had done his doctoral dissertation on Peter Ruckman, circulated a letter across the country openly accusing Pensacola Christian College of being Ruckmanites.[8] It seemed as though anyone who would deviate from the critical text must be a Ruckmanite. Unfortunately, many Fundamentalists have been similarly confused.

There Has Been Little Exposure to the Received Text Position

As the twenty-first century has begun, perhaps the most significant reason many Fundamentalists are confused is that they have never been exposed to the problems of the critical text. Moreover, most are illiterate as to why the Received Text position is to be preferred. Up until just recently, there were very few Fundamentalist institutions of higher learning which questioned the critical text. It was considered to be the domain of extremists and Peter Ruckman to deviate from the critical text position. One classic example of this problem is illustrated in a book released in 1999 entitled *From the Mind of God to the Mind of*

---

[8]That pastor was R. L. Hymers. He, however, has since informed this author that he does hold to and believe in the Received Text position.

Man.⁹ The book was published by Fundamentalists who purported it to be neutral and a comprehensive statement on the transmission of the Bible. However, the book clearly was an apologetic for the critical text and any modern-language translation of the Bible based on it.

Moreover, as was noted in an earlier chapter of this volume, the bibliographies of that book contained almost no references to works supporting the Received Text. In the last quarter of the twentieth century, there has been a profusion of books written attacking the critical text position, supporting the Received Text, and defending the King James Version. Many of these works have exhibited genuine scholarship and historical research. Yet, because their conclusions have not supported the prevailing party line, they have largely been ignored. But the evidence has not gone away nor will it. Proper understanding will never come when the truth is suppressed and that is exactly what has gone on for far too long.

Pride Is an Issue

Over the last half of the twentieth century, significant amounts of political capital have been expended by Fundamentalist institutions in defending the critical text position. In some cases, they have staked their credibility to this issue. However, even though evidence has continued to mount indicating that they have been wrong, a nasty five-letter word hinders many from admitting the error of their way. That word is *p-r-i-d-e*. Pride makes it difficult to publicly admit one has been wrong, especially when political adversaries have openly accused one of being wrong. Many therefore stubbornly cling to the critical text and the translations which result therefrom.

---

[9] James B. Williams, general ed., *From the Mind of God to the Mind of Man* (Greenville, S.C.: Ambassador—Emerald International, 1999).

The Issue Today

The Admission of Frank Logsdon

Fundamentalists sympathetic to the critical text often favor the New American Standard Bible (NASB). However, there is a poignant story connected to the New American Standard Bible of which many Fundamentalists are unaware.

The New American Standard Bible was originally produced by the Lockman Foundation of La Habra, California. During the 1950s, Frank Dewey Lockman realized that he could obtain the copyrights for the 1901 American Standard Version (ASV). In 1957, he therefore asked Frank Logsdon to come to his home and explore with him the feasibility of creating a new translation of the Bible based upon the American Standard Version of 1901. Upon completing a feasibility study, Logsdon advised him to proceed. Ironically, without the support of Frank Logsdon, the New American Standard Bible would never have been produced.

Frank Logsdon is on record as noting that "at that time, I thought that the Westcott and Hort text was correct."[10] Accordingly, the New American Standard Bible was produced from the then current critical text which was based upon the Westcott and Hort Greek text. Logsdon wrote the format for the New American Standard Bible. He interviewed the translators and he sat with them when they wrote the preface thereof. The preface of the New American Standard Bible is essentially the work of Frank Logsdon. When the New American Standard Bible was published, Logsdon received copy number seven of the fifty deluxe copies which were printed.

Meanwhile, David Otis Fuller, a close friend of Dr. Logsdon, sat down with him and pointed out what he felt were the problems with the critical text. Logsdon's first reaction was immediate suspicion, thinking his friend had "gone off the deep end" on this King James stuff. However, as Logsdon began to research the issue, he confided to his wife, "I am afraid I am in trouble with the Lord. I cannot refute these argu-

---

[10] Les Garrett, *Westcott & Hort: The Occult Connection*, 10.

ments."[11] He went on to say regarding his own project, the New American Standard Bible, "It is wrong. It is terribly wrong. It is frightfully wrong and I do not know what I am going to do about it."[12] For four months, he wrestled with the matter and finally sat down and wrote to his friend, Frank Lockman. In that letter, he wrote: "You will always be my friend but I can no longer ignore the criticisms. I cannot refute them, and dear brother I have not a thing against you, but the only thing I can do under God is to renounce every attachment to the New American Standard Bible."[13] Mr. Lockman wrote back and said that he was shocked beyond words to put it mildly. He said that he would write him further in several weeks. He did not because he died shortly thereafter.

Frank Logsdon had the courage and conviction to admit he was wrong. In realizing the problems and apostasy connected with the critical text, he separated himself therefrom. It meant disassociating himself from one of the major accomplishments of his life. Yet, he had the courage to do so. Would to God Fundamentalists across the land would have the courage to separate from the work and influence of many apostates regarding the critical text with its resultant translations.

As has been documented throughout this volume, the critical text has been tainted with apostasy from its inception to its current manifestation. The origin of Vaticanus and Sinaiticus was in ancient Alexandria, Egypt. With the proliferation of Gnosticism and Platonism prevalent there, a red flag ought to go up at the start of this issue for a Fundamentalist. The influence of Origen and Eusebius and their budding apostasy should put up another. The fact that the chief representatives of the Alexandrian forerunner of the critical text, Sinaiticus and Vaticanus, were hidden from view for 1500 years ought to bring more pause for concern. While persecuted, believing brethren such as the Waldenses were being martyred for use of Received-Text-based translations of the Bible, these two famous pillars of the critical text were

---

[11]Ibid.

[12]Ibid.

[13]Ibid.

hidden in the bowels of the Vatican and a monastery at Mount Sinai. While the Reformation blossomed across Europe, Vaticanus and Sinaiticus remained shrouded from view.

Why would God hide the best representation of His Word in such places of spiritual darkness for 1500 years if it in fact most closely represents the autographa? Why would those preaching the truth throughout the Dark Ages and the Reformation be denied the real text of Scripture? The answer should be apparent. Vaticanus, Sinaiticus, and their other small number of allies are not the true representation of the Word of God.

In 1809, Joseph Stevens Buckminster, an early American Liberal, urged Harvard College to publish an American edition of Griesbach's critical Greek New Testament. His rationale was that he saw its value in promoting text criticism. In his opinion, it also was "**a most powerful weapon to be used against the supporters of verbal inspiration.**"[14] Why can Liberals clearly see this but many Fundamentalists cannot?

The lineage of almost all eighteenth- and nineteenth-century textual critics is deeply rooted in German Higher Rationalism. This is the genesis of modern theological Liberalism. Yet, the critical text has developed from this corrupt seed bed. Why will some Fundamentalists ignore this documented history?

The chief architects of the modern critical text, Westcott and Hort, have a documented history of apostate associations in the Broad Church movement in England. Their writings, particularly in their private correspondence, clearly identify them as apostates. Try though they may to deny it, the unforgiving facts for many Fundamentalists are that Westcott and Hort *were* involved in occult activities through much of the time they were developing their new Greek text of the New Testament. Their own writings question and belittle the doctrine of inspiration and inerrancy. They demanded that a Christ-rejecting Unitarian be kept upon their revision committee. They were apostates. How can a true

---

[14]Theodore Letis, *The Ecclesiastical Text* (Philadelphia: Institute for Renaissance & Reformation Biblical Studies, 1997), 2.

Fundamentalist have anything to do with them or their major contribution, the modern critical text?

In the twentieth century almost all of the major editors of the critical text have been card-carrying theological Liberals. This is true for Kurt Aland, Bruce Metzger, and Eugene Nida, not to mention Cardinal Carlo Martini of the Roman Catholic Church. Why are Fundamentalists willing to ignore this?

The United Bible Societies is the chief publisher of the modern critical text. Yet, the United Bible Societies is deeply involved with the Roman Catholic Church and the World Council of Churches. Its lineal predecessor, the British and Foreign Bible Society (BFBS), was apostate from its beginning, stubbornly protecting Unitarian supporters thereof. In contrast, conservatives in England founded the Trinitarian Bible Society in reaction against the British and Foreign Bible Society. The Trinitarian Bible Society has from its beginning stood upon the Trinity and the Deity of Christ, the Received Text, and the King James Version. The British and Foreign Bible Society and its successor, the United Bible Societies, have long advocated the critical text and its concomitant, modernistic translations. Why will Fundamentalists support the side of Unitarians and the World Council of Churches against those who have stood for the Trinity and the Deity of Christ?

The translations of choice by New Evangelicals and Liberals in the last quarter of the twentieth century have been anything but the King James Version. They delight in using that which has been based upon the critical text. Why will many Fundamentalists do the same thing?

The apostle wrote, "Come out from among them and be ye separate, saith the Lord." But he also wrote, "and touch not the unclean *thing*." The principle of separation thus applies to not only unholy personalities, but also to unholy **things**. A thesis of this writer is that the critical text is unholy through its manifold associations with apostasy.

"What concord hath Christ with Belial? Or what part hath he that believeth with an infidel?" In the appendices at the end of this volume is documentation of the deletions and alterations in some of the popular versions of the Bible based upon the critical text. What is most alarming is the diminution of the person of Christ. That in itself ought to be enough to separate from the versions based upon the critical text. The scriptural principle of separation remains. What part have we which believe with the work of infidels (apostates)? If the principle of separation remains valid, then it must apply to the textual and translational issue.

Review Questions for Further Study

1. What well-known study Bible has added confusion to the textual issue?

2. What are some of the events in the twentieth century which diverted attention from the textual issue.

3. What is the name of the "ism" many Fundamentalists have erroneously assumed to be a defense of the King James Version?

4. Has there been widespread exposure to the problems of the critical text in the past century?

5. What is a five-letter word which has hindered many Fundamentalists from fully understanding the textual issue?

6. Who was Frank Logsdon and what did he repudiate?

APPENDIX A

PROBLEMS IN THE NEW AMERICAN STANDARD BIBLE

The New Testament of the New American Standard Bible (NASB) was first published in 1960 by the Lockman Foundation. It was conceived as a modernization and revision of the American Standard Version of 1901. Later, the Old Testament was included with it. The New Testament portion of the New American Standard Bible followed the twenty-third edition of the Nestlé-Aland Greek text which was the latest manifestation of the critical text in the 1950s.[1]

There are literally hundreds of places where the New American Standard Bible deviates from the King James Version and the text upon which it was based (the Textus Receptus). Many Fundamentalists have been led to believe that the New American Standard Bible is the best translation. However, what may be shocking for many Fundamentalists is the diminution of the person of Jesus Christ by the New American Standard Bible as compared to the King James Version. This has been done by deleting many references to the Lordship of Jesus or otherwise diminishing titles such as *Christ* when compared to the King James Version. Again, the textual base for the New American Standard Bible is the critical Greek text from which it was translated. Its translators only followed the text set before them. The data produced below is summarized and based upon research done by Australian researcher Les Garrett in his book *Which Bible Can We Trust?*

In John 20:13, Mary stood weeping before the empty tomb of Jesus. Upon that occasion, the angels said, "Woman, why weepest thou?" Her answer was, "Because they have taken away my Lord." Yet, this is pre-

---

[1] The NASB was translated primarily from the 23rd edition of the Nestle Greek New Testament. Editorial Board, New American Standard Bible (Carol Stream, Ill.: Creation House, 1960), vii.

cisely what the New American Standard Bible has done. Based upon the critical text, the New American Standard Bible deletes many references to the person of our Lord that are in the King James Version (based on the Received Text). In the New Testament alone, references to Jesus as *Lord* have been taken away in **thirty-nine** places. The title *Christ* has been eliminated in **fifty-two** places. The name of *Jesus* has been eliminated in **eighty-seven** places. And, 617 *words* spoken by Jesus Christ have been deleted![2] Though there certainly are other problems in the New American Standard Bible, when the person of our Lord is diminished, ought that not raise a red flag? Has not this been the objective of the evil one from the mists of antiquity?

Examples of Deletions

Let us look at some examples of these deletions. We will use the King James Version as a point of reference and then note the word deleted from the New American Standard Bible as follows: for example, Lord. If the reader cares to verify, he may then check the New American Standard Bible and will find that the noted word has in fact been removed and in some cases something else has been substituted.

The Lordship of Christ

Matt. 13:51	"They say unto him, Yea Lord."
Mark 9:27	"And said with tears Lord, I believe.
Mark 11:10	"Blessed *be* the kingdom of our father David, that cometh in the name of the Lord."
Luke 22:31	"And the Lord said, Simon, Simon, behold, Satan hath desired *to have* you."
Luke 23:42	"And he said unto Jesus, Lord, remember me

---

[2]Les Garrett, ed., *Which Bible Can We Trust?* (Queensland, Australia: Christian Center Press, 1982), 2.

	when thou comest into thy kingdom."
Acts 7:30	"There appeared to him . . . an angel ~~of the Lord~~."
Acts 9:5	"And ~~the Lord~~ said, I am Jesus."
Acts 9:6	"And the ~~Lord~~ *said* unto him."
Acts 9:29	"And he spake boldly ~~in the name of the Lord~~ Jesus."
Acts 15:17	"~~Saith the Lord~~, who doeth all these things."
Acts 22:16	"Calling on the name ~~of the Lord~~."
Rom. 1:3	"Concerning his Son ~~Jesus Christ our Lord~~."
Rom. 6:11	"Alive unto God through Jesus Christ ~~our Lord~~."
Rom. 14:6	"~~To the Lord~~ he doth not regard *it*."
Rom. 16:24	"~~The grace of our Lord Jesus Christ *be* with you all. Amen~~."
1 Cor. 10:28	"~~For the earth *is* the Lord's, and the fulness thereof~~."
1 Cor. 11:29	"For he that eateth and drinketh unworthily, eateth and drinketh damnation to himself, not discerning ~~the Lord's~~ body."
1 Cor. 15:47	"The second man *is* ~~the Lord~~ from heaven.
2 Cor. 4:10	"Always bearing about in the body the dying of ~~the Lord~~ Jesus."
Gal. 6:17	"For I bear in my body the marks of ~~the Lord~~ Jesus."
Eph. 3:14	"For this cause I bow my knees unto the Father ~~of our Lord Jesus Christ~~."
Col. 1:2	"Grace *be* unto you, and peace, from God our Father ~~and the Lord Jesus Christ~~."
1 Tim. 1:1	"By the commandment of God our Saviour, and ~~Lord~~ Jesus Christ, *which is* our hope."
1 Tim. 5:21	"I charge *thee* before God, and ~~the Lord~~ Jesus Christ."
Titus 1:4	"Grace, mercy, *and* peace, from God the Father and ~~the Lord~~ Jesus Christ."

Heb. 10:30	"I will recompense, ~~saith the Lord~~."
Rev. 19:1	"Alleluia; Salvation, and glory, and honour, and power, unto ~~the Lord~~ our God."

These are only a sampling of the places where the Lordship of Christ is diminished in the New American Standard Bible. A significant number of other deletions pertain to the Lordship of Christ.

The Name of Jesus

Again using the King James Version as a point of reference, let us take note of *some* of the places where the New American Standard Bible deletes the name of Jesus.

Matt. 4:12	"Now when ~~Jesus~~ had heard that John was cast into prison."
Matt. 4:18	"And ~~Jesus~~, walking by the sea of Galilee, saw two brethren."
Matt. 8:3	"And ~~Jesus~~ put forth *his* hand, and touched him, saying, I will; be thou clean."
Matt. 8:5	"And when ~~Jesus~~ was entered into Capernaum, there came unto him a centurion, beseeching him."
Matt. 8:7	"And ~~Jesus~~ saith unto him, I will come and heal him."
Matt. 9:12	"But when ~~Jesus~~ heard *that*, he said unto them, They that be whole need not a physician, but they that are sick."
Mark 1:41	"And ~~Jesus~~, moved with compassion, put forth *his* hand, and touched him, and saith unto him, I will; be thou clean."
Mark 2:15	"And it came to pass, that, as ~~Jesus~~ sat at meat in his house."

Mark 5:13	"And forthwith ~~Jesus~~ gave them leave. And the unclean spirits went out."
Luke 7:22	"Then ~~Jesus~~ answering said unto them, Go your way."
Luke 23:43	"And ~~Jesus~~ said unto him, Verily I say unto thee, To day shalt thou be with me in paradise."
John 3:2	"The same came to ~~Jesus~~ by night, and said unto him, Rabbi, we know that thou art a Teacher come from God."
John 5:17	"But ~~Jesus~~ answered them, My Father worketh hitherto, and I work."
John 8:20	"These words spake ~~Jesus~~ in the treasury, as he taught in the temple."
Acts 3:26	"Unto you first God, having raised up his Son ~~Jesus~~."
Acts 8:37	"And he answered and said, ~~I believe that Jesus Christ is the Son of God~~."
Acts 9:29	"And he spake boldly ~~in the name of the Lord Jesus~~."
Acts 19:10	"So that all they which dwelt in Asia heard the word of the Lord ~~Jesus~~."
Rom. 1:3	"Concerning his Son ~~Jesus Christ our Lord~~, which was made of the seed of David according to the flesh."
Rom. 15:8	"Now I say that ~~Jesus~~ Christ was a minister."
Rom. 16:18	"For they that are such serve not our Lord ~~Jesus~~ Christ."
1 Cor. 12:3	"No man can say that ~~Jesus is the Lord~~, but by the Holy Ghost."
1 Cor. 16:22	"If any man love not the Lord ~~Jesus Christ~~, let him be Anathema Maranatha."
2 Cor. 4:6	"For God, who commanded the light to shine out of darkness, hath shined in our hearts, to *give* the light of the knowledge of the glory of God in the face of ~~Jesus~~ Christ."

2 Cor. 5:18	"Who hath reconciled us to himself by ~~Jesus~~ Christ."
Eph. 3:9	"And to make all *men* see what *is* the fellowship of the mystery, which from the beginning of the world hath been hid in God, who created all things ~~by Jesus Christ~~."
Eph. 3:14	"For this cause I bow my knees unto the Father of ~~our Lord Jesus Christ~~."
Col. 1:2	"Grace *be* unto you, and peace, from God our Father ~~and the Lord Jesus Christ~~."
Col. 1:28	"Whom we preach, warning every man, and teaching every man in all wisdom; that we may present every man perfect in Christ ~~Jesus~~."
1 Thess. 1:1	"Grace *be* unto you, and peace, ~~from God our Father, and the Lord~~ Jesus ~~Christ~~."
2 Tim. 4:22	"The Lord ~~Jesus Christ~~ *be* with thy spirit."
Philem. 6	"That the communication of thy faith may become effectual by the acknowledging of every good thing which is in you in Christ ~~Jesus~~."
1 Pet. 5:10	"But the God of all grace, who hath called us unto his eternal glory by Christ ~~Jesus~~."
1 Pet. 5:14	"Peace *be* with you all that are in Christ ~~Jesus~~. Amen."

The references deleting the name of Jesus from the New American Standard Version listed above represent fewer than one half of the **eighty-seven** times that blessed name is eliminated therefrom. Our purpose has been to provide a representative sampling.

Jesus as Christ

Again using the King James Version as a point of reference, let us notice a sampling of the places that the New American Standard Bible deletes references to Jesus as Christ.

Matt. 23:8	"But be not ye called Rabbi: for one is your Master, ~~even Christ~~; and all ye are brethren."
John 4:42	"Now we believe, not because of thy saying: or we have heard *him* ourselves, and know that this is indeed the ~~Christ~~."
John 6:69	"And we believe and are sure that thou art ~~that Christ~~, the Son of the living God."
Acts 2:30	"Therefore being a prophet, and knowing that God had sworn with an oath to him, that of the fruit of his loins, according to the flesh, ~~he would raise up Christ~~ to sit on his throne."
Acts 8:37	"And Philip said, If thou believest with all thine heart, thou mayest. And he answered and said, ~~I believe that Jesus Christ is the Son of God~~."
Acts 19:4	"That they should believe on him which should come after him, that is, on ~~Christ~~ Jesus."
Rom. 1:3	"Concerning his Son ~~Jesus Christ our Lord~~, which was made of the seed of David according to the flesh."
Rom. 1:16	"For I am not ashamed of the gospel ~~of Christ~~."
Rom. 16:20	"And the God of peace shall bruise Satan under your feet shortly. The grace of our Lord Jesus ~~Christ~~ *be* with you. Amen."
1 Cor. 5:4	"In the name of our Lord Jesus ~~Christ~~, when ye are gathered together, and my spirit, with the power of our Lord Jesus ~~Christ~~." *(Editor's note: Christ is eliminated twice in one verse.)*
1 Cor. 9:18	"What is my reward then? *Verily* that, when I preach the gospel, I may make the gospel of

Touch Not the Unclean Thing

~~Christ~~ without charge, that I abuse not my power in the gospel."

Gal. 3:17 "And this I say, *that* the covenant, that was confirmed before of God ~~in Christ~~, the law, which was four hundred and thirty years after, cannot disannul, that it should make the promise of none effect."

Gal. 6:15 "For ~~in Christ Jesus~~ neither circumcision availeth any thing, nor uncircumcision, but a new creature."

Eph. 3:9 "And to make all *men* see what *is* the fellowship of the mystery, which from the beginning of the world hath been hid in God, who created all things ~~by Jesus Christ~~."

Eph. 3:14 "For this cause I bow my knees unto the Father ~~of our Lord Jesus Christ~~."

Col. 1:2 "Grace *be* unto you, and peace, from God our Father ~~and the Lord Jesus Christ~~."

Col. 3:13 "If any man have a quarrel against any: even as ~~Christ~~ forgave you, so also *do* ye."

1 Thes. 1:1 "Grace *be* unto you, and peace, from God our Father, ~~and the Lord Jesus Christ~~."

2 Thes. 2:2 "That ye be not soon shaken in mind, or betroubled, neither by spirit, nor by word, nor by letter as from us, as that the day of ~~Christ~~ is at hand."

1 Tim. 2:7 "Whereunto I am ordained a preacher, and an apostle, (I speak the truth ~~in Christ~~, *and* lie not;) a teacher of the Gentiles in faith and verity."

2 Tim. 4:22 "The Lord ~~Jesus Christ~~ *be* with thy spirit."

Heb. 3:5 "Wherefore, holy brethren, partakers of the heavenly calling, consider the Apostle and High Priest of our profession, ~~Christ~~ Jesus."

1 John 1:7 "But if we walk in the light, as he is in the light, we have fellowship one with another, and the blood of Jesus ~~Christ~~ his Son cleanseth us from all sin."

2 John 9 "Whosoever transgresseth, and abideth not in the doctrine of Christ, hath not God. He that abideth in the doctrine of ~~Christ~~, he hath both the Father and the Son."

The references above deleting *Christ* represent about one half of the total number eliminated from the New American Standard Bible. In all, there are about 178 places in the New American Standard Bible where references to Jesus by name, Him as Lord, or as Christ have been deleted as compared to the Received Text! To be sure, the New American Standard Bible has not *removed* the doctrine of Christ. However, can any one dispute that it has been *diminished* and *diluted*?

In all fairness, the diminution of the person of the Lord Jesus Christ is not unique to the New American Standard Bible. Other popular versions based upon the critical text (the NIV, RSV, The Jehovah Witnesses' Bible—the New World Translation, Good News for Modern Man, et al.) all have similar deletions.

One thing which is common to all cults is a diminution of the person of Jesus Christ. That certainly is true of the Jehovah's Witnesses. It is true of the Mormons. It is even true of the Church of Rome as Mary is worshiped more than Jesus. Is it not foreboding when the critical text and the popular versions translated therefrom, in principle, follow the same practice?

APPENDIX B

PROBLEMS IN THE NEW INTERNATIONAL VERSION

The problems of the New International Version (NIV) are similar in nature to that of the New American Standard Bible, though the New International Version has idiosyncrasies unique to itself. Not only have many references to our Lord been diminished, the source of the New International Version (the NAE) should manifest concern for Fundamentalists. In addition, the New International Version also has a large number of entire verses removed, and its translational character is loose.

The National Association of Evangelicals and the New International Version

According to the Preface of the New International Version, the National Association of Evangelicals (NAE) was the organization that conceived the New International Version in 1965. The National Association of Evangelicals has been a flagship organization of the New-Evangelical movement in the last half of the twentieth century in America. If separation from compromise remains a hallmark of Fundamentalism, the involvement of the National Association of Evangelicals itself should raise a red flag.

Textual Deletions

The New International Version deletes **seventeen** entire verses outright from the New Testament when compared to the text used by the church of Jesus Christ for nineteen centuries. These include the following.[1]

Matt. 17:21	"Howbeit this kind goeth not out but by prayer and fasting."
Matt. 18:11	"For the Son of man is come to save that which was lost."
Matt. 23:14	"Woe unto you, scribes and Pharisees, hypocrites! for ye devour widows' houses, and for a pretence make long prayer: therefore ye shall receive the greater damnation."
Mark 7:16	"If any man have ears to hear, let him hear."
Mark 9:44	"Where their worm dieth not, and the fire is not quenched."
Mark 9:46	"Where their worm dieth not, and the fire is not quenched."
Mark 11:26	"But if ye do not forgive, neither will your Father which is in heaven forgive your trespasses."
Mark 15:28	"And the scripture was fulfilled, which saith, And he was numbered with the transgressors."
Luke 17:36	"Two *men* shall be in the field; the one shall be taken, and the other left."
Luke 23:17	"(For of necessity he must release one unto them at the feast.)"
John 5:4	"For an angel went down at a certain season into the pool, and troubled the water: whosoever then first after the troubling of the water stepped in was made whole of whatsoever disease he had."
Acts 8:37	"And Philip said, If thou believest with all thine heart, thou mayest. And he answered and said, I believe that Jesus Christ is the Son of God."

---

[1] The King James Version is used as the basic point of reference.

Acts 15:34	"~~Notwithstanding it pleased Silas to abide there still.~~"
Acts 24:7	"~~But the chief captain Lysias came *upon us*, and with great violence took *him* away out of our hands.~~"
Acts 28:29	"~~And when he had said these words, the Jews departed, and had great reasoning among themselves.~~"
Rom. 16:24	"~~The grace of our Lord Jesus Christ *be* with you all. Amen.~~"
1 John 5:7	"~~For there are three that bear record in heaven, the Father, the Word, and the Holy Ghost: and these three are one.~~"

After Mark 16:8, the New International Version interrupts the text with the following statement: "The two most reliable early manuscripts do not have Mk. 16:9-20." Thus, doubt is clearly cast upon these **twelve** verses. After John 7:52, the New International Version again interrupts the text with a similar announcement: "The earliest and most reliable manuscripts do not have John 7:53-8:11." Thus, another **twelve** verses are cast in doubt. The New International Version also clearly questions the integrity of another **four** verses in Matt. 12:47, 21:44, and Luke 22:43-44.

Therefore, a total of **forty-five** verses are either omitted from the text of the New International Version or are openly doubted as to their integrity. Furthermore, there are another **147** verses in the New International Version where significant portions of the verses are missing as compared to the Received Text. Together, there are a total of **192** verses in the New International Version which are either directly deleted, openly doubted, or have significant portions missing. Can anyone claim that there is no substantial difference between the New International Version and the King James Version?

Dynamic Equivalence

The New International Version translators followed a translational style called *dynamic equivalence* developed by Eugene Nida of the United Bible Societies. Whereas the American Standard Version of 1901 followed strict *formal equivalence*, the New International Version translators were much more loose in their translating.

All translating from one language to another is a mixture of literal rendering as well as allowance for cultural idioms and forms of syntax. This is true in both the language of origin as well as the language into which something is translated. The King James translators for the most part utilized formal equivalence in translating both the syntax and idioms of the original biblical languages.

However, the translators of the New International Version utilized dynamic equivalence to the degree that their work is almost a running paraphrase and not a translation. Dynamic equivalence therefore allows for a great deal of subjectivity on the part of the translators to interpret the biblical text. From purely a technical point of view, the New International Version therefore is a poor translation. In large measure, it is "loosely translated." The subjective opinions of the translators are therefore emphasized more than if they had been conservative in their style of translation.

The perspective of the New International Version's translators seemingly is the understanding of the *reader* rather than "What saith the Scripture" or "Thus saith the Lord." The focus thus is *man-centered* rather than God-centered. The New International Version therefore represents a watered-down, dumbed-down version of the Bible.

APPENDIX C

PROBLEMS WITH THE NEW KING JAMES VERSION

The New King James Version (NKJV) is significantly different from most modern language versions of the Bible. To its credit, the New Testament portion thereof is translated from the Textus Receptus. Moreover, its translators rejected the system of dynamic equivalence using rather what they called "complete equivalence in translation." The New King James Version also included *"The Translators to the Reader"* from the 1611 edition of the King James Version which is a benefit.

However, there are problems with the New King James Version as a *translation*. Listed below are seven areas of difficulty. The problems listed below are a summary of the work of D. K. Madden and his booklet *"Remarks on the New King James Version."*[1]

Absence of Certain Distinctive Pronouns

The translators of the New King James Version made an editorial decision not to use the old-English, second-person pronouns such as "ye," "thou," "thine," and others. Rather, they substituted more modern second-person pronouns such as "you" for "ye" and "thou." Where the King James Version presented "thy" or "thine," the New King James Version substitutes "your" and "yours."

The problem is that "thou" is second person *singular* and "ye" reflects second person *plural*. The New King James Version makes no

---

[1] D. K. Madden, *Remarks on the New King James Version* (Tasmania, Australia: privately printed, 1989).

distinction in number when it uses the generic "you." It therefore is less accurate in its translation than the old King James Version.

Capitalizing Pronouns Relating to God

The translators of the New King James Version also made an editorial decision to capitalize pronouns which refer to Deity. The old King James Version does not. Though there is nothing wrong in principle with thus denoting pronouns of Deity, the problem is that the New King James Version has either been inconsistent in so doing or has become interpretive rather than merely translational. There are places where pronouns have been traditionally assumed to refer to a member of the Godhead but they were not capitalized in the New King James Version. In most cases, the capitalization is correct, but there are some places where a pronoun apparently referring to a member of the Trinity is not capitalized.

One example of this problem is found in Ps. 89:27 where the old King James Version reads, "*Also I will make him my firstborn, higher than the kings of the earth.*" Most conservative commentators have ascribed the "him" here to be Jesus Christ. However, the New King James Version renders the verse as follows: "*Also I will make him My firstborn, the highest of the kings of the earth.*" Notice here that "My" is capitalized indicating God the Father. However, "him" is not. There either was editorial carelessness or an interpretive decision that the "him" here is not Christ.

Translators can get into trouble when they seek to be interpretive. That evidently is what the New King James Version translators have done here. The old King James Version translators were wise in sticking to translation and avoiding being interpretive.

Subject Headings

Most Bible editions will have some sort of chapter or section headings which briefly summarize the contents of a section. These are not inspired and are inserted by editors or translators to assist the reader. There is nothing wrong in principle with such comments. The problem in the New King James Version is that some of their subject headings deviate from traditional, conservative views regarding a given portion of Scripture. For example, in headings for the Song of Solomon, there is nary a word about any figure or application to Jesus Christ. The view of the editors here is solely human in its perspective. Or for example, the heading for Rom. 8:1 in the New King James Version says, *"Free from Indwelling Sin."* However, virtually all conservative commentators would suggest the section pertains to freedom from the condemnation of sin. Reflected is weak editorial perspective.

Weak Translations

To a certain degree, all translation is subjective. However, there seems to be a number of places in the New King James Version which are poorly translated when compared to centuries of long-standing thought. For example, the old King James Version renders 1 Cor. 1:18 as, *"For the preaching of the cross is to them that perish foolishness; but unto us which are saved it is the power of God."* The New King James Version ends the verse, *"but to us who are **being** saved it is the power of God."* There certainly are theological implications to both readings. The New King James Version at this point implies that salvation is a process rather than a completed work of God. The overwhelming body of conservative biblical scholars for the past five hundred years supports the reading of the old King James Version.

Another example of a poor translation is found in Rev. 19:8. The old King James Version reads, *"And to her was granted that she should be arrayed in fine linen, clean and white: for the fine linen is the righteousness of the saints."* The New King James Version reads, *"for *the fine linen is the **righteous acts** of the saints.*" There clearly is a difference and the implications are significant. Some might argue that these and other examples are subjective in nature and within the parameters of judgment for the grammar and syntax in translating the text. That may be true. However, once again the judgment of the translators seems to go against the grain of centuries of accepted thought regarding the proper sense of the text. Because the New King James Version is based upon the Textus Receptus, the issue is not textual as is the case for most modern versions based upon the critical text. Here, the translators chose to deviate from what most scholars through the centuries have agreed was proper translation.

Handling of Miracles

In the New King James Version, there is a tendency to translate the Greek word σημειον (semeion) as "sign(s)." The old King James Version more frequently translates the word as "miracle(s)." It is true that the word can be rendered either way. However, when the context clearly portrays a "miracle," why not use that word? There are implications to both of the words *miracle* and *sign*. "Miracle" has a supernatural implication. "Sign" does not necessarily have that connotation.

Creation by Jesus Christ

In the New Testament where creation is linked to Jesus Christ, in every instance, the New King James Version translates the Greek preposition "δια" (dia) as "through" instead of "by." See John 1:3,10; 1 Cor. 8:6; Eph. 3:9; Col. 1:16; and Heb. 1:2. There is a fine line between the two, but there certainly is a nuance of distinction. Implied is that Jesus Christ was involved in creation but was not the Creator. This is again an area of subjective choice of words in translation, but it has profound implications. The New King James Version is weak at this point.

Footnotes

The New King James Version as noted earlier, is based upon the Textus Receptus. However, in a number of places, marginal notes or footnotes refer the reader back to the critical text. The reader is left to believe that the critical text is a viable alternative to the Textus Receptus. In principle, therefore, the New King James Version directs the reader to the apostasy connected with the critical text. Examples of this may be found in footnotes for 1 Tim. 3:16, a classic variant in the critical text which diminishes the Deity of Christ. Other examples (among many) referring the reader to the critical text may be found for Rom. 14:10, Matt. 27:24, and Matt. 18:11. Sadly, the New King James Version gives no warning of the serious problems in the several critical editions of the Greek New Testament it recommends to the reader.

In summary, the New King James Version is a significantly better translation than any version based upon the critical text. However, all in all, it is a weak translation. It removes precise pronouns found in older English. It is inconsistent in its use of capitalized pronouns referring to Deity. Its chapter headings at times are weak. There are places where the choice of vocabulary transgresses centuries of careful biblical scholarship. It is weak in the way it relates Jesus Christ to creation. Finally, and perhaps worst of all, it directs the reader back to the critical text in its footnotes.

APPENDIX D

WEAKENED DOCTRINE IN THE CRITICAL TEXT

A standard defense of the critical text (and versions based thereupon) is that though it has differences with the Received Text, no doctrine is eliminated or changed. On its face, that statement is more or less true. However, in the critical text and its concomitant translations, major doctrine is *weakened or diluted.* This is generally true in the wider scope of New Testament doctrine. However, it is particularly true as it pertains to the doctrine of Christ and of salvation. Though there is a fairly widespread pattern of doctrinal truth being *diluted* in the critical text, we will focus our attention only upon that which pertains to Jesus Christ, salvation, and related doctrine. Accordingly, let us take note how the critical text *weakens* the doctrine of heaven and hell, the doctrine of salvation, and worst of all, the doctrine of Christ. The material listed below has been gleaned from research done by D. A. Waite.[1]

The Critical Text Weakens the Doctrines of Heaven and Hell

The biblical doctrines of heaven and hell are not eliminated from the critical text (or in the translations based thereupon). However, as will be demonstrated below, they clearly are *diluted and weakened.* Once again, we will use the King James Version as a reference point and note the portions deleted (by strikeout) in the critical text and its popular translations.

---

[1] D. A. Waite, *Defending the King James Bible* (Collingwood, N. J.: Bible for Today, 1992), 131-183.

Dilution of the Doctrines of Hell
and Eternal Judgment

- Mark 3:29 — But he that shall blaspheme against the Holy Ghost hath never forgiveness, but is in danger of eternal ~~damnation~~.
- Mark 9:44 — ~~Where their worm dieth not, and the fire is not quenched.~~
- Mark 9:46 — ~~Where their worm dieth not, and the fire is not quenched.~~
- John 3:15 — That whosoever believeth in him ~~should not perish~~, but have eternal life.
- 2 Pet. 2:17 — These are wells without water, clouds that are carried with a tempest; to whom the mist of darkness is reserved ~~for ever~~.

In the five passages noted above, the doctrine of hell and eternal judgment surely is weakened. In each of the five cases, some aspect of eternal judgment is diluted by the critical text.

Weakening of the Doctrine of Heaven

- Luke 11:2 — And he said unto them, When ye pray, say, Our Father ~~which art in heaven~~, Hallowed be thy name. Thy kingdom come. Thy will be done, ~~as in heaven~~, so in earth.
- Heb. 10:34 — For ye had compassion of me in my bonds, and took joyfully the spoiling of your goods, knowing in yourselves that ye have ~~in heaven~~ a better and an enduring substance.
- 1 John 5:7 — For there are three that bear record ~~in heaven, the Father, the Word, and the Holy Ghost: and these three are one~~.

- Rev. 16:17　And the seventh angel poured out his vial into the air; and there came a great voice out of the temple ~~of heaven~~, from the throne, saying, It is done.

The doctrine of heaven is not eliminated from the critical text and its translations. But as noted in the examples cited above, it surely has been diminished.

The Critical Text Weakens the Doctrine of Salvation

In similar fashion, the doctrine of salvation and related truths are weakened in the critical text and in translations based thereupon.

- Mark 9:42　And whosoever shall offend one of *these* little ones that believe ~~in me~~, it is better for him that a millstone were hanged about his neck, and he were cast into the sea.
- John 6:47　Verily, verily, I say unto you, He that believeth ~~on me~~ hath everlasting life.
- Rom. 1:16　For I am not ashamed of the gospel ~~of Christ~~: for it is the power of God unto salvation to every one that believeth; to the Jew first, and also to the Greek.
- 1 Cor. 5:7　Purge out therefore the old leaven, that ye may be a new lump, as ye are unleavened. For even Christ our passover is sacrificed ~~for us~~.
- Gal. 4:7　Wherefore thou art no more a servant, but a son; and if a son, then an heir of God ~~through Christ~~.
- Gal. 6:15　For ~~in Christ Jesus~~ neither circumcision availeth any thing, nor uncircumcision, but a new creature.
- Col. 1:14　In whom we have redemption ~~through his blood~~, *even* the forgiveness of sins.
- 1 Tim. 6:19　Laying up in store for themselves a good foundation against the time to come, that they may lay hold on ~~eternal~~ life.

•1 Pet. 4:1	Forasmuch then as Christ hath suffered ~~for us~~ in the flesh, arm yourselves likewise with the same mind: for he that hath suffered in the flesh hath ceased from sin.
•Rev. 21:24	And the nations ~~of them which are saved~~ shall walk in the light of it: and the kings of the earth do bring their glory and honour into it.

In the passages of Scripture listed above, it should be apparent that the integrity of the doctrine of salvation through faith in Jesus Christ has been weakened. It has not been eliminated from the critical text, but it has been eroded. Pause and consider the implications of each of these passages with the noted portions removed as they appear in the critical text. Part of the problem that Fundamentalists have in seeing these is that they are aware of what the King James Version says. These verses are still in the back of their minds and therefore, they are not as alarmed as they ought to be. However, consider those never exposed to the full doctrine of the King James Version. They don't know what has been deleted. Of necessity, their understanding is thus diluted.

The Critical Text Weakens the Doctrine of Christ

Perhaps the most serious doctrinal declension in the critical text and translations based thereupon is the dilution and weakening of the doctrine of Christ. The casual reader likely will not notice the various places where these deletions and diminutions take place. However, when viewed together as a list, the composite weakening of the doctrine of Christ is shocking.

The Doctrine of Christ

- 2 John 9   Whosoever transgresseth, and abideth not in the doctrine ~~of Christ~~, hath not God. He that abideth in the doctrine of Christ, he hath both the Father and the Son.

The Virgin Birth of Christ

- Matt. 1:15   And knew her not till she had brought forth her ~~firstborn~~ son: and he called his name JESUS.
- Luke 2:33   And ~~Joseph~~ and his mother marvelled at those things which were spoken of him.[2]

The Eternality of Christ

- John 1:18   No man hath seen God at any time; the only begotten ~~Son~~, which is in the bosom of the Father, he hath declared him.[3]
- Rev. 1:8   I am Alpha and Omega, ~~the beginning and the ending~~, saith the Lord, which is, and which was, and which is to come, the Almighty.

---

[2] It should be noted that the popular modern translations such as the New International Version and the New American Standard Bible follow the critical text precisely in substituting his father for Joseph. This clearly implies that Joseph was the father of Jesus thus substantially weakening the doctrine of the virgin birth.

[3] It should also be noted that the critical text substitutes the word *God* for *Son*. Though the Son certainly was begotten, God the Father was not. This is utter confusion and diminishes the historic teaching regarding the eternality as well as the incarnation of Christ. It is significant that Gnosticism, prevalent in the first and second centuries, held that Christ was one of many gods. The critical text favors the Gnostic position and hints that those holding such a view may have been responsible for this change.

•Rev. 1:11	Saying, ~~I am Alpha and Omega, the first and the last~~: and, What thou seest, write in a book, and send it unto the seven churches.[4]
•Rev. 5:14	And the four beasts said, Amen. And the four and twenty elders fell down and worshipped ~~him that liveth for ever and ever~~.
•Rev. 11:17	Saying, We give thee thanks, O Lord God Almighty, which art, and wast, ~~and art to come~~; because thou hast taken to thee thy great power, and hast reigned.
•Rev. 16:5	And I heard the angel of the waters say, Thou art righteous, O Lord, which art, and wast, ~~and shalt be~~, because thou hast judged thus.

The Omnipresence of Christ

•John 3:13	And no man hath ascended up to heaven, but he that came down from heaven, even the Son of man ~~which is in heaven~~.[5]

God's Manifestation in the Flesh

•1 Tim. 3:16	And without controversy great is the mystery of godliness: ~~God~~ was manifest in the flesh, justified in the

---

[4]It should be noted in the two passages noted above that the eternality of Jesus Christ is clearly diminished by deleting the words indicated.

[5]Though acknowledging that Jesus Christ came down from heaven, the critical text at this point will not allow that He was still in heaven and thus omnipresent.

- 1 John 4:3 Spirit, seen of angels, preached unto the Gentiles, believed on in the world, received up into glory.⁶
 And every spirit that confesseth not that Jesus ~~Christ is come in the flesh~~ is not of God: and this is that spirit of antichrist, whereof ye have heard that it should come; and even now already is it in the world.⁷

Creator

- Eph. 3:9 And to make all men see what is the fellowship of the mystery, which from the beginning of the world hath been hid in God, who created all things ~~by Jesus Christ~~.

Worship of Christ

- Luke 24:52 And they ~~worshipped him, and~~ returned to Jerusalem with great joy.

---

⁶Popular manifestations of the critical text such as the New International Version and the New American Standard Bible substitute the word *he* for God. Who the *he* is is left up to the reader to determine. This clearly is a weakening of the doctrine of the incarnation.

⁷Gnosticism, prevalent in the first and second century, denied that Christ had a physical body because of its adherents' belief that the material world was evil. Does not this change of the text suggest Gnostic influence?

Jesus as Son of God

•John 6:69	And we believe and are sure that thou art that ~~Christ, the Son of the living God~~.[8]
•John 9:35	Jesus heard that they had cast him out; and when he had found him, he said unto him, Dost thou believe on the Son of ~~God~~?[9]
•Acts 8:37	~~And Philip said, If thou believest with all thine heart, thou mayest. And he answered and said, I believe that Jesus Christ is the Son of God~~.[10]
•John 8:28	Then said Jesus unto them, When ye have lifted up the Son of man, then shall ye know that I am he, and that I do nothing of myself; but as my Father hath taught me, I speak these things.[11]
•John 8:38	I speak that which I have seen with my Father: and ye do that which ye have seen with your father.[12]
•John 10:32	Jesus answered them, Many good works have I shewed you from my Father; for which of those works do ye stone me?[13]
•John 14:28	Ye have heard how I said unto you, I go away, and come again unto you. If ye loved me, ye would rejoice,

---

[8]Critical text translations substitute holy one for Christ, the Son of the living God.

[9]The critical text substitutes the word *man* for *God*.

[10]The critical text eliminates this verse altogether. See Rev. 22:19.

[11]The critical text substitutes the word *the* for *my*. By implication, the personal relationship of Jesus as Son of the Father is eliminated.

[12]The critical text substitutes the for my implying that Jesus is not the Son of the Father.

[13]Again, the critical text substitutes the word *the* for *my* implying that Jesus is not the Son of the Father.

Weakened Doctrine in the Critical Text

	because I said, I go unto the Father: for ~~my~~ Father is greater than I.[14]
•John 16:10	Of righteousness, because I go to ~~my~~ Father, and ye see me no more.[15]
•Eph. 3:14	For this cause I bow my knees unto the Father ~~of our Lord Jesus Christ~~.[16]

Jesus' Mission to Save the Lost

•Matt. 18:11	~~For the Son of man is come to save that which was lost.~~[17]
•Luke 9:56	~~For the Son of man is not come to destroy men's lives, but to save them.~~ And they went to another village.[18]

Jesus' Bodily Resurrection

•Luke 24:12	~~Then arose Peter, and ran unto the sepulchre; and stooping down, he beheld the linen clothes laid by~~

---

[14]The critical text once again substitutes the word *the* for *my* implying that Jesus is not the Son of the Father.

[15]The critical text continues to substitute the word *the* for *my* implying that Jesus is not the Son of the Father.

[16]The critical text again diminishes the Father-Son relationship between the Father and Jesus weakening the doctrine that Jesus is the Son of God.

[17]The critical text eliminates this verse. See Rev. 22:19.

[18]Notice how the critical text eliminates the spiritual essence of this great verse and simply notes that they went to another village.

	themselves, and departed, wondering in himself at that which was come to pass.[19]
•Luke 24:40	And when he had thus spoken, he shewed them his hands and his feet.[20]
•Acts 2:30	Therefore being a prophet, and knowing that God had sworn with an oath to him, that of the fruit of his loins, according to the flesh, he would raise up Christ to sit on his throne.[21]

The Lordship of Christ

As noted in appendix A, the word *Lord*, as it relates to Christ, has been eliminated in thirty-nine places in the New American Standard Bible. There are a similar number of deletions in the New International Version. The reason is simple—the modern critical text greatly diminishes the number of times Jesus is referred to as Lord!

Jesus as Lord

As noted in appendix A, the name of Jesus has been eliminated in eighty-seven places in the New American Standard Bible. Once again, this version is credited with being the most careful translation of the critical text. The real problem is that the modern critical text eliminates the name *Jesus* eighty-seven times.

---

[19]Though retaining this verse, the New American Standard Bible, adds this marginal note, "Some ancient mss omit verse 12."

[20]The New American Standard Bible deletes this verse which so graphically describes the bodily resurrection of our Lord. It thus weakens the doctrine of the bodily resurrection of Christ.

[21]The critical text herein clearly dilutes the doctrine of the bodily resurrection of Christ.

All Things through Christ

• Philip. 4:13 I can do all things through ~~Christ~~ which strengtheneth me.[22]

The Judgment Seat of Christ

• Rom 14:10 But why dost thou judge thy brother? or why dost thou set at nought thy brother? for we shall all stand before the judgment seat of ~~Christ~~.[23]

Conclusion

We will concede that the critical text does not *eliminate* or directly change long-established doctrine. However, as documented above, it certainly *dilutes* crucial New Testament doctrine, especially as it pertains to the person of our Lord Jesus Christ. As documented above, such foundational doctrines as the virgin birth of Christ, the eternality of Christ, the omnipresence of Christ, the incarnation of Christ, Jesus as Creator, worship of Jesus, His coming to save that which is lost, the bodily resurrection of Christ, His Lordship and others **have all been diminished, diluted, or weakened in the critical text**. This charge is indisputable to anyone who will examine the data.

---

[22] The critical text substitutes him for Christ. Once again, the person of Jesus Christ is either diminished or weakened in the critical text.

[23] There are only two places in the Bible that the judgment seat of Christ is mentioned. The critical text eliminates one of them. In the mouth of two or three witnesses shall every word be established (2 Cor. 13:1). The greater point is that the critical text has thus removed one half of the references to the bema seat of Christ.

APPENDIX E

EVIDENCES OF A HISTORICAL CONNECTION BETWEEN THE WALDENSES AND THE KING JAMES VERSION

A thought which is intriguing for Bible-believing Baptists is the possibility that there may be a link between the ancient Waldenses, their forerunners, and the King James Version. Jean Leger was a Waldensian pastor and leader in the seventeenth century. In 1669, he wrote "that since the time of the Apostles, or their closest successors, the torch of the gospel was lit among the Vaudois. . . . It was never completely extinguished."[1] Clearly stated is the assertion by Leger that his movement—the Waldenses (or Vaudois)—had existed from apostolic times. (The word *vaudois* is the French equivalent of the Alpine term *waldens* or the Italian *valdesi*. In each case, the words simply mean "valleys." The Waldenses [or the Vaudois] were Bible-believing churches of the valleys of the Alps and Piedmont regions of northern Italy and southeastern France.)

Leger also quoted Theodore Beza regarding the Vaudois. Beza was John Calvin's successor at Geneva and considered an authority of the Reformation era. Beza is quoted as having said, "The Vaudois were so called due to their staying in the Valleys, and narrow places of the Alps, and one could say that they are the remainder of the most pure primitive Christian church."[2] That is a remarkable statement from one of the leaders of the Reformation. Implicit is that the Vaudois reflected true biblical Christianity going back to apostolic times.

---

[1] Jean Leger, *Histoire de Piemont des Eglises Evangeliques des Vallees de Piemont*, trans. Lauri Stiles (Leyde: J. Le Carpentier, 1669), 164.

[2] Ibid., 167.

Evidences of a Historical Connection Between the Waldenses and the King James Version

Reformation-era church historian Peter Boyer also wrote a history of the Vaudois in the year 1692.³ Boyer asserts that the pre-Vaudois churches (the Italic churches) not only go back to apostolic times, but were in fact founded by the apostle Paul himself.⁴ Whether Paul had any direct connection with the Italic churches of the first century is surely uncertain. However, what does seem to be clear is that there were churches in the Piedmont region of northern Italy as early as the end of the first century.

The Italic churches later came to be known as the Vaudois and by the twelfth century were more commonly known as the Waldenses. These churches were never a "denomination" or hierarchical in nature. They rather were an ongoing historical movement located in the valleys of northern Italy and the sub-Alpine regions of what later would be called France, Italy, and Switzerland. Because of their isolation and relatively widespread dispersion across this region, they remained more of a movement of autonomous churches rather than an organized, regional "Church." One thing these churches all had in common was a strong resistance to the corruptions of the Roman Catholic Church. In fact, the Roman Church fiercely persecuted these simple, Bible-believing churches during its infamous inquisitions. Though some of the Vaudois and Waldensian churches eventually drifted into sacramentalism and even forms of heresy, there is ample evidence that there were always churches of this region which were biblical in faith and practice.⁵ (An analogous church movement in the twentieth century would be Baptists in

---

³Boyer was commissioned by King William III of England to write an official history of the Vaudois for his majesty.

⁴Peter Boyer, *The History of the Vaudois* (London: Three Bibles in St. Paul's Church Yard, 1692), 6.

⁵Thomas Williamson, *The Waldenses Were Independent Baptists: An Examination of the Doctrines of This Medieval Sect* (Bloomfield, N.Mex.: Historic Baptist, 1996), 1-4.

America. Many have been biblical in their faith and practice. Some are apostates. Others are somewhere in between. So were the Waldenses.)

The Waldenses and their lineal predecessors are remarkable because they evidence a lineage of churches which for the most part remained true to the Word of God from apostolic times up through the Reformation. Though the Waldenses of the Reformation era were influenced by Calvin and Beza, they existed as a movement for fourteen centuries before the Reformers exploded across Europe in the sixteenth century. Eventually, the Waldenses became pedobaptists (baby baptizers) through their association with the Reformation and still exist today in Italy as a more or less "Protestant" church. However, that was not the case for the first fourteen centuries of their illustrious history.

However, what is germane to the primary purpose of this book is the possible connection between the Waldenses and the lineage of the Received Text. Martin Luther is reputed to have ascribed the Old Latin translation to the Italic churches of the Piedmont by A.D. 157. This version which was otherwise known as the Italic (sometimes called the Itala) followed the Received Text.[6]

Leger also wrote in 1669 that the Vaudois (Waldenses) have "*always* had the entire joy and fruition of the celestial treasure of the true *preserved* holy Scriptures" (emphasis mine).[7] What is absolutely astounding about this quotation is that Leger claimed that the Waldenses (or Vaudois) had *always* possessed the Word of God. Moreover, he referred to the Scriptures as *preserved*. Clearly implicit is that even in the seventeenth century the Waldenses were cognizant of the preservation of the Word of God.

Coming into the second millennium after Christ, there is specific historical record of Waldensian translations into the dialects of the valleys of the Piedmont and sub-Alpine regions of France and Switzer-

---

[6]Jack Moorman, ed., *Forever Settled: A Survey of the Documents and History of the Bible* (Johannesburg, South Africa: privately printed, 1985; reprint, Collingswood, N.J.: Bible for Today, 1997), 107.

[7]Leger, *Histoire de Piemont des Eglises Evangeliques*, 164.

Evidences of a Historical Connection Between the Waldenses and the King James Version

land.[8] There is record of such translations from A.D. 1100 onward.[9] The fact that there were Waldensian translations clearly implies a translation source.

The textual form of several of the Waldensian translations suggests that they were translated from Greek manuscripts because they followed the book arrangements of the Byzantine Bible and not that of the Latin Vulgate.[10] Moreover, because of their aversion to Rome and anything pertaining to Rome, the Vaudois likewise shunned the Latin Vulgate. What may be reasonably concluded therefore is that, in some cases, Waldensian translators worked from ancient Greek manuscripts of the Received Text. Though vigorously denied by some, there is record that some Waldenses did in fact know and use Greek.[11] Moreover, because of their unique heritage and their separatism from the Roman Catholic Church, it may well be *assumed* that the Waldensians had in their possession long-treasured ancient manuscripts of the New Testament. Leger also wrote of them being in possession of "extremely old parchments" of the Scriptures.[12]

The Roman Catholic inquisition turned its wrath against the separatist, dissident churches of the valleys (i.e., the Waldenses) beginning in 1488. This merciless persecution reached its climax when the Catholics almost exterminated the Waldenses in the massacre of 1655.

---

[8]These translations were in Provencal and Romaunt. The former was a Latin based dialect of the Alps used by many Waldenses. The latter was another dialect of Latin used throughout southern Europe in the centuries prior to the Renaissance.

[9]Emilio Comba, *History of the Waldenses of Italy from Their Origin to the Reformation*, trans. Teofilo E. Comba (London: Truslove & Shirley, 1889), 167.

[10]Ibid., 176.

[11]J. A. Wylie, *History of the Waldenses* (London: Cassell & Co., 1860), chapter 10, p. 2, of Internet edition (http://www.pbtseminary.com/Baptists/J.%20Wylie/the_waldenses.htm), September 9, 2000.

[12]Leger, *Histoire de Piemont des Eglises Evangeliques*, 164.

Because the Catholic Inquisition against the Waldenses lasted for almost two hundred years, it is reasonable to assume that these Bible-believing brethren sought safe havens for their records and treasured manuscripts. There in fact is *specific* historical record that Leger, the Waldensian pastor and church historian, sent manuscripts to Geneva in 1662 for safe keeping from the intensifying Catholic Inquisition.[13] If this was the case then, is it unreasonable to conclude that such refuge was not sought earlier for records and manuscripts? In the massacre of 1655, most other Waldensian records were destroyed by the Catholics.

History has recorded that the King James translators worked primarily from Theodore Beza's fifth edition of the Received Text produced in 1598.[14] Of course, Beza did his textual work from Geneva. Moreover, there had developed a bond of kinship between the Reformers at Geneva and many of the Waldensians because of their mutual adversary, the Roman Catholic Church. Of further interest is that John Calvin was related by marriage to Waldensian church leaders.[15]

One old historian by the name of Edgar, who has otherwise been lost to antiquity, directly asserts that Beza in Geneva used Waldensian Greek manuscripts in preparing his Greek New Testament. Edgar is reputed to have said that Beza "'astonished and confounded the world' with the Greek manuscripts which he unearthed. This later edition of the Received Text is in reality a Greek New Testament brought out under Waldensian influence."[16] This writer has not been able to find further corroboration of this assertion at the time of this writing. However, one historian certainly is on record as affirming this. Morever, it certainly is

---

[13]Ibid., 167.

[14]Frederick Henry Scrivener, *The New Testament in Greek: According to the Text Followed in the Authorized Version Together with the Variations Adopted in the Revised Version* (London: Cambridge University Press, 1881), vii.

[15]Leger, *Histoire de Piemont des Eglises Evangeliques,* 167.

[16]"Our Authorized Bible Vindicated" in *Which Bible?* ed. David Otis Fuller (Grand Rapids: Grand Rapids International Publications, 1970), 210.

plausible to assume that if Leger brought manuscripts to Geneva in 1662 for safe keeping that other Waldenses did so earlier. Beza produced his Greek New Testament of the Received Text in Geneva at this general time. Though there is no conclusive evidence that Beza used Waldensian manuscripts, circumstances allow theories to arise suggesting the possibility.

If this is the case, then there could be a direct lineage of the Received Text from the end of the first century through the Italic churches to the Vaudois to the Waldenses to Beza to the King James's translators. And *if* this is the case, then there may be a historical lineage of the Received Text down through the ages through *believing* churches to the present hour. Though proof of this theory cannot be established at the time of this writing, it is a fascinating prospect nevertheless.

SELECTED BIBLIOGRAPHY

This bibliography is divided into two sections: Books and Articles. The Books section also includes unpublished class notes. The Articles section includes articles from periodicals and essays in books.

Books

Aland, Kurt. *The Problem of the New Testament Canon*, London: A. R. Mowbray, 1962.

Aland, Kurt, and Barbara Aland, eds. *Kurzgefasste Liste der grieschen Handscriften des Neuen Testaments*. Hawthorne, N. Y.: Walter de Gruyter, 1994.

_____. *The Text of the New Testament: An Introduction to the Critical Editions to the Theory and Practice of Modern Textual Criticism*, 2d ed. Grand Rapids: W. B. Eerdmans, 1989.

Aland, Kurt, Matthew Black, Bruce M. Metzger, and Allen Wikgren, eds. *The Greek New Testament*, 3d ed. London: United Bible Societies, 1966.

Anderson, G. W., and D. E. Anderson. *The English Bible, Its Preservation and Blessing*. Grand Rapids: Trinitarian Bible Society, n.d.

Ashbrook, John. *Separation from Apostasy*. Columbus, Ohio: Ohio Bible Fellowship, 1975.

_____. *Separation from Brethren*. Sundbury, Ohio: Ohio Bible Fellowship, n.d.

Selected Bibliography

Bauder, Kevin. *The Bible Version Debate: A Reply to the PCC Proposal*. Plymouth, Minn.: Central Baptist Theological Seminary, 1998.

Baird, Henry Martyn. *Theodore Beza: The Counsellor of the French Reformation*. New York: G. P. Putnam's Sons, 1899.

Bell, Rod. *Manifesto on Biblical Separation*. Virginia Beach, Virginia: Fundamental Baptist Manifesto, n.d.

Bob Jones University faculty. *Biblical Separation*. Greenville, S.C.: Bob Jones University, n.d.

Boyer, Peter. *The History of the Vaudois*. London: Three Bibles in St. Paul's Church Yard, 1692.

Brown, Andrew. *The Word of God among All Nations*. London: Trinitarian Bible Society, 1981.

Burgon, John. *A Brief Summary of the Causes of the Corruption of the Traditional Text of the Holy Gospels*. Collingswood, N. J.: Summarized by the Bible for Today, 1997.

_____. *The Causes of Textual Corruption*. Original publisher unknown. Reprint, Collingswood, N.J.:, Dean Burgon Society, n.d.

_____. *Inspiration and Interpretation*. London: J. H. & Jas. Parker, 1861. Reprint, Collingswood, N.J.: Bible for Today, 1984.

_____. *The Revision Revised*. Original publisher unknown, 1883. Reprint, Collingswood, N.J.: Dean Burgon Society, n.d.

_____. *The Traditional Text of the Holy Gospels*. London: George Bell & Sons, 1896. Reprint, Dean Burgon Society, 1998.

Burgon, John, and Edward Miller. *The Causes of the Corruption of the Traditional Text of the Holy Gospels*. London: MacMillan Co., 1897.

Cathcart, William. *The Ancient British and Irish Churches*. Philadelphia: American Baptist Publication Society, 1894.

Ciarrocca, Richard. *Testimony of Dr. Frank Logsdon*. Elkton, Md: Observations, 1994.

Clearwaters, R. V. *The Conservative Baptist Manifesto*. Portland, Oreg.: n.p., 1953.

Cloud, David. *Myths about the Modern Bible Versions*. Oak Harbor, Wash.: Way of Life Literature, 1999.

_____. *Unholy Hands on God's Holy Book: A Report on the United Bible Societies*. Oak Harbor, Wash.: Way of Life Literature, 1985.

Comba, Emilio. *History of the Waldenses of Italy from Their Origin to the Reformation*. Translated by Teofilo E. Comba. London: Truslove & Shirley, 1889.

Coston, Stephen. *King James Unjustly Accused?* St. Petersburg, Fla.: Konigswort, 1996.

Dean Burgon Society (1978-1994). "Messages from the 16th Annual Meeting, August 1994." Collingswood, N.J.: Bible for Today, 1994.

Durston, Christopher. *James I*. London: Routledge, 1993.

Ecumenism and the United Bible Societies. London: Tyndale House, 1985.

Selected Bibliography

Emerton, Ephraim. *Desiderius Erasmus of Rotterdam*. New York: G. P. Putnam's Sons, 1899.

Ehrman, Bart D. *The Orthodox Corruption of Scripture*. New York: Oxford University Press, 1993.

Freeman, Paul. *Bible Doctrines Affected by Modern Versions*. Catasauqua, Pa.: Race Street Baptist Church, n.d.

_____. *Why I Stand on the King James Version*. Pekin, Ill.: privately printed, n.d.

Friesen, Abraham. *Erasmus, the Anabaptists, and the Great Commission*. Grand Rapids: Eerdmans Publishing Co., 1998.

Fuller, David Otis. *The Battle for the Word of God*. Grand Rapids: Institute for Biblical Textual Studies, n.d.

_____. *The Crowd Can Be Wrong*. Grand Rapids: Institute for Biblical Textual Studies, n.d.

_____. *The Impregnable Rock of Holy Scripture*. Grand Rapids: Institute for Biblical Textual Studies, n.d.

_____. *Is the King James Version Nearest to the Original Autographs?* Grand Rapids: Institute for Biblical Textual Studies, 1972.

_____. *A Position Paper on the Versions of the Bible*. Grand Rapids: Institute for Biblical Textual Studies, n.d.

_____, ed. *Counterfeit or Genuine — Mark 16? John 8?* Grand Rapids: Grand Rapids International Publications, 1975.

_____, ed. *True or False?* Grand Rapids: Grand Rapids International Publications, 1973.

_____, ed. *Which Bible?* Grand Rapids: Grand Rapids International Publications, 1970.

Garrett, Les. *A Concordance of the Destruction of the Two and Three Witnesses in the Bible.* Queensland, Australia:Voice of Thanksgiving, 1999.

_____. *Westcott & Hort: The Occult Connection and New Greek Text.* Queensland, Australia: Voice of Thanksgiving, 1997.

_____, ed. *Which Bible Can We Trust?* Queensland, Australia: Christian Center Press, 1982.

Gauld, Alan. *The Founders of Psychical Research.* New York: Schocken Books, 1968.

Gifis, Steven H. *Law Dictionary.* 2d ed. New York: Barrons, 1984.

Gilly, William Stephen. *Waldensian Researches during a Second Visit to the Vaudois of Piemont.* London: C. J. G. & F. Rivington, 1831.

Graham, Mac. *Should the Church Be Concerned about Bible Translations?* Grand Rapids: Institute for Biblical Textual Studies, n.d.

Grant, Robert. *A Historical Introduction to the New Testament.* New York: Harper & Row, 1963.

Greenlee, J. Harold. *Introduction to New Testament Textual Criticism.* Grand Rapids: Eerdmans Publishing Co., 1964.

Grisanti, Michael, ed. *The Bible Version Debate.* Minneapolis: Central Baptist Theological Seminary, 1997.

Selected Bibliography

Gromacki, Robert. *New Testament Survey*. Grand Rapids: Baker Book House, 1974.

Hills, Edward F. *Believing Bible Study*. 3d ed. Des Moines, Iowa: Christian Research Press, 1991.

──────. *The King James Version Defended*. Des Moines: Christian Research Press, 1956.

Hort, Arthur Fenton. *Life and Letters of Fenton John Anthony Hort*. Vol. 2. London: MacMillan & Co., 1896.

Hort, Fenton John Anthony. *The New Testament in the Original Greek*. 2d ed. New York: Harper, 1882.

Hoskier, Herman. *Codex B and Its Allies: A Study and an Indictment*. London: Bernard Quaritch, 1914.

Huizinga, John. *Erasmus and the Age of Reformation*. New York: Harper & Row, 1924.

Hymers, R. L. *Ruckmanism Exposed*. Los Angeles: Fundamentalist Baptist Tabernacle, 1998.

Jackson, Paul. *The Position, Attitudes, and Objectives of Biblical Separation*. Schaumburg, Ill.: General Association of Regular Baptist Churches, n.d.

Johnson, Dell. "Notes on New Evangelicalism." Pensacola, Fla.: Pensacola Christian College, unpublished class notes, 1999.

Kelly, Balmer H., and Donald G. Miller, eds. *Tools for Bible Study*. Richmond: John Knox Press, 1956.

Kenyon, Frederic. *Handbook to the Textual Criticism of the New Testament.* 2d ed. Grand Rapids: Eerdmans Publishing Co., 1951.

_____. *Our Bible and the Ancient Manuscripts.* 4th ed. New York: Harper Bros., 1895.

_____. *Recent Developments in the Textual Criticism of the Greek Bible: Schwieich Lectures of the British Academy.* London: Oxford University Press, 1932.

_____. *The Text of the Greek Bible: A Student's Handbook.* London: Duckworth, 1937.

Kinder, Gordon. *Cassiodoro de Reina, Spanish Reformer of the Sixteenth Century.* London: Tamesis Books, 1975.

Ladd, George Eldon. *The New Testament and Criticism.* Grand Rapids: W. B. Eerdmans Publishing Co., 1967.

Lake, Kirsopp. *The Text of the New Testament.* London: Rivingtons, 1904.

Lee, Maurice Jr. *Great Britain's Solomon: James VI & I in His Three Kingdoms.* Champaign, Ill.: University of Illinois Press, 1990.

Leger, Jean. *Histoire de Piemont des Eglises Evangeliques des Vallees de Piemont.* Translated by Lauri Stiles. Leyde: J. Le Carpentier, 1669.

Letis, Theodore. *The Ecclesiastical Text.* Philadelphia: Institute for Renaissance & Reformation Biblical Studies, 1997.

_____. *The Majority Text: Essays and Reviews in the Continuing Debate.* Philadelphia: Institute for Renaissance & Reformation Biblical Studies, 1987.

———. *A New Hearing for the Authorized Version*. Philadelphia: Institute for Renaissance & Reformation Biblical Studies, 1997.

Lindsell, Harold. *The Battle for the Bible*. Grand Rapids: Zondervan, 1976.

———. *The Bible in the Balance*. Grand Rapids: Zondervan, 1979.

Madden, D. K. *Remarks on the New King James Version*. Tasmania, Australia: privately printed, 1989.

Marsden, George. *Reforming Fundamentalism: Fuller Seminary and the New Evangelicalism*. Grand Rapids: Wm. B. Eerdmans Publishing Co., 1987.

———. *Understanding Fundamentalism and Evangelicalism*. Grand Rapids: Wm. B. Eerdmans Publishing Co., 1991.

Martin, Alfred. "A Critical Examination of the Westcott-Hort Textual Theory." Th.D. thesis, Dallas Theological Seminary, 1951.

Mauro, Philip. *Which Version? Authorized or Revised?* Boston: Scripture Truth Depot, 1924.

McClure, Alexander. *The Translators Revisited*. Original publisher unknown, 1858. Reprint, Litchfield, Mich.: Maranatha Bible Society, n.d.

McDowell, Josh. *Evidence That Demands a Verdict*. San Bernadino, Calif.: Campus Crusade for Christ International, 1972.

Metzger, Bruce M. *The Text of the New Testament: Its Transmission, Corruption, and Restoration*. New York: Oxford University Press, 1964.

_____, ed. *The Reader's Digest Bible: Condensed from the Revised Standard Version, Old and New Testaments*. Pleasantville, N. Y.: Reader's Digest Association, 1982.

Miller, Edward. *A Guide to the Textual Criticism of the New Testament*. Original publisher unknown, 1886. Reprint, Collingswood, N.J.: Dean Burgon Society, 1979.

Moorman, Jack, ed. *Forever Settled: A Survey of the Documents and History of the Bible*. Johannesburg, South Africa: privately printed, 1985. Reprint, Collingswood, N.J.: Bible for Today, 1997.

Morris, Henry. *A Creationist's Defense of the King James Bible*. El Cajon, Calif.: Institute for Creation Research, 1996.

Neander, Augustus. *The History of the Christian Religion and Church during the First Three Centuries*. Translated by Henry John Rose. Philadelphia: James M. Campbell & Co., 1843.

Nida, Eugene. *Message and Mission: The Communication of the Christian Faith*. New York: Harper, 1960.

Nolan, Frederick. *An Inquiry into the Integrity of the Greek Vulgate: or, Received Text of the New Testament*. London: F. C. & J. Rivington, 1815.

Ottley, Richard. *A Handbook to the Septuagint*. London: Methuen, 1920.

Paine, Gustavus. *The Men behind the KJV*. Grand Rapids: Baker Book House, 1959. Reprint, Collingswood, N.J.: Bible for Today, n.d.

Paisley, Ian. *My Plea for the Old Sword*. Belfast, Northern Ireland: Ambassador Productions, 1997.

Selected Bibliography

Pickering, Ernest. *Biblical Separation: The Struggle for a Pure Church*. Schaumburg, Ill.: Regular Baptist Press, 1979.

———. *The Tragedy of Compromise*. Greenville, S.C.: Bob Jones University Press, 1994.

Pickering, Wilbur, *The Identity of the New Testament Text*. Nashville: Thomas Nelson, 1977. Reprint, Collingswood, N.J.: Bible for Today, n.d.

Quebedeaux, Richard. *The Worldly Evangelicals*. San Francisco: Harper & Row, 1978.

Radmacher, Earl, and Zane Hodges. *The NIV Reconsidered*. Dallas: Kerugma, 1990.

Reynolds, M. H. *Modern Bible Versions Are Dangerous*. Grand Rapids: Institute for Biblical Textual Studies, n.d.

Riley, W. B. *Divinely Ordered Divisions*. Reprint, Minneapolis, Minn.: Central Seminary Press, n.d.

Riplinger, G. A. *New Age Bible Versions*. Munroe Falls, Ohio: AV Publications, 1994.

Rockwood, Perry. *Bible Separation*. Halifax, Canada: Peoples Gospel Hour, n.d.

Ruckman, Peter S. *The Christian's Handbook of Manuscript Evidence*. Pensacola, Fla.: Pensacola Bible Institute, 1970.

Salter, W. H. *The Society for Psychical Research: An Outline of Its History*. London: Tavistock Square, 1948.

Sawyer, J. W. *The Legacy of our English Bible.* Montesano, Wash.: n.p., 1990.

Schaff, Philip. *Theological Propaedeutic: A General Introduction to the Study of Theology, Exegetical, Historical, Systematic, and Practical, Including Encyclopaedia, Methodology, and Bibliography: A Manual for Students.* 8th ed. New York: Charles Scribner's Sons, 1909.

Scofield, C. I. *The Scofield Reference Bible.* New York: Oxford University Press, 1909. Reprint, 1945.

Scrivener, Frederick Henry. *A Full Collation of the Codex Sinaiticus.* Original publisher unknown, 1864. Quoted in David Cloud, *Myths about the Modern Bible Versions*, 192. Oak Harbor, Wash.: Way of Life Literature, 1999.

———. *The New Testament in Greek: According to the Text Followed in the Authorized Version Together with the Variations Adopted in the Revised Version.* London: Cambridge University Press, 1881.

———. *A Plain Introduction to the Criticism of the New Testament.* Vol. 2. 2d ed. Cambridge, Deighton, Bell, & Co., 1874.

———. *A Supplement to the Authorized English Version of the New Testament.* London: William Pickering, 1845.

Sightler, James. *A Testimony Founded For Ever: The King James Bible Defended in Faith and History.* Greenville, S.C.: Sightler Publications, 1999.

———. *Tabernacle Essays on Bible Translation.* Greenville, S.C.: Tabernacle Baptist Church, 1993.

Selected Bibliography

Smith, George Vance. *Texts and Margins of the Revised New Testament Affecting Theological Doctrine Briefly Reviewed* (original publisher unknown), 47. Quoted in David Cloud, *Myths about the Modern Bible Versions*, 198-199. Oak Harbor, Wash.: Way of Life Literature, 1999.

Smith, Preserved. *Erasmus: A Study of His Life, Ideals and Place in History*. New York: Dover Publications, 1962.

Sorenson, David. *Why We Use the King James Version*. 4th ed. Duluth, Minn.: Northstar Baptist Ministries, 2000.

Spence, O. Talmadge. *Scriptural Separation*. Greenville, S.C.: International Committee for the Propagation & Defense of Biblical Fundamentalism, 1982.

Spinka, Matthew. *Advocates of Reform: From Wyclif to Erasmus*. Philadelphia: Westminster Press, 1953.

Sturz, Harry A. *The Byzantine Text-Type and New Testament Textual Criticism*. Nashville: Thomas Nelson Publishers, 1984.

Teachout, Raymond. *Breaking Down the Walls: The Subversive Work of Evangelical Inclusivism*. Ste-Foy, Quebec: Études Bibliques pour Aujord' hui, 1999.

Trinitarian Bible Society. *Ecumenism and the United Bible Societies*. London: Trinitarian Bible Society, n.d.

Tulga, Chester. *The Case for Separation in These Times*. Little Rock: Challenge Press, 1952.

Turner, Charles V. *Why the King James Version: The Preservation of the Word of God by Faithful Churches*. Bowie, Tex.: Baptist Bible Translators, n.d.

Van Bruggen, Jakob. *The Ancient Text of the New Testament.* Winnipeg: Premier Printing 1976.

Van Kleeck, Peter. *Fundamentalism's Folly: A Bible Version Debate Case Study.* Grand Rapids: Institute for Biblical Textual Studies, 1998.

Vincent, Marvin. *A History of the Textual Criticism of the New Testament.* New York: Macmillan Co., 1899.

Waite, D. A. *The Authorized Version 1611 Compared to Today's King James Version.* Collingswood, N.J.: Bible for Today, 1985.

_____. *A Brief Analysis of the NIV Inclusive Language Edition.* Collingswood, N.J.: Bible for Today, 1997.

_____. *Central Seminary Refuted on Bible Versions.* Collingswood, N.J.: Bible for Today, 1999.

_____. *Defending the King James Bible.* Collingswood, N.J.: Bible for Today, 1998.

_____. *Foes of the King James Bible Refuted.* Collingswood, N.J.: Bible for Today, 1997.

_____. *Fundamentalist Distortions on Bible Versions.* Collingswood, N.J.: Bible for Today, 1999.

_____. *Heresies of Westcott and Hort.* Collingswood, N.J.: Bible for Today, 1998.

_____. *Westcott's Denial of Christ's Bodily Resurrection.* Collingswood, N.J.: Bible for Today, 1983.

Warfield, Benjamin. *Presbyterian Review 3*. N.p., 355. Quoted in Theodore Letis, *The Ecclesiastical Text*, 17. Philadelphia: Institute for Renaissance & Reformation Biblical Studies, 1997.

Watts, Malcolm. *The Lord Gave the Word: A Study of the History of the Biblical Text*. London: Trinitarian Bible Society, 1998.

Westcott, Arthur. *Life and Letters of Brooke Foss Westcott*. Vol. 1. London: MacMillan & Co., 1903.

Westcott, B. F. *The Epistle to the Hebrews: The Greek Text with Notes and Essays*. 3d ed. London: Macmillan, 1920.

_____. *The Epistles of St. John: The Greek Text with Notes and Essays*. 2d ed. Cambridge: Macmillan, 1886.

_____. *The Gospel According to St. John: The Authorized Version with Introduction and Notes*. London: John Murray, 1892.

_____. *The Gospel of Life*. London: Macmillan & Co., 1888.

_____. *The Revelation of the Risen Lord*. New York: Macmillan & Co., 1891.

Westcott, Brooke Foss, and Fenton John Anthony Hort. *Introduction to the New Testament in the Original Greek with Notes on Selected Readings*. London: Macmillan & Co., 1882. Reprint, Peabody, Mass.: Hendrickson, 1988.

_____. *The New Testament Text in the Original Greek*. 4th ed. New York: Macmillan Co., 1940.

White, James R. *The King James Only Controversy*. Minneapolis: Bethany House Publishers, 1995.

Williams, James B., general ed. *From the Mind of God to the Mind of Man*. Greenville, S.C.: Ambassador—Emerald International, 1999.

Williamson, Thomas. *The Waldenses Were Independent Baptists: An Examination of the Doctrines of this Medieval Sect*. Bloomfield, N.Mex.: Historic Baptist, 1996.

Wilson, David. *King James VI & I*. New York: Oxford University Press, 1956.

Wylie, J.A. *History of the Waldenses*. London: Cassell & Co., 1860.

Articles

Colas, Ralph. "Perspectives." *Review* (Sellersville, Pa.: Independent Baptist Fellowship of North America), February 2000, 2.

Downey, Paul W. "Canonization and Apocrypha." In *From the Mind of God to the Mind of Man*, ed. James B. Williams, 31-64. Greenville, S.C.: Ambassador—Emerald International, 1999.

Elliott, J. K. "The Original Text of the Greek New Testament." *Fax Theologica* 8 (1988): 6.

Epp, E. J. "The Twentieth Century Interlude in New Testament Textual Criticism." *Journal of Biblical Literature* 93 (1974): 403.

Glenny, W. Edward. "Defining the Terms." In *The Bible Version Debate*, ed. Michael Grisanti, 41-69. Minneapolis: Central Baptist Theological Seminary, 1997.

⎯⎯⎯. "The Preservation of Scripture." In *The Bible Version Debate*, ed. Michael Grisanti, 71-106. Minneapolis: Central Baptist Theological Seminary, 1997.

Selected Bibliography

Hodges, Zane. "The Greek Text of the King James Version." In *Which Bible?* ed. David Otis Fuller, 25-38. Grand Rapids: Grand Rapids International Publications, 1970.

Houghton, Myron. "The Preservation of Scripture." *Faith Pulpit* (Ankeny, Iowa: Faith Baptist Theological Seminary), August 1999, 2.

Huffman, Jerry. "Michigan Church Leaves GARBC." *Calvary Contender* (Huntsville, Ala.: Calvary Baptist Church), 15 May 2000, 2.

Keylock, Leslie. "The Bible That Bears His Name." *Moody Monthly*, July/August 1985, 87-89.

Kilpatrick, G. D. "The Transmission of the New Testament and Its Reliability." *Bible Translator* 9 (July 1958): 128-29. Quoted in Wilbur Pickering, *The Identity of the New Testament Text*, 114. Nashville, Tenn.: Thomas Nelson, 1977. Reprint, Collingswood, N.J.: Bible for Today, n.d.

Lake, Kirsopp. "The New Testament in the Original Greek." *Harvard Theological Review* 21 (1928): 345-46.

McCune, Roland D. "Doctrinal Nonissues in Historic Fundamentalism." *Detroit Baptist Seminary Journal* 1, no. 2 (fall 1996): 177.

Mincy, John C. "The Making of the King James Version." In *From the Mind of God to the Mind of Man*, ed. James B. Williams, 129-146. Greenville, S.C.: Ambassador—Emerald International, 1999.

Minnick, Mark. "Let's Meet the Manuscripts." In *From the Mind of God to the Mind of Man*, ed. James B. Williams, 65-98. Greenville, S.C.: Ambassador—Emerald International, 1999.

Parvis, M. M. "The Goals of New Testament Textual Studies." *Studia Evangelical* 6 (1973): 406.

Smallman, William H. "Printed Greek Texts." In *From the Mind of God to the Mind of Man,* ed. James B. Williams, 169-184. Greenville, S.C.: Ambassador—Emerald International, 1999.

Sumner, Robert. "Sumner's Incidents and Illustrations—Were Westcott and Hort Members of a Ghost Society?" *Target* 9 no. 1 (January 1994): 7.

"The Bible Societies." *Trinitarian Bible Society Quarterly Record,* Jan.-Mar. 1979, 13-14.

Thompson, D. A. "The Controversy Concerning the Last Twelve Verses of the Gospel according to Mark." Surrey: Bible Christian Unity Fellowship, 39-40; reprint of an article which appeared in *Bible League Quarterly.* London 1973.

Williams, James B., "Introduction: The Issue We Face." In *From the Mind of God to the Mind of Man,* ed. James B. Williams, 1-12. Greenville, S.C.: Ambassador—Emerald International, 1999.

Wojan, Karen Ann. "The Real King James." *Moody Monthly,* July/August 1985, 87-89.

General Index

Abbot, George, 208
Ablondi, Alberto, 124
Abrio, Francisco, 203
Aglionby, John, 209
Aland, Kurt, 22, 28, 65, 117, 118, 132
Aland, Barbara, 132
Alexandria, Egypt, 89, 93, 95, 96, 97, 98
Alexandrian textual family, 23, 25, 49, 51, 99, 100
American Standard Version, 130, 217, 221
American Bible Society, 130
American Council of Christian Churches, 184
Anabaptists, 188, 191, 192, 193, 211
Andrews, Lancelot, 205
Anglican Church, 167, 170, 181, 193, 200, 210, 211
Anglican translators, 210
Apollonides, 139
Arianism, 25
Arinze, Francis, 124
Arius, 98
Asclepiades, 139
Ashbrook, John 154
Athanasius, 98, 156, 157

Balfour, Lord Arthur, 176
Baptist Bible Fellowship, 153
Basilikon Doron, 197, 198
Bass, Clarence, 159
Bethel Theological Seminary, 159
Beza, Theodore, 31, 45, 70, 71, 78, 92, 187, 195, 256, 258, 260, 261
Beza's Greek New Testament, 83, 92, 187
Bibliology, 6

Bishops' Bible, 45, 46, 83
Black, Matthew, 117
Blavatsky, Helena, 178
Blayney, Benjamin, 17,
Bodmer and Chester Beatty Papyri, 64, 138
Bois, John, 209
Bombasius, 91, 188
Boyer, Peter, 257
Brabant, 91
Brainthwaite, William, 209
Brett, Richard, 208
British and Foreign Bible Society, 117, 122, 123, 125, 224
Broad Church Party, 106, 107, 116, 170, 223
Buckminister, J. S., 108, 223
Burgon, John, 21, 50, 81, 102, 104, 132, 136, 168, 213, 215
Burkitt, F. C., 80, 81
Byzantine Church, 88
Byzantine Text, 38, 49, 76, 88, 89, 93

Calvin, John 29, 45, 71, 78, 195, 256, 258
Cambridge University, 91, 106, 166, 172, 175, 204, 206
Cambridge Edition, 18, 19
Catechical School of Alexandria, 97, 98
Celtic Church, 83
Central Baptist Theological Seminary, 2, 17, 51, 55
Chaderton, Lawrence, 207
Chatauqua Bible Conferences, 152
Chester Beatty Papyrus, 138
Church of England, (See also Anglican Church) 167, 181, 193, 200, 210, 211
Clark, Richard, 206
Clark, Kenneth, 63
Clearwaters, Richard V., 215, 216
Clement of Alexandria, 97
Cloud, David, 117

General Index

Codex Alexandrinus, 35
Codex Sinaiticus, 24, 25, 26, 27, 40, 41, 45, 50, 72, 91, 96, 98, 99, 100, 101, 102, 104,
Codex Vaticanus, 24, 25, 26, 27, 28, 35, 40, 41, 45, 49, 69, 72, 91, 92, 95, 96, 98, 99, 100,
Codex W, 83
Coggan, Lord, 125
Colas, Ralph, 184
Coleridge, Samuel, 106, 112, 176
Colwell, Ernest, 64
Communist Party, 158
Complutensian Polyglot, 83
Conservative Baptist Association, 2, 4, 153
Constantine the Great 24, 26, 99
Constantine, manuscripts for, 100
Coston, Stephen, 202
Council of Nicea, 98
counting of texts, 132
Coverdale Bible, 45, 83
Coverdale, William, 45
critical text, Alexandrian origin of the, 96
critical text, logic of the 60, 128
critical text, rationalism of the, 61
critical text, subjectivity of the, 62
critical text, contradictions of the, 63
critical text, uncertainly of the, 65
critical text position, 20 *ff*

Dallas Theological Seminary, 109
Darwin, Charles, 112, 179, 182
Deity of Christ, 98, 116, 163, 170, 181, 217, 224, 244
Devries, Ed, 16
Dillingham, Francis, 207
Diodati Version, 84
double stream, the, 43

Duoay Version, 46
Durston, Christopher, 202
dynamic equivalency, 121, 240

Ecclesiastical Text, 39, 40
Edes, Richard, 208
electic text, 3, 22, 41
Ellerton, John, 112
Elliott, J, K., 51
Elzivir brothers, 31
Elzivir's Greek New Testament, 83
English Bibles, 44
English Revised Version, 105, 180, 181
Eranus Club, 176
Erasmus, Desiderius, 31, 45, 69, 70, 83, 90, 91, 137, 186, 187, 188, 189, 190, 191, 193, 211
Erasmus and Vaticanus, 90, 91
Estiennes, see Stephens, Robert
Eusebius, 26, 98, 99, 100, 125
evolution, theory of, 111, 112, 179
exemplars, 134, 135, 136, 137

Farstad, Arthur, 39
Fawkes, Guy, 201
Fosdick, Harry Emerson, 152; 155, 156
Friesen, Arthur, 191
Fuller Theological Seminary, 157, 159, 218
Fuller, David Otis, 5, 216, 221
Fundamental Baptist Fellowship, 155
Fundamental Baptist perspective, 1
Fundamentalism, a brief history of, 150 *ff*
fundamentalism, essence of, 3
Fundamentalism, its summum bonum, 5
Fundamentalist defined, 154

General Index

Gaius, 139
Gallic Church, 83
Garrett, Les, 171, 179
General Association of Regular Churches, 4, 153
Geneva Bible, 45, 46, 83
German (Higher) Rationalism, 93, 100, 106, 107, 109, 115, 125, 149, 150, 162, 163, 164, 166, 210, 223
Ghostly Guild, 172, 173 174, 177, 178, 180
Glenny, W. Edward, 51, 77
Gnosticism, 96, 97, 114, 222
Good News for Modern Man, 235
Gothic Version, 30, 81
Graham, Billy, 158
Greenlee, J. H., 167
Griesbach, J. J., 61, 71, 73, 100 109, 163, 164, 165, 166, 223
Gromacki, Robert, 51

Harvard College, 108, 223
Hermes Club, 175
Hermophilus, 139
Hills, Edward, 64, 80, 136, 215, 216
Hodges, Zane, 39, 60
Holland, Thomas, 207
Hort, Arthur, 168, 175, 176
Hort, F. J. A., 73, 80
Hoskier, Herman, 215
Hubmaier, Balthasar, 192
Hymers, R. L., 219

inclusivism, 182
Independent Baptist Fellowship of North American, 184
Inquisition, 260
inspiration, thought, 7, 64
inspiration, verbal, 6, 8
Institute for New Testament Textual Research, 118

intentional corruption, 137
International Committee for the Propagation and Defense of Biblical Fundamentalism, 160
Irenaeus, 137
Itala (Italic) Version 30, 47, 78, 79, 258
Italic Version, 47, 258
Italic Church, 78, 258

Jehovah's Witnesses, 26, 235
Johnson, Dell, 216

Kenyon, Frederic, 77, 79, 82, 103
Kilpatrick, G. D., 138
King James translators, 204 *ff*
King James VI, 193, 195
King James Only position, 15-19, 30
King James I, 186, 193, 194, 197, 198, 199, 200, 201, 202
Knox, John, 29

Lachmann, Karl, 100 164, 165, 166
Lake, Kirsopp, 135
Latin Vulgate, 19, 189, 259
Lawrence University, 62
Laws, Curtis Lee, 3
Lee, Maurice, 202
Leger, Jean, 256, 258, 259, 260
Letis, Theodore, 39, 107, 216
Lightfoot, J. B., 109, 176
Lively, Edward, 206
Lockman, Frank, 221, 222
Logsdon, Frank, 221, 222
Lovik, Olaf, 2
Luther, Martin, 29, 187, 189, 190, 258
Luther's German Bible, 83

Machen, J. Gresham, 159
Madden, D. K., 240
majescules, 37
Majority Text, 15, 39, 133
manuscript types, 35
manuscript terms, 34
Marsden, George, 160
Martin, Alfred, 109, 215
Martini, Carlo, 28, 28, 124, 224
Masoretic Hebrew Text, 19
Matthew Bible, 45, 83
Matthew, Thomas, 45
Maurice, F. D., 107
Mauro, Philip, 104
McClure, Alexander, 204
Metzger, Bruce 28, 95
Meyers, Frederic, 175
Miller, Edward, 77, 213, 215
miniscules, 37, 136
Moody Bible Institute, 109
Moody Monthly, 194
Moorman, Jack, 63, 135
Mount Athos, 88
Muralt, Leonhard von, 191

N/U Text, 117, 125
Napoleon, 103
National Association of Evangelicals, 236
National Council of Churches, 51, 119, 120
Neo-orthodoxy, 66
Nestle, Eberhard, 28, 29
Nestle-Aland Greek Text, 117, 125, 132, 159, 167, 227
New International Version, 8, 9, 125, 235, 236, 238, 239
New American Standard Bible, 2, 10, 124, 221, 227, 228, 230, 232, 233, 235, 236, 254

New King James Version, 10, 240
New English Bible, 124
New Evangelicalism, 157 *ff*
Niagra Falls Bible Conferences, 152
Nida, Eugene, 121, 224
Nolan, Frederic, 79
Norris, J. Frank, 217
Northern Baptist Convention, 2, 3, 4, 152, 153, 155
Northwestern College, 51, 77, 153

Ockenga, Harold, 157
Ohio Bible Fellowship, 154
Old Latin Text, 79, 258
Origen, 26, 98, 99, 110, 125
Orr, James, 61
Oxford Edition, 18, 19

Pantaenus, 97
Parvis, M. M., 50
Pensacola Christian College, 219
Peshitta Version, 30, 79, 81
Pickering, Wilbur, 135, 138, 167
Pickering, Ernest, 152, 156, 159
Pierpont, William, 39
Pillsbury Baptist Bible College, 2
Plato, 96, 97
Platonism, 98, 222
Pontifical Biblical Institute, 121
Pope Sixtus, 92, 103
Pope Leo X, 189
Preservation through the Received Text, 31
Preservation through the church, 30, 58
Preserved Text position, 30 *ff*
Princeton Theological Seminary, 119
Providential preservation, 52, 55 *ff*

Puritans, 205, 208

Rabbula, 81
Rationalism, see German Rationalism
Reader's Digest Condensed Bible, 119, 120
Received Text position, 38
Reformation, 131, 187, 189, 256, 258
Reina Cassiodoro de, 203
Reina-Valera Version, 203
resurrection, physical, 28
Reuchlin, John, 188
Revised Standard Version, 119, 120, 124, 235
Reynolds, John, 205
Richardson, John, 206
Riley, W. B., 4, 217
Riplinger, Gail, 171
Riverside Church, 152, 155
Robinson, Maurice, 39
Rockefeller, John D., 152
Rockwood, Perry, 154
Roman Catholic Church, 19, 24, 28, 41, 46, 55, 78, 85, 92, 93, 103 104, 120, 122, 123, 124, 125, 149, 158, 186, 189, 190, 191, 193, 194, 224, 235, 260
Romaunt, 259
Ruckman, Peter, 15, 218, 219

Saint Catherine's Monastery, 24, 101
Salter, W. H., 178
Saravia, Hadrian, 205
Schaff, Phillip, 130
Scofield, C. I., 214, 216, 218
scriptoriums, 88
Scrivener, F. H. A., 102, 137
Semler, J. S., 107, 108, 163, 166
separation, scriptural principle of, 4, 143 *ff*

Septuagint, 101
Sidgwick, Arthur, 175, 176
Sightler, James, 110, 172
Sixtine Edition, 92, 103
Smith, George Vance, 180, 181
Smith, Preserved, 188
Smith, Miles, 208
Society for Psychical Research, 176, 178, 179, 180
Sorenson, Henry, 2
Spanish Version, 83
Spence, O. Talmadge, 160
Spurgeon, Charles Haddon, 154, 214
Stalsett, Gunnar, 125
Stephanus, see Stephens, Robert
Stephanus Greek New Testament, 83
Stephens, Robert, 31, 70, 92, 187
Stuart, James, 193, 194, 195, 200, 203, 211
Stunica, 137
substitutionary atonement, 28
Sumner, Robert, 173
Syrian Church, 81
Syrian Text, 76, 80

Taverner's Bible, 83
textual criticism, two types of, 69
textual criticism based in belief, 69
textual criticism based in Rationalism, 71
textual editors, liberalism of, 162
Theodotus, 139
Theosophical Society, 178
Thomson, Giles, 209
Tischendorf, Frederic, 24, 92, 99, 100, 101, 103, 117, 166
Today's English Version, 125
translations, American Indian, 85
translations, Asian and other, 86

General Index

translations, modern European, 84
translations, early European, 83
translations of the early church, 78
Tregelles, Samuel, 103, 165, 166
Trinitarian Bible Society, 124, 126, 224
Tubingen, 150, 162
two textual philosophies, 52
two textual bases, 48
two types of Bibles, 44
Tyndale, William, 29, 44, 188

Ulfilas, 82
Uncials, 37
Unitarians, 106, 107, 122, 123, 149, 150, 163, 180, 182, 223
United Bible Societies, 28, 29, 65, 72, 117, 118, 120, 121, 122, 123, 124, 125, 167, 224, 239
University of Oxford, 204, 209
University of Alexandria, 96
Van Bruggen, Jakob, 63, 131, 133, 216
Vaudois, see Waldenses

Waite, D. A., 17, 19, 25, 83, 116, 216, 245
Waldenses, 30, 47, 78, 90, 222, 256, 257, 258, 259, 260, 261
Waldensian Bibles, 47
Waldensian manuscripts 71, 259, 260
Warfield, 23, 62
weighting of texts, 129
Weiss Greek Text, 117
Weldon, Sir Anthony, 200, 201, 202
Westcott and Hort's theory, 72
Westcott and Hort's mentors, 107
Westcott and Hort Greek Text, 117, 123, 168, 180, 181, 223, 214, 221
Westcott and Hort's collation, 105
Westcott and Hort, liberalism of, 167, 170

Westcott and Hort and Darwin, 179 *ff*
Westcott and Hort, 23, 25, 27, 61-63, 66, 71, 72, 76, 95, 105-114, 116, 125, 128, 163, 164, 166-182, 210, 211, 223
Westcott, B. F., 111, 112, 113, 114, 115, 117, 130, 172, 174, 175
Westminster Abbey, 204
Wheeler, N. M., 62
Whittingham, William, 45
Wikgren, Allen, 117
Williams, J. B., 174
World Baptist Fellowship, 154
World Council of Churches, 28, 224
Wotton, Sir Henry, 199
Wycliffe, John, 44, 46, 188

Young, Peter, 195

SCRIPTURE INDEX

Genesis 3:1 — 146

Exodus 20:1 — 13

Psalm 1:1 — 146
Psalm 11:3 — 7
Psalm 12:6 — 67
Psalm 19:9 — 59
Psalm 89:27 — 241
Psalm 105:8 — 54
Psalm 119:89 — 53
Psalm 119:103 — 67
Psalm 119:152 — 53
Psalm 119:160 — 54

Proverbs 3:5-6 — 56
Proverbs 30:5-6 — 8, 67

Isaiah 40:8 — 54

Matthew 1:15 — 249
Matthew 4:12 — 230
Matthew 4:18 — 230
Matthew 5:18 — 13
Matthew 8:3 — 230
Matthew 8:5 — 230
Matthew 8:7 — 230
Matthew 9:12 — 230
Matthew 13:51 — 228
Matthew 16:18 — 189

Matthew 17:21 — 237
Matthew 18:11 — 237, 244, 253
Matthew 23:8 — 233
Matthew 23:14 — 237
Matthew 24:35 — 52, 53
Matthew 27:24 — 244
Matthew 28:18-20 — 191

Mark 1:41 — 230
Mark 2:15 — 230
Mark 3:29 — 246
Mark 5:13 — 231
Mark 7:16 — 237
Mark 9:27 — 228
Mark 9:42 — 247
Mark 9:44 — 237, 246
Mark 9:46 — 237, 246
Mark 11:10 — 228
Mark 11:26 — 237
Mark 15:28 — 237
Mark 16:9 — 214

Luke 7:22 — 231
Luke 9:56 — 253
Luke 11:2 — 246
Luke 17:36 — 237
Luke 21:33 — 8
Luke 22:31 — 228
Luke 23:17 — 237

Luke 23:42 — 228
Luke 23:43 — 231
Luke 24:12 — 253
Luke 24:39 — 114
Luke 24:40 — 254
Luke 24:52 — 251

John 1:1 — 115
John 1:3 — 243
John 1:10 — 243
John 1:15 — 115
John 1:18 — 249
John 1:28-29 — 110
John 3:2 — 231
John 3:13 — 250
John 3:15 — 246
John 4:1 — 115
John 4:42 — 233
John 5:4 — 237
John 5:17 — 231
John 6:44 — 233
John 6:47 — 247
John 6:69 — 252, 233
John 7:53-8:11 — 91, 214
John 8:20 — 231
John 8:28 — 252
John 8:38 — 252
John 8:44 — 145
John 9:35 — 252
John 10:32 — 252
John 14:28 — 252
John 16:10 — 253
John 16:13 — 57
John 17:17 — 57, 59
John 20:13 — 227

Acts 2:30 — 233, 254
Acts 3:26 — 231
Acts 7:30 — 229
Acts 8:37 — 231, 233, 237, 252
Acts 9:5 — 229
Acts 9:6 — 229
Acts 9:29 — 229, 231
Acts 15:17 — 229
Acts 15:34 — 238
Acts 19:4 — 233
Acts 19:10 — 231
Acts 22:16 — 229
Acts 24:7 — 238
Acts 28:29 — 238

Romans 1:3 — 229, 231, 233
Romans 1:16 — 233, 247
Romans 6:11 — 229
Romans 8:1 — 242
Romans 14:6 — 229
Romans 14:10 — 244, 255
Romans 15:8 — 231
Romans 16:17 — 148, 149
Romans 16:18 — 231
Romans 16:20 — 233
Romans 16:24 — 229, 238

1 Corinthians 1:18 — 242
1 Corinthians 5:4 — 233
1 Corinthians 5:7 — 247
1 Corinthians 8:6 — 243
1 Corinthians 9:18 — 233
1 Corinthians 10:28 — 229
1 Corinthians 11:29 — 229
1 Corinthians 12:3 — 231

Scripture Index

I Corinthians 15:47 — 229
1 Corinthians 16:22 — 231

2 Corinthians 2:17 — 21
2 Corinthians 4:6 — 231
2 Corinthians 4:10 — 229
2 Corinthians 5:18 — 232
2 Corinthians 6:14-18 — 143, 144

Galatians 3:17 — 234
Galatians 4:7 — 247
Galatians 6:15 — 234, 247
Galatians 6:17 — 229

Ephesians 3:9 — 243, 232, 234, 251
Ephesians 3:14 — 229, 232, 234, 253

Philippians 2:10 — 181
Philippians 4:13 — 255

Colossians 1:2 — 229, 232, 234
Colossians 1:14 — 247
Colossians 1:16 — 243
Colossians 1:28 — 232
Colossians 3:13 — 234

1 Thessalonians 1:1 — 232, 234
1 Thessalonians 4:18 — 8

2 Thessalonians 2:2 — 234
2 Thessalonians 3:6 — 147

2 Thessalonians 3:14 — 147, 148

1 Timothy 1:1 — 229
1 Timothy 2:7 — 234
1 Timothy 3:15 – 58
1 Timothy 3:16 — 244, 250
1 Timothy 4:1 — 173
1 Timothy 5:21 — 229
1 Timothy 6:19 — 247

2 Timothy 3:16 — 6
2 Timothy 4:13 — 36
2 Timothy 4:22 — 232, 234

Titus 1:4 — 229

Philemon 6 — 232

Hebrews 1:2 — 111, 243
Hebrews 2:9 — 114
Hebrews 3:5 — 234
Hebrews 7:10 — 111
Hebrews 10:30 — 230
Hebrews 10:34 — 246

1 Peter 4:1 — 248
1 Peter 5:10 — 232
1 Peter 5:14 — 232

2 Peter 1:21 — 6
2 Peter 2:17 — 246
2 Peter 3:12-13 — 53

1 John 2:12 — 111, 114

1 John 4:3 — 251
1 John 5:7 — 91, 215, 238, 246

2 John 9 — 235, 249

Revelation 1:11 — 250
Revelation 5:14 — 250
Revelation 11:17 — 250
Revelation 16:5 — 250
Revelation 16:17 — 247
Revelation 19:1 — 230
Revelation 19:8 — 242
Revelation 21:24 — 248
Revelation 22:18-19 — 119

VITA OF DAVID H. SORENSON

David H. Sorenson was born on June 25, 1946, in Stillwater, Minnesota, to Henry C. and Viola H. Sorenson. The author is a third-generation, Fundamental Baptist pastor. His father and maternal grandfather were Fundamental Baptist pastors for about fifty years each.

The educational background of the author includes graduation from Pekin Community High School of Pekin, Illinois, in 1964. He graduated from Pillsbury Baptist Bible College in 1969 with a bachelor of arts degree. He graduated *cum laude* from Central Baptist Theological Seminary of Minneapolis in 1972 with a master of divinity degree. In 2001, he received an earned doctor of ministry degree from Pensacola Theological Seminary. This book is an adaptation of the major project for that degree.

Some of his ministry experiences include having served as an assistant pastor under Richard V. Clearwaters at Fourth Baptist Church from 1970-72. He then assisted his father as associate pastor at the Faith Baptist Church in Pekin, Illinois, from 1972-82. The author then became the senior pastor of the First Baptist Church of Brainerd, Minnesota, from 1982-87. From 1987-89, he served as the pastor of the Sara Bay Baptist Church in Bradenton, Florida. In early 1989, after a definitive call of God, the author went to Duluth, Minnesota, to start (from scratch) the Northstar Baptist Church in that city. He has continued as the pastor of that Fundamental, independent Baptist church since that time.

During the 1970s, David Sorenson also wrote several books pertaining to church bus ministries. More recently he has written several popular books. One is entitled *Training Your Children to Turn Out Right* (1995), published by the American Association of Christian Schools and now in its third printing. Another book written by David Sorenson is *The Art of Pastoring* (1998), published by Northstar Baptist Ministries. It is used by a number of Christian colleges around the country in their ministerial classes and is in its second printing. The most recent book written by David Sorenson is entitled *Have a Heavenly Marriage* (2000), published by the Sword of the Lord.

Additional copies of this book
may be obtained from:

Northstar Baptist Ministries
1820 West Morgan Street
Duluth, MN 55811

218-726-0209
davidsorenson@juno.com